In Quest of Dali

By the same author

LIFE WITH PICASSO
(with Françoise Gilot)

A DICTIONARY OF MODERN PAINTING *(ed.)*

CONFESSIONS OF A LITERARY ARCHAEOLOGIST

In Quest of Dali

by Carlton Lake

Paragon House

New York

First Paperback edition, 1990

Published in the United States by

Paragon House Publishers
90 Fifth Avenue
New York, NY 10011

Library of Congress Cataloging-in-Publication Data

Lake, Carlton.
  In quest of Dali / by Carlton Lake. — 1st paperback ed.
    p.   cm.
  ISBN 1-55778-386-1   : $12.95
    1. Dali, Salvador, 1904-   .   2. Artists—Spain—Biography.
I. Title.
N7913.D35L3   1990
759.6—dc20
[B]   *90-34296*
                                                          CIP

Manufactured in the United States of America

10   9   8   7   6   5   4   3   2   1

For Ned, who started it all

Illustrations follow pages 128 and 224.

F O R E W O R D

During the winter of 1964, New England Merchants National Bank of Boston bought a large painting by Salvador Dali, which they planned to display in their new headquarters office in the Prudential Center in Boston. One of the bank's officers, an old friend of mine, asked me if I would take a look at the picture, at the Knoedler galleries in New York, and write a short article about it which the bank could print in a booklet designed to explain to their customers just who this man Dali was and what his painting was all about.

At first I hesitated. Like a good many others, I had been put off by the tiresome publicity the press has devoted to Dali. And yet I had occasionally wondered just how accurately that kind of news story reflected the man himself and to what extent it mirrored the taste and insight of those writers and editors for whom Dali is, apparently, prime copy. I had read his early books and seen serious accounts of lectures he had given at the Sorbonne and elsewhere, and they had aroused my interest in some of his ideas. Behind the bizarre façade of the public personage there was, obviously, an exceedingly sharp and original mind. I wanted to know more about that mind. And so I decided I would go to New York and look at the bank's picture; also, if the occasion presented itself, at the man. What happened when I did is a long story—long in evolution and long in clarification—but perhaps it will help others understand better this strange, provocative, unique phenomenon called Dali.

CARLTON LAKE

"I want everybody to talk about Dali—
even if they speak well of him."

—SALVADOR DALI

PART ONE

The man from Knoedler's handed me the catalog of Dali's exhibition. *Hommage à Crick et Watson,* the cover proclaimed. Above the title was a photograph of a three-dimensional model of DNA—deoxyribonucleic acid, the material which carries the genetic code that determines the development of all living things. Its twin helices twisted around each other in the appropriate symbolic manner. Dali had apparently touched up the model's stick-and-ball components in the photograph with gouache so that some of the upper elements in the two chains suggested soldiers with rifles being exploded by the giant-sized splattered signature *Dali* that crowned the composition. But the model had been reoriented—whether deliberately or unwittingly I had no way of knowing—so that its vertical axis was now horizontal. In the upper corners were photographs of the two Nobel Prize-winning scientists of the title, identified by the *Time*-like captions "Watson: A model builder" and "Crick: Life is a three-letter word."

"Number one in the catalog," Mr. Leary, the man from Knoedler's, informed me.

I turned to No. 1 and read its title: GALACIDALACIDESOXIRI-
BUNUCLEICACID (*Hommage* [sic] *to Crick and Watson*). I looked
up questioningly at Mr. Leary, a tall, well-fed fellow of sixty
or thereabouts, with glasses, a reddish complexion, and the
jovial urbanity appropriate to a man who must often find himself in the position of justifying a price in six figures attached
to the paintings he shows. The price of this one had been widely
reported in the press as $150,000; the buyer, New England Mer-
chants National Bank of Boston, had neither confirmed nor de-
nied the report.

"You'll find more of an explanation farther on," Mr. Leary
said. I turned two pages and read:

At a time when the titles of pictures are rather short (i.e. "Picture
No. 1" or "White on White") I call my Hommage to Crick and
Watson: GALACIDALACIDESOXIRIBUNUCLEICACID. It is my longest title
in one word. But the theme is even longer: long as the genetical
persistance [sic] of human memory. As announced by the prophet
Isaiah—the Saviour contained in God's head from which one sees
for the first time in the iconographic history his arms repeating the
molecular structures of Crick and Watson and lifting Christ's dead
body so as to resuscitate him in heaven.

"Mr. Dali has promised to write out a statement of just what
the picture represents," Mr. Leary said. "I'll turn that over to
you when we get it. But he should be here any minute. I called
him just a little while ago to remind him you were coming."

With the catalog analysis more or less firmly in mind, I
walked over directly in front of the picture. It was ten feet high
and thirteen and a half feet wide, I had been told. It looked
even larger, perhaps because, having been rolled for storage, it
now hung loosely without frame or stretcher against the velvet-
lined wall. In spite of its monumental dimensions it had a subdued air about it. It had been painted with few colors, and
those, with the exception of a few small touches of red above
the head of a woman shown back-to in the center foreground,

had very subtle tonal gradations: a pale gray, a gray-blue, and ocher, ranging from a near-brown to a slightly burnished golden yellow. At first glance the composition seemed to consist mainly of an infinite expanse of rolling plain with low-lying mountains at the left and in the background and billowing clouds above. In both upper corners, dark gray-blue areas set off sharply a glowing light reflected in the clouds between them. I could make out two shadowy kneeling figures in the upper right-hand corner, and at the very center of the top, a small angel with wings spread in flight. Farther to the left, I saw a gray-blue and brown bearded patriarchal figure holding out, toward the center, a partially unrolled scroll on which I read, with some difficulty, the opening syllables of the picture's title. Below the patriarch's feet, wisps of fleecy white cloud caught the light, and directly below that area was a more finished version of the DNA model reproduced on the catalog cover: small round balls connected by slender sticks. In places the balls appeared to be human heads attached to the upper parts of torsos, the sticks to be lances or rifles in the hands of fighting men. Underneath, the terrain was mountainous and its masses glowed in a deep golden-beige mist. Directly below, in the lower left-hand corner, the mountains grew darker, but a bit of the light picked up what appeared to be an irregularly rectangular sheet of paper signed *Dali 1963.*

At the lower right were geometric elements arranged in more orderly and figurative fashion. Small standing figures—apparently Arab riflemen wearing burnouses—formed cubes, each one aiming his rifle toward the man at his left, with the heads of four kneeling figures beneath them reinforcing the cubic structure. In the center foreground, back to the viewer, stood (or, possibly, kneeled; it was impossible to tell, since only the upper two-thirds of the body showed) a woman draped with a white cloak, her brown hair, like the cloud areas, catching the light from an invisible sun. I assumed this figure to be Gala,

Dali's wife. He has painted her into so many of his pictures that, even back-to, she is readily identifiable.

As I studied the picture, I saw that the upper central cloud area was more than just clouds. For one thing, I could make out, near the bearded figure with the scroll in the upper left-hand corner, what seemed to be the top of a head looking down toward the plain beneath. And on the head, what had first appeared to be a luxuriant growth of curly hair revealed, the longer I studied it, at least two figures: one standing and, from its fullness, apparently female; the other seated and indistinct. I was wishing I had Dali's statement to guide me across this vast mystical expanse when Mr. Leary came back into the room and said, beaming, "Here's Mr. Dali now."

Dali came quickly over to me and shook hands. He was wearing a black greatcoat with astrakhan collar, carrying a black Homburg and a short stick with an antique enameled-silver head. He took off his coat, set it down, with his hat, on a bench at the far end of the room, and came back to me, still holding firmly to his stick. He was wearing a pinstripe double-breasted black suit, black buckle shoes, and a tie woven of black and gold threads set off by an antique stickpin. He unbuttoned his suit jacket and stuck one thumb in a pocket of his waistcoat, a particularly magnificent weave sewn with lavish overlays of heavy gold thread. His black hair was pommaded, and his waxed mustache, somewhat shorter than I had seen it in photographs, curled upward for about three inches on either side. He was followed by Leary and a lean young man whom Leary introduced as Mr. Abbott, an architect from the decorating firm responsible for the installation of the picture at the bank's new headquarters in Boston after its scheduled stopover at the Spanish Pavilion in the New York World's Fair.

Dali pointed with his stick to an enormous storage tube at the far end of the room, from which the Knoedler people had removed the painting.

"Ees no good to roll, unroll, like that."

"Right. Right," Leary said. "We won't do it very often. Once more, but that's all."

"All right. You put een fair, then after thee fair, ees feeneesh, no?"

"Yes. Yes. Understood," Leary said. "Now then, Mr. Dali, we were just saying—do you remember you made the suggestion you were eventually going to write out, for the bank—"

"Yes, ees almos' ready now. Een French. Somebody translate eento Eengleesh. No beeg. One page."

I could see that communication would bog down badly if Dali and I had to talk in English. I suggested we speak in French and told him not to bother to have his explanatory statement translated. While I was working on the booklet for the bank, I'd take care of the translation of his text, too.

"*Parfait, parfait,*" Dali said, with much rolling of the *r*'s. "I will send it to you . . ." He hesitated. "How long are you staying in New York?"

A couple of days, I told him; then I had to return to Boston.

"*Alorrrs* . . . I'll give that to you tomorrow at . . . about five o'clock. Five o'clock? Come to tea at five o'clock. I'll give it to you in French that won't be completely French."

I told him I thought I could cope with it satisfactorily.

"*Parfait,*" he said and gave a careful twist to one side of his mustache. He pointed to the painting. "Would you like to have me tell you a little right now?"

I told him I would indeed. I assumed from the catalog description that the bearded figure in the upper left-hand corner holding the partially unfurled scroll was the prophet Isaiah, but what about the winged figure at top center?

"Yes," Dali said, "that is Isaiah, and that"—he pointed with his stick toward the vaguely headlike mass at the left of the cloud area—"is God, but he doesn't have wings. The winged figure in the center of the body of God is there because in the beginning I had painted a Greek figure without arms and then I put in the angel where the arm is cut off. You see it or not?"

I told him I could see that the left arm of the God figure was missing.

"That is right," he said. "God has no wings and no left arm. His right arm is all that part there." He indicated a diaphanous right arm which came down from a shoulder just below the head of God, along the misty mountainous area at the left side of the picture, toward the female figure in the center foreground. "The arm is holding the dead Christ." He pointed to a trickle of red oozing out of an incision in the left side of the body of Christ, just below the area where the right arm of God supported the dead body. "That is the blood running out of Christ. That is a shoulder. There is Christ's arm and his head. *Bon.* All this is the body. There are his thighs coming down to the knees. You can even see the belly button." I walked closer to the canvas and searched what seemed the appropriate area. "No, no," Dali said. He tapped a spot in the mist just to the left of the female head. "There is the belly button—right there. That is the reason why, at the fair, there will be a light to clarify all these figures. It will come on gradually, then fade away just as slowly. Then on again and off again. It is very important to have the lighting just right."

He went over once more the particulars of the body of Christ. "You feel the heaviness of the body and of the sacrifice, don't you? That's what I want to stand out—God taking Christ up to heaven."

I referred to the statement in the catalog that the arms of God were repeating for the first time in iconographic history the molecular structures of Crick and Watson. Dali pointed to the little balls at the left of the body of Christ. "They form two spirals," he said, "like that, like that"—and he made the appropriate circular gestures with his stick. "Like one of those little stairways. Like a corkscrew. And the rhythm of that part is carried out in the upward movement of Christ in the arm of God. It is mathematically exact."

He walked over to the canvas and peered at the cubes formed

by the groups of Arab riflemen shooting one another. I asked him the significance of the Arabs. "They are there because I am Spanish," he said. "In the history of Spain you cannot separate our civilization from that of the Arabs. There is a sort of phenomenon of symbiosis. When the library at Alexandria was burned, all the great mathematical writings of antiquity were lost, and it was the Arabs who preserved them for us. In the Escorial you will find documents that have an extraordinary importance because they are the ones that served as the basis of the metaphysics of Ramón Lull. For me he is the greatest man who ever lived. He was stoned to death by Arabs, but he is the one who inherited and passed along to us all the culture of the Arabs. The finest book on geometry ever written is the one by Juan de Herrera, the builder of the Escorial, called *Discurso sobre la forma cúbica.* He was the first Cubist, and his book was inspired by the archangelic Ramón Lull. Herrera took the mathematical knowledge of Ramón Lull and made a marvelous metaphysical and aesthetic treatise, much finer than the one by Fra Luca Pacioli, the contemporary of Raphael. So whenever I can, in my paintings, I like to pay tribute to the Arabs. Then, too, they say that I have Arab blood, descended from Dali Mami, a contemporary of Cervantes." He waved his stick across the plains and mountains at the center of the canvas. "I always paint those vast sandy expanses that go on as far as the eye can see. I don't know why; I have never even been in North Africa. I suppose it's an atavism of the Arab blood. Here the Arabs represent a kind of destruction, like minerals in the process of annihilating themselves. It is the molecular structure of minerals. Whereas that"—he pointed back to the spirals formed by the circles at the left—"is the persistence of memory. Everything is based on that. It is the contrary of the cubes."

One of Dali's best-known canvases, painted in 1931 and now in the Museum of Modern Art in New York, bears the title *The Persistence of Memory* and includes, among its pictorial symbols, three "soft" watches, one of which is draped over the lone branch of a defoliated tree. I mentioned that painting.

"That is extraordinary, isn't it?" he said. "I foresaw the whole idea and now they are getting around to proving it scientifically. It is in the genes—the key to life, the genetic code which transmits to each living cell."

Dali turned to Abbott and broke into English again. "I myself een vairy airly time paint thees een melting watches. Everybody thought a game but now they know eet already exeest. Now thees must be lighted *pour que le* people see thees all dtheesappear zlowly thee two seelhouettes every ten meenutes."

I said the lighting looked to me like a difficult job, in view of the subtlety of the color. "No, no, no, no, no," Dali said. "Thee light ees general light. We eencrease thee light on painteeng. Thee public theenk eet sees a veesion and believe they have painted thee peecture. They feel flattered."

Abbott looked unconvinced. "But when we hang the picture in the bank, our problem is going to be complicated by the fact that we must control the lighting on the painting as the outside light changes. The bank is a glass building."

"But thees ees posseeble control," Dali said. "You weell see." He turned back to me and in French said, "This was painted with only three colors. The whole painting. But people won't realize it. Mars brown, a golden yellow, ultramarine blue, and that's all. It is in the spirit—oh, it is different, of course, but it has that same dreamlike quality—of Watteau's painting *The Embarkation for Cythera*. Not the one in the Louvre; the one in Berlin. There is the same feeling in the crowd of figures that spiral upward toward the top of the canvas."

I asked about the two shadowy figures at the upper right. "Those? They are monks in adoration before God," Dali said. He walked up close to the painting and examined it carefully. "I wish they wouldn't keep on rolling and unrolling it," he said. "It was painted so recently it could be easily damaged."

I asked him about the two figures in the head of God. "The

larger one is a Virgin—a Madonna. The shadowy figure in the
center is Christ. Christ always existed in the head of God." He
pointed to the figure I took to be Gala. "That is my wife, Gala,
who stares, not at God, not at Christ, but at the blood. The
blood is not coming out of the arm of God but out of the body
of Christ, just at the spot where the two spirals touch."

One of the most interesting details was the texture of Gala's
hair. In color it ranged from the golden yellow of its highlights
to a chestnut brown but it had the texture of one of those
rounded loaves of French bread known as *pain de campagne*.
Dali has made several paintings of bread over the years. In one
of them two pieces of bread are shown "expressing the sentiment of love." Here in Gala's hair I saw the tones and texture
of those earlier pictures, but applied with greater range and
variety. I mentioned that to Dali.

"That is exact," he said. "For me those bread pictures have
a Eucharistic significance. Here the hair takes on the same
meaning by—shall we say?—contagion, because of its proximity
to the body of Christ. What you notice about its remarkable
texture results from my having given it a vibrancy in the mate-
rialization of its structure. That is entirely intentional. It has
a suppleness and a fluidity that run the full gamut from soft
bread crumbs to the dark outer crust." He fanned his fingers
over the hair. "It is *really* bread."

I asked him about the houses and other details of the landscape. "Those are local touches reminiscent of the countryside
around Cadaqués on the Costa Brava, where I live and paint
from June until November. They are not exactly copies but it
exists like that." He turned to Abbott. "Sorry to speak een
French like thees."

"That's perfectly all right," Abbott said. "I've had the pleasure." Leary, I noticed, had left the room.

"By thee way," Dali said, speaking to Abbott, "what weell
thee painteeng be set off against?"

"The molding?" Abbott asked. Dali looked puzzled. Abbott

rephrased his question: "You mean what frame will be put on it?"

"No," Dali said. "Thee wall. Thee wall."

"It's going to be travertine marble," Abbott said.

"What color? *Clair?*" Dali asked.

"Warm beige," Abbott said.

"But clear *ou* dark?" Dali insisted.

"*Clair,*" Abbott said.

Dali frowned and considered the painting. "*Je crois que* thees painteeng ees better weeth one dark part of wall. Brown ees vairy good. But I don't theenk ees good weeth theengs *trop claires, vous ne trouvez pas?* Because thee painteeng ees *très claire.* Thee painteeng ees vairy light. And ees much more eeffecteeve weeth *le* light all een thee painteeng and thee wall behind, dark. Not too much clear around."

Abbott said he would go get a sample of the molding *and* the wall to give Dali a better idea, and he left. Dali took another look at his painting. When he turned again to me, he looked more satisfied with the situation.

"This is, in any case, the contrary of everything being done in painting today," he said. "It is based entirely on nuances and transitions that are almost imperceptible, both in the tension of its figures and in the gradations of its tones. It is the opposite of brutality. Today people like things that hit them between the eyes, that give the same kind of shock you get from drinking three martinis, one right after another. But if you keep on looking at that kind of painting, after a while, just as when you keep downing the martinis, you can't see the painting any longer. It makes a great effect when you first look at it, one of those violent things, but afterwards it's very tiring. But a painting like this is something that grows and becomes full of meaning for you because of its depth and its nuances."

I had just been up at the Guggenheim Museum looking at the prizewinners and other entries in their biennial survey of painting. It was hard not to feel surfeited before the tour was over, I told him.

"Of course. The shock, really, is the best part of those things. But to live with them! Can you imagine having to spend the rest of your life in that place?" Dali's eyes rolled upward and his nostrils flared. "The one virtue they have is the wallop they give you, but after you have been hit over the head a certain number of times you don't feel anything more. That is why people are all excited about Pop Art. At least Pop Art gives them something concrete. And that is why Huntington Hartford's Gallery of Modern Art is going to be a big success. Bouguereau and Gustave Moreau will give them the pleasure of letting them see an honest-to-God belly button and a mouth they can believe in."

I thought back to some of the objects Dali had created in the 1930's—the forerunners of some of today's Pop Art objects. I reminded him of them.

"Most of the Pop artists admit they are descended from Marcel Duchamp and me," he said. "I painted concrete objects that, even in appearing irrational, were real and understandable. Take that drawing of mine, for example, showing a woman's body with drawers opening out of it. Those drawers include everything—Freud, Christianity, the possibility of penetrating into the interior of a human being with its secret compartments all full of meaning. Then, too, that dinner jacket I made, covered with little *pousse-café* glasses filled with peppermint, dead flies, and straws. Now people say it was a stroke of genius, but when I made it, no one paid any attention to it. All those objects I made that were completely irrational sold so badly. My wife brought here that siphon bottle I had built. It was fifty feet long and held up by a crutch. When I showed it at the Julien Levy gallery, they thought it was something to laugh at, but nobody saw the importance that lay in building such a difficult irrational object. Now all the galleries here are filled with subproducts of things like that. There's one fellow who spends all his time making siphon bottles: one an inch long, another an inch and a half, another in plastic, and so on. Then there's Arman, whose specialty is cutting things in half. I did that in the Surrealist period. I exhibited a shoe I had cut in half, but at that time nobody paid any attention to it. We were the avant-garde. What they're doing today is really old hat." He pointed to his painting. "Look at that painting. People will call it *pompier*—academic, too conservative. Actually, it is fifty years ahead of its time."

Dali's reference to *pompier* art reminded me of another of the pictures listed in the Knoedler catalog under No. 5: *Small Battle of Tetuán,* which I had not seen but assumed to be a study for one of his large paintings in Huntington Hartford's Gallery of Modern Art. In the "Analysis" section of the catalog I had read the following explanation:

It was said with malice that Dali was surrealism's Meissonier. What happiness if it were true and were I able to paint photographs of my dreams by hand as well as Meissonier painted his anecdotes.

I asked Dali if this represented his true feeling about Meissonier.

His eyes opened wide. "But Meissonier is a very great painter," he said. "Not so great as Fortuny. Fortuny in Spain did sublime things, but still, Meissonier is great and is going to be considered great once again. Why, just compare his work to that garbage you saw at the Guggenheim Museum. That is going to pass away—pass away so fast. It has a quality of shock and surprise at first, but as soon as the newness wears off, one comes to understand there is very little to see in all that. Then the reaction sets in. We've had abstract expressionism—all those spots and all that violence—and how does it end up? In Pop Art, with those people who only copy exactly a comic strip without changing a thing. It's just a reaction away from the kind of painting whose objective was to show the artist's temperament in every brushstroke and toward something completely standardized—a nostalgia for the object. I told Roy Lichtenstein the other day, 'You are a romantic. When you paint an ice cream soda, you don't make it the way it looks today. In a drugstore today they put it into a paper cup, not any longer into the kind of glass you show. That is finished. So what you are painting is a romantic remembrance of the kind of ice cream soda you had as a boy, like Proust with his *madeleine*. So you Pop artists choose things with a sentimental value that puts them in a class with Proust's tea cake. Actually, Vermeer was much more classical a Pop artist than you. He looked at life in Delft. He didn't change a thing. He painted it just as it was, just like a photographer, and he painted some of the most immortal masterpieces in the history of painting. It wasn't the romantic side—Delft as he had known it when he was a little boy. He was there, he looked, and he painted what he saw. All Vermeer is like that. His whole work is the record of the passage of his eye. It is sublime. But after all, there is only one Vermeer. It takes a kind of religious vocation to paint like that.' "

In a number of Dali's paintings, such as the *Crucifixion* in the Metropolitan Museum and *The Sacrament of the Last Supper* in the National Gallery in Washington, theological themes have replaced the Freudian ones of his earlier work. I asked him what brought him to that pass.

"I had no religious ideas at first," he said. "During my adolescence I was an atheist because my father was one. He was a kind of anarchist. First I was interested in Freud and then in the sciences—biology and nuclear physics. The more I studied the sciences, the more I realized that everything religion tells us is true. Theoretically, that was fine. But I still lacked that grace which is faith. That is more difficult. I have the feeling it will come in a surer form, but I don't know just when. It comes and it goes. It oscillates."

Abbott came into the room carrying a foot-long piece of pale-beige travertine marble and a piece of dark-brown velvet. He held the marble against the side of the painting.

"Ees too light," Dali said. "Weell they put a deeferent one een thee lobby?"

"This piece has the same intensity as the painting," Abbott said.

"Exactly," Dali said. "Ees for that ees wrong."

"This is the material that the ninety-foot wall is to be made of," Abbott continued. "It's perfectly possible, though, now that the bank has bought this painting instead of having a mural done for the area as they originally planned, that we'll redesign the wall. Now, you mentioned before that it might be a good idea for the painting to be set back."

"Ees posseeble."

"In that case, in the setback the wall could be made out of a darker material."

Dali thought. "I theenk a reech texture, a material like a moiré, for instance. No velvet but moiré." He turned to me and said, in French, "I am now doing a painting based on the scientific background of moiré. I will tell you about it later— maybe tomorrow." Then, to Abbott, "Those two theengs together of thee same eentensity, ees not posseeble. Now wiz thees light ees eemposseeble because too white."

Abbott placed his strip of dark-brown velvet between the painting and the travertine, juggling them back and forth until the proportions satisfied him.

"Thees ees good. Good proportion," Dali said. "Now wiz some material, more dark, behind painting, before *le* wall, become vairy beautiful. But ees no posseeble put together immediatel. Ees much better. I believe ees no necessary frame. You put material, no frame at all, *ou* black, gold, vairy t'in, almost eenveeseeble."

That tied it up. Dali seemed satisfied with his interim solution. He looked at his watch and decided he was late for another appointment. He picked up his coat.

"Have you seen the latest Picassos?" he asked me. Not the very latest, in any case, since I'd been in America for several months, I told him. "Knoedler's bought four. You could ask to see them," he said. I asked him what he thought of them. "In his variations on Velásquez, there were some interesting things," Dali said. "But in the *Luncheon on the Grass* series, much less. Just a few comments and all that repetition. Of course, you have to bear in mind, he is very old." He picked up his hat, stick, and gloves. "Well," he said, "don't forget tomorrow. Let's say—not five—six o'clock at the St. Regis."

Shortly after six the next evening—a Sunday—I entered the St. Regis lobby. When I inquired for Dali, the man at the desk told me he was in the hotel's King Cole Bar. I walked into the bar and saw him sitting at a large round table, surrounded by a group of eight: three girls and five men. He saw me approaching the table, rose, and pulled over another chair from one of the adjoining tables. He was dressed, as he had been the day before, in a double-breasted pinstripe black suit. The gold waistcoat was clearly visible. He introduced me to his friends: the three girls seemed to have no names other than Mademoiselle. Two were taffy-colored blondes, one of them with an impressive coiffure in the ascensional tradition of the Dalinian spiral; the third, a sultry brunette. All three were exceedingly decorative.

One of the men, seated between two of the girls at Dali's left, a short, stocky fellow with a round face and a meridional accent, was Arman, the Pop artist Dali had referred to in our conversation at Knoedler's the day before as the man whose "specialty is cutting things in half." Next was a Mr. Carlos Alemany, an

Argentinian who has executed unusual precious-stone jewelry designed by Dali, examples of which I had seen exhibited in Paris several years earlier. To the right of Dali were three men: a bald, bespectacled man in his sixties named Colin, who, I was told, ran an actor's studio in Carnegie Hall where—among others—Marlon Brando and Rod Steiger had been trained; a small, middle-aged, worried-looking man in a dark-blue suit, a Paris publisher named Foret; and a tall, slender, slightly stooped, graying man of forty or so, wearing rimless glasses. His name was Field, Dali said, and he was preparing the complete catalog of Dali's work.

Dali seated me at his right and beckoned to a waiter hovering nearby, who came over and took my order. Field, at my right, asked me where I was from. Generally Paris, I told him, but when I was in the States, Boston. He smiled politely.

"In that case we can talk," he said. "I went to Harvard." He spoke in a precise, meticulous manner that I had not associated with Harvard since well before its goldfish- and phonograph-record-eating period. He handed me an 8½-by-11-inch sheet headed "The Salvador Dali Catalog." It listed Albert Field, with an address in Queens, as "compiler" and carried the following typed announcement:

It is important that the catalog of my work be complete and accurate. I will appreciate your supplying Mr. Field with all possible information.

It was signed, in reproduction, by a Dali signature and date (1956) that covered about half the sheet. Knowing the years of effort that had gone into Zervos' catalog of Picasso's work—still far from complete, or even up-to-date—I complimented Field on his ambition.

He bowed. "I expect it will be a long job," he said.

I asked him if he was an art historian.

"No, I am a schoolteacher. I teach science and English in the ninth grade, in Queens."

I asked him what he thought of Dali's preoccupation with scientific subjects in his recent painting.

"He is very serious about it," Field said. "Are you writing about Dali, by the way?"

I hadn't completely made up my mind about that, I told him.

"You should," he said. "He's a very interesting man—more interesting than anyone realizes."

Colin leaned across the table and in what I took to be a central European accent said, "That is right. I used to be a scientist and I am constantly amazed at the perception he has in talking with men of science. They are, too. His interest is more than serious; it is profound."

Dali turned to me. "You know museum people in Boston. Can't you do something for Foret?" The worried-looking little man began to cheer up visibly. I asked Dali what needed to be done.

"He has produced the biggest and most valuable book in the world—a masterpiece," Dali said. "It belongs in an American museum. You should see it."

The waiter returned with drinks of one kind or another for everyone but Dali. Colin started talking to Foret and Field in French.

Dali asked me what I was writing at the moment. A book about Picasso, I told him. He sat up straighter.

"That won't amount to anything," he said. "It can't. He doesn't give himself to anybody. Not the way I do. *Moi, je me livre,*" he said, almost fiercely.

I knew, of course, that Dali's relations with Picasso, as with most of the other artists who had befriended him in the 1920's and 1930's, had deteriorated badly over the past twenty-five years. I had read statements Dali had made or written about Picasso in newspaper interviews, magazine articles, and books, in which he sometimes seemed to be combining the roles of rebellious son and jealous lover—goading, provocative statements designed principally, perhaps, to draw not blood but a reply. As far as I knew, Picasso had always ignored them.

"He gave himself this time," I said.

Dali shrugged. "It's hard to believe. But we'll see when the book comes out."

I asked Dali about the paper he was to give me. He looked blank. The one relating to the bank's picture, I said.

"*Ah, oui*," he said slowly. "I have given it to Monsieur Field. He will translate it into English."

I told him that wasn't necessary. I would take care of that. Besides, I preferred it in the original.

"But he must make a copy for his records," Dali said. "He keeps a record of everything relating to me. Then he will send it to you. Monsieur Field," he called out. Field looked up from his conversation with Colin and Foret. Dali repeated the substance of his story. Field nodded soberly.

I asked Field how long it would take him to translate Dali's paper. He shrugged. "A day or so. I can send it to you in Boston if you will give me your address." I wrote it on a page of a pocket reminder and gave it to him. He read it, folded it neatly, and filed it carefully away in the inner recesses of his wallet, in the exact spot, I felt, that he had long since assigned to papers of its kind in accordance with a definite and undeviating policy. I asked him how he had become involved in cataloging the complete works of Dali. He cleared his throat.

"I have to go back to 1941 to answer that question," he said. "One day I took a guided tour of the galleries at the Museum of Modern Art. I thought most of the stuff I saw was trash, badly done by incompetent people, out to fool the public. I felt that some of it was actually conscious fraud, and the rest merely incompetence trying to pass itself off as inspiration. You can't make art by splashing a can of paint on canvas and calling it something. I said so to the young lady who took us around. I said I thought Miró was a fraud, Mondrian was a fraud—Dali agrees with me on that—and others too. She was horrified. It had never occurred to her to doubt any of the gods of so-called modern art. I was obviously a philistine of the worst type. But there was a possibility that I *might* be saved because I did like the things by Dali that I saw. There were two things about them that I loved, and still do. One was his technical ability. Whatever he paints looks as though that was exactly what he wanted to paint, instead of being the nearest he could get to it, which is true of many artists. His work always looks finished, right—even some of his hasty sketches.

"The other thing I liked was that his subjects were interesting. Not every one of the perhaps two thousand works of his that I've seen is equally interesting, but very few fail to express *something*. Most of them have something to say: not a message —that's another kind of art, and I'm not sure I like that, either— but some expression of his subconscious or of the subconscious of man or of the feeling one has in a situation which can't be put well in words but can sometimes be expressed on canvas. And these two qualities, both of which I happen to like, seem at their peak in him. There are other artists who have one quality but, I think, without the other. I'm sure Picasso can draw well, although I didn't discover it until about six years ago because I think all his recent stuff is absolute trash, the kind that without the name of Picasso could not be sold for two cents. People would not take it home to put on their walls if it had not been 'a Picasso.' And I've seen a lot of it."

I asked him if he had in mind any particular recent work of Picasso's.

"Let's start with the one at the UNESCO building in Paris, which is—well, I haven't seen anything as bad as that in the school where I teach, where beginners are told to splash their souls on the paper and they do. Picasso said once that he was laughing at the world, and I think he's laughing at his customers before all others. He wrote this in something. I don't remember in just what, but I saw it."

I told Field he had probably read an account, or perhaps

even excerpts, of a book by Giovanni Papini, called *Il Libro Nero,* a collection of imaginary interviews published in 1951, in which Papini had his subjects tell him the sort of thing about themselves that he would have liked to hear them say. In Picasso's case, Papini "quoted" him as saying that ever since Cubism he had been amusing the public—and the critics—with all the queer games and gags that popped into his head, that the less they understood, the more they admired, and that, as a result, he had grown rich as a public entertainer who had cashed in on the vanity and imbecility of his contemporaries. Papini had explained in a foreword that this talk was pure invention on his part, but apparently few had bothered to read the foreword, because quotations from that "interview" keep cropping up in newspapers all over the world. I assumed that Field had read one of those.

Field pursed his lips. "You may be right," he said. "I swallowed it easily because I couldn't see why anybody who *could* do better would deliberately do things that badly. And he gets paid for it! That horrifies me. Then there are other artists who have imagination but don't seem able to get what they want to express onto canvas so that other people will feel it too. So I started to notice everything I could find of Dali's. I saw paintings of his in galleries and museums and kept track of him through the newspapers and art magazines. Then, about six or seven years ago, I went to the library at the Museum of Modern Art and asked if there was a good iconography. I wanted to know what I had missed. I wanted to be more efficient in looking at Dali's works, not just haphazard. They told me there was no such thing. I said, 'That's absurd. He's the second-best-paid painter alive'—Picasso, I believe, earns more—'and there ought to be.' The librarian, who did the bibliography for the museum catalogs, said, 'Of course there ought to be, but who's going to do it?' So I went to see Dali and asked him if someone was doing it—an iconography and bibliography combined—and he said no. I showed him my three-by-five index cards and all my notes. I said, 'I've been trying to make a catalog. I have this much done: here are the paintings, who owns them, where they've been exhibited, in which book they've been illustrated —that sort of thing.' He said, 'Pairfect. Pairfect. You are thee catalog,' and he clapped his hands. So I am the catalog. Each winter, when he returns to New York, I show him my new discoveries. Every photograph that I have, or any reproduction, I have checked with him personally, so that whatever I say is his, in the catalog, is there because *he* has said it is his."

I asked him where he had collected the photographs and other reproductions.

"First, from the catalogs of art exhibits held all over the United States and Europe. Libraries in New York—one or another of them—get the catalogs of most exhibitions. Then there are the reviews in the various art magazines, American and French particularly. That takes care of current work. For the older things, I've checked the collections of Surrealist and other avant-garde magazines in the Museum of Modern Art here—*Cahiers d'Art, Minotaure,* and so on. And from time to time I get to Paris and search out the same sort of thing there. I've had to track down quite a number of people who had dropped out of sight, and look up heirs sometimes, but there are still many paintings that I have not been able to check off the list. For example, each time I come across an exhibition catalog—let's say it's one for an exhibition at the Pierre Colle gallery in Paris in 1932—I make a list of all the titles it includes. Every title that is already in *my* catalog—the Salvador Dali catalog, that is—I encircle. Then I set out to find the ones that are left over. The paintings are enough of a problem by themselves, but the drawings"—Field shook his head despairingly— "they're next to impossible. They were almost never listed individually in the exhibition catalogs. No one knows how many he's done or what they are or where they are, and I think no one ever will. Eventually we may get within three hundred of what he's done. I don't think we can hope to get any closer than that. However, if we find two thousand drawings, I won't be surprised."

I turned to where Dali had been. His chair was empty.

"The trouble is," Field continued, "Dali doesn't have any archives that would be of help. Gala has some records, but they are incomplete and she will allow no one else to refer to them. There are paintings at their home in Port Lligat that she has never allowed anyone to see; others in storage in Paris and quite a collection stored in New York."

I asked him why the secrecy.

He shrugged. "You'll have to ask Gala that. Each time the question of seeing them has come up, she's tired or busy or just doesn't feel like it. Of course, if Dali should die before Gala, she will have a collection of tremendous value, because she has some magnificent things in storage in those three places."

I asked him if he knew how old Gala was.

"I've heard she is about ten years older than Dali, but she could easily pass for forty-five," he said cautiously.

I knew Dali was born in 1904. If Field's hearsay was correct, Gala would be at least seventy. I asked him where Gala was now.

"In their suite, I suppose. She doesn't like the New York climate and she wasn't very well awhile back. She's better now, though. But to get back to the catalog, I suppose it will go on and on. Then, some year when there's nothing else coming out about Dali, Dali will say, 'Let's get the catalog out and see what happens.' Because it will be as complete as of that moment as I can make it."

It sounded like an expensive book to produce, I said.

"I don't know. That depends on whether one attempts to illustrate it."

I said I didn't see what utility it would have if it wasn't illustrated.

Field thought for a moment. "Yes, I think you're right. But in some cases the illustrations I have are so bad, to print them

would be a horror. Descharnes has a good collection, though."
And who was Descharnes?

Field reached into an open briefcase beside his chair and took
out a quarto volume I had seen displayed in a number of book-
shop windows: *The World of Salvador Dali.* The glossy cover
was illustrated with a blown-up detail of a photograph of Dali's
face, in which a watch dial with one "melting" hand was
painted into the eye.

"Descharnes wrote this book," Field said. "He's a brilliant
photographer. The book is really a combination of color photography and layout with incidental text. I translated it into
English, except for Dali's explanatory captions for the paintings. They were translated by Haakon Chevalier. I don't know
how many photographs of Dali and his work Descharnes has
made—thousands. Fortunately he has been able to photograph
most of the works that are in Spain. He has traced them to
owners in Barcelona, Cadaqués, Figueras, and other places. He
has even found some that I failed to find. I say 'even' because I
started ahead of him. Sometimes people would show me the
paintings of Dali that they had and then later on Descharnes
would talk to them, over a beer somewhere, and after a while
they'd come up with another one. I can't speak Spanish and he
can, you see. He was able to get at some things that Dali himself had forgotten about. Dali doesn't remember well the pre-
Surrealist work until he sees it, and then it comes back to him.
He has a magnificent visual memory. Almost always he can say
something about a painting beyond the fact that it's his. And
he's often a great help with the titles. You see, one problem I've
had in checking out the titles left over from the exhibition catalogs is that many Surrealist titles don't describe the subject of
the painting. What are you going to do with a title like *The
Meeting of the Illusion and the Arrested Moment?* What *can*
you do with it? Nothing. But sometimes there is a clue. One
picture I came across recently shows something that appears to
be a raindrop at the end of something else that is absolutely in-

definable. Well—it's Surrealist. I showed Dali a photograph of it, and it turned out to be *Vestige atavique après la pluie*. The raindrop put us on the right track."

It was time for me to leave. I reminded Field to send along Dali's paper about the bank's picture to me in Boston. Foret, who had been sitting so quietly and unobtrusively on the other side of Field as to have become almost invisible, stood up as I did, stuck out his hand, and said "Foret." As I acknowledged the reintroduction, he handed me a small four-page folder headlined, in French, "The book that astonishes the entire world: The Apocalypse." Underneath the title, in somewhat smaller characters, was the name "Joseph Foret," and beneath that, in smaller type, "Text by St. John, illustrated by seven great painters." The "painters," in strict alphabetical order, were Bernard Buffet, Salvador Dali, Léonor Fini, Foujita, Georges Mathieu, Trémois, Zadkine.

"I'd like to show you my book," Foret said. "It took three years to produce. It weighs nearly five hundred pounds and it's valued at over four hundred thousand dollars." He opened the folder in my hand and pointed to a photograph that looked like a French working-class funeral procession. It was captioned, "Seven men are needed to carry this precious burden." On the facing page were quotations from the French press. "Who knows," said one of them, "perhaps future generations will study this book the way we study the Great Pyramid." Another, from a paper unfamiliar to me, said, "Many go to the exhibition with skepticism, mistrusting the spell cast by publicity, but all come away convinced and shaken."

"The book has been exhibited all over France. People visit it just the way they do a monument," Foret said, quoting a caption at the bottom of page three. "I came here to arrange exhibitions in the United States. I came on a seventeen-day economy flight because I planned to be here only four days. I thought that would be time enough to make all the arrangements. But Americans take so long to make up their minds.

I've been here a month already. I'm going to wait one more week, but that's the limit."

I told him I wished I could do something to help, but I just didn't know anybody I could sell his idea to. He nodded as though he had expected that answer all along.

"I hope you will come visit my collection of Dali iconography," Field said. I told him I'd like to, and perhaps would on my next trip to New York. In using the word "iconography" I stumbled over it slightly. He corrected me gently. "Like bib-li-og-ra-phy," he said, syllabicating with precision. He issued a similar invitation to Foret.

Foret looked unhappier still. "I'm like a prisoner in my room. I'm tied to the telephone. I don't dare to go out in case someone should call while I'm gone. You can't ever rely on the switchboard operators to get a message straight."

Someone tugged at my arm. It was Dali. "Can you come see me tomorrow morning?" he asked. "There won't be all these people. We'll have a chance to talk."

What would be a good time?

"At nine thirty *je suis à vous,*" he said. We shook hands; then, grasping his silver-handled stick in one hand and the taffy blonde with the spiral coiffure in the other, he headed for the door.

Monday morning at 9:30 I rang up Dali from the St. Regis lobby. After a long wait he answered. His voice sounded fogbound. "I am in the process of getting up," he said. He asked me to wait for him in the lobby. In about twenty minutes he arrived, freshly shaved, mustache waxed, the same golden waistcoat gleaming out from beneath the same double-breasted pinstripe jacket. He was carrying a small armload of notebooks and file folders stuffed with papers.

"We'll go upstairs," he said. "Not to my suite: Madame Dali is there. Everything is in disorder. It's very complicated." We took the elevator to the seventeenth floor, walked half the length of the main corridor, and then Dali unlocked a door and let us into a sitting room. He tossed his notebooks and papers onto a coffee table and sat down on the divan. I sat down opposite him.

"I told you at Knoedler's the other day that I was doing a painting based on the principle of moiré," he said briskly. "I consider that the great discovery of my life. I had been doing research in that direction for five years when I read, in the *Sci-*

entific American, a paper by Dr. Gerald Oster and a Japanese colleague on moiré patterns, setting forth approximately the same conclusions I had reached."

I told Dali I knew of moiré in a form called watered silk used as doublures in some types of bookbinding. Was that material related to his discovery?

"That is the origin of it," he said. "The wavy, shimmering look of the fabric you're familiar with is created by folding over the ribbed cloth onto itself, with the parallel cords slightly misaligned. You exert pressure, which causes the pattern of one to be superimposed onto the other. When you open up the material, you have a new formal pattern resulting from the combination of the two. You get a comparable effect by placing together any two similarly periodic structures with alternating solid and open areas. The principle has widespread scientific application in optics, acoustics, crystallography, and many other fields."

But how did that apply to his painting?

"I'm working now," he said, "on a large painting based on the dollar sign. First of all, I adore money. After Madame Dali that is what I love the most, because I am a mystic. In the Middle Ages the mystics were often alchemists, who tried to transform base metals into gold. Then, too, I am the incarnation of Mercury and also of Pollux, so I have the right, like them, to bear the caduceus. And that, when you analyze it, is the dollar sign: two parallel vertical columns with that sinuous inscription which is a reference to the serpent.

"In Crete they represented the Dioscuri—Castor and Pollux—by two vertical bars bound together by a serpent, very much like the American dollar sign. And that is the true graphism of moiré: two vertical lines with a serpent between them—to put it in very simplified fashion. In this painting, for the first time, there will really be three dimensions—what Velásquez tried to do in *Las Meninas—The Maids of Honor.* I remember Cocteau was once asked what he would carry away if the Louvre were burning. He answered, 'I'd carry away the fire.' Later, some journalists in Madrid asked me what I would carry away if the Prado were burning. I told them I would carry away the air—specifically the air contained in Velásquez's *Meninas,* because it is air such as no one else ever painted. But now, with my studies of moiré, I can really create an optical illusion, completely physical, of a third dimension. Because I have discovered, along with Dr. Oster, that those nearly microscopic geometric structures in a moiré pattern act on the eye in exactly the same manner as mescalin or LSD. So Dali's public will be drugged with infinitely jesuitical hypocrisy because these things are invisible to the eye but react on the same part of the eye that LSD affects chemically."

I told Dali I assumed he had worked up to his conclusions on a different basis from Dr. Oster's.

He nodded. "Oster used mathematical equations. I had been studying all kinds of variations in pearl and mother-of-pearl, based on the research of Stéphen Leduc. Mother-of-pearl is a kind of equivalent of moiré. It consists of a series of layers, very near to one another, that break down the light and produce the phenomenon of iridescence. I had been experimenting with iridescence, carrying it further than anyone else had ever done, because I'm planning to produce a liquid television. I've been working on it for several years. But this will give you an idea of the adaptation of the moiré principle to painting." He reached into a notebook on the coffee table and took out a piece of stiff, crimson material, about four by six inches, with a slightly fuzzy textured finish and a subdued allover *semis* pattern. In addition to its two normal dimensions it seemed to have considerable depth. "Touch it," he said. I pressed a finger against it, and the finger appeared to sink into its surface, like a foot into a deep-pile rug, but the surface was flat and resistant with no thickness behind it. "You see?" Dali said triumphantly. "It's only an optical illusion. That's the principle of moiré. The material has all kinds of decorative uses—to put on a wall, cover a book, and so on. But up until now no one has understood the transcendent importance of that principle for painting. After all, what is this process called oil painting, invented by the Van Eycks? It is a series of layers, each one with a different geometric form resulting from its chemical content. The possibilities are infinite. It is possible to create any effect one can imagine." He pointed to the ashtray on the coffee table. "People who take LSD see this ashtray sinking into the table. They reach for it but can't touch it. The world they know suddenly becomes impossible. They are drawn to this fairy tale world but it is a complete distortion of weight and the density of matter. That is the effect I am after in my painting, but without any drug—with these almost microscopic structures."

In other words, an extension of *trompe-l'oeil*, I said.

"Exactly. And the *trompe-l'oeil* side of painting fascinates me more and more. Real painting began only with oil painting. Before then it was simply iconography. They had no means of rendering the atmosphere, the air that surrounded the objects they painted. The miraculous thing is that with earth products you can absolutely reconstitute space. That is why modern painting has gone off the track: because it has abandoned the illusionistic side, which is painting's most sublime power. Modern painting has left behind Vermeer and, instead, has set about doing things that are like posters. When you start talking about squirting paint out of the tube directly onto the wall, it becomes an absurdity. The whole spiritualizing process of art is lost. Matter itself doesn't count until it disappears to give way to an illusion of reality. The brief vogue for abstract expressionist painting—in fact the entire range of modern painting since the time of Ingres—will one day be seen as a total disaster.

"The whole Impressionist movement is nothing more than a caricature, and that holds for everything that followed it. But each little ism came up with some tiny fragment of truth. The Impressionists put the accent on the phenomenon of light. Vermeer's light was better expressed than theirs, but in their painting, light drowned out everything else, even though they didn't know what they were doing, because no Impressionist painter had a very profound understanding of what the process of painting was all about. They mixed opaque colors with transparent ones. Their paintings are just so many garbage pails. Look at them today. So many of them which were supposed to be models of luminosity have become yellow and ugly, because those painters had no sense of métier. From the point of view of technique the movement was absolute anarchy.

"After that, there was a series of reactions. People were tired of the Impressionists' formlessness of light, so we had the Cubist reaction. The Cubist partition of form was a return to a kind of Platonic classicism, but it, too, was just another caricature, much too exaggerated. Then, as a reaction against Cubist formalism, came Surrealism, which was really a kind of Romantic caricature. The subject became the protagonist of the painting, but a subject which came out of dreams, via Freud. Then another reaction—this time against the idea of the subject as the important element—abstract art. Now after forty years of that, people are so tired of spots and splashes they reach out for concrete images, but way out of context, and so we have the craze for Pop Art, in which an artist copies minutely a Coca-Cola poster. But, as I said, in all those movements there is a little fragment of truth, however much it may be distorted. Like the story Raimu told one day at the Berkeley restaurant in Paris. He started out by saying, 'When I was twenty-two years old, one night I made love twenty-four times.' Everyone hooted at him until finally, looking very sad, he said, 'Maybe not, but even so, there's a seed of truth in it. It wasn't me; it was my sister.' 'But twenty-four times!' someone objected. 'Oh, yes,' he said. 'That was the business she was in.' So all these art movements have *something* to them, some little bit of truth. But what's the result? A terrible spiritual crisis. Artistically we're in the midst of a tremendous decadence. You'd wonder how it is people could be taken in by so many different forms of nonsense, each one less meaningful than the last.

"I went to see Picasso one day while he was painting *Guernica*. He was working on the horse. He said, 'You ought to paint that horse for me. I want it to be so realistic—just like in Caravaggio—that you can smell the sweat. But I'm too old. Besides I wouldn't know how to do it. I'd rather give the ideas. If there's some good in them, someone else will take them over later on.' He's always been a creator of ideas, each day inventing something new, but he doesn't have the patience to sit down and carry them out, because if you want to be a really good painter, you need a lot of métier—things he never knew. The things he was doing in the Blue Period were fairly well drawn but not like Vermeer. That kind of painting you have to sweat out when you're young, first putting on a coat of Naples yellow, letting it dry, then adding a golden yellow to give it more transparency—all the secrets of the métier that are known to the 'official' painters, the ones that are out of fashion today, like Bouguereau or Meissonier. Why, Meissonier is a colossus from the point of view of technique. Never in a lifetime could Picasso make a decent copy of a painting by Meissonier. He wouldn't know how to go about it. That is literally true. He knows nothing about all that. Even I am not a great technician. Meissonier painted much better than Dali. If someone gave me a little painting of Meissonier's to copy, I wouldn't be able to do it. Let's not even talk about a really great painter like Vermeer. That's why I always say, although modesty is not my specialty, that if I compare myself to Velásquez or someone like that, my work is a complete catastrophe. But if I compare myself to present-day painters, I'm way up on the pinnacle. There's no need to talk about my genius; it's just that the others are so bad and they have so little grasp of métier—none, really. Not Matisse or Picasso or any of those people would have been capable of going to the Louvre and making even a mediocre copy like so many unknowns who are there doing just that. Obviously that's because they set out to do something else. We are living through a total crisis of conscience. As Rimbaud wrote and Picasso used to repeat, 'I seated Beauty on my knees and I found her bitter.' So Picasso plunged into ugliness, thinking he'd find a stronger emotion there than in beauty, which had been done and overdone since time began. He's frightened to death of being considered *pompier*—old-fashioned. I remember one day, Gala had bought three little Cubist collages. Picasso was looking at them in our apartment, a little uneasily, because he realized they weren't great works of art. He knows what Velásquez and Vermeer represent. 'Well, at any rate,' he said, 'that's a long way from Bouguereau.' And from the defensive way he said it, I knew then that he was afraid of Bouguereau. I, on the contrary, have never made any secret of the fact that it was my ambition to paint as well as Bouguereau and Meissonier. I'll never achieve it, but that's my ideal. Meanwhile, I am Dali, with a technique that may never equal Bouguereau's but is still unique because it is coupled with my own process of presenting candid snapshots of irrational imagery. I say 'irrational' because I discovered long ago that the world hasn't yet the means of distinguishing between rational and irrational; so during this transitional period we have to consider them irrational.

"You see, this *is* a period of crisis. First of all, painters have lost faith in technique. And they aren't sufficiently familiar with science to unite scientific knowledge with their aesthetic possibilities. As for religion, there are many young people who are beginning to believe once again, or who have a kind of religious feeling. Politically, they are largely disillusioned with Communism. They may have a vaguely monarchistic point of view, as I did when I was young, or like Mathieu, who is a fervent monarchist. But the temper of our times has been set by that period a little further back when artists believed in nothing, not in religion or the family or aesthetics or technique. That's very abnormal. When you don't believe in anything, you're not capable of painting anything. And that's the point we've reached. And so they wind up by painting something all black or all white—anything at all—that they subjectively endow with the notion that here is the cosmos. It's the story of *Le Chef-d'oeuvre inconnu* of Balzac: great anxiety and a terrible drive toward the Absolute. They're smitten with the cosmos, but they have no means of handling it or of achieving anything at all. That is why we are reaching the end of an epoch. In my own case, it was only when I began to believe in science, and through that in eternity and the existence of God, that I saw where I was going. Until now nobody had believed in realism for a very long time. It had been too worn out by academicism. But once painters rediscover it, through either a mystical state or a new feeling for the object, then we'll have a real renaissance. Because all these so-called revolutions we have lived through from Ingres until now, all that is useful. The realist painter who comes to dominate his period after all that won't be like Bouguereau; he'll be something different, someone who will incorporate spiritually all the adventures, all the failures, all the drama of modern art, and he will have been able to sublimate all the *élan vital* that implies in a new classical wrapping. Now, the mediocre abstract painters only paint the microcosmos. Look in a scientific magazine and you'll see photographs of the chromosomes, the trajectory of a proton, or the collision of a particle with an antiparticle—all with a strong resemblance to what the abstract painters are doing. But the true painter must paint the macrocosmos—your nose and your mouth. What would be fascinating would be for painters to paint the macrocosmos, but with the experience of the microcosmos behind them. What distinguishes our age from the Renaissance is that now for the first time we realize that matter, instead of being something continuous, is discontinuous. As Eddington pointed out, if one wanted to give an accurate representation of a table, instead of being compact the table should resemble something like a swarm of flies. That is the true understanding of matter, and some artists have sensed it. Impres-

sionism led to the Pointillism of Seurat, the Divisionism of the
touch, which was already a foretaste of the discontinuity of matter. After that, Cubism began to divide up form in its own
special way, and that, too, is a reference to the discontinuity of
matter. But until now we have only been fragmenting matter.
That is why the paintings of Velásquez are so fascinating. When
you study one of them closely, you can say that this canvas was
painted with so-and-so-many brushstrokes, because each stroke
is separate from every other. Velásquez is a great precursor. And
he is the precursor of my painting of the dollars. When you
analyze the pattern of his brushstroke closely, you see that there
are always two vertical lines and then a curved line. His vertical
lines define the object, and the curved line rounds it off and
creates the space around it. We might say that Velásquez was
already painting the dollar sign at that time. He was *the* great
painter of the Spanish imperial period, with that melancholy
that came to him from his Portuguese side and that adds to
Spanish painting, which is too dry, a kind of moist quality that
is absolutely sublime. Quevedo has written some wonderful
things about Velásquez. In one passage he made what amounts
to a complete analysis of what today we call *tachisme*. He said
that Velásquez painted with *chafarrinadas*, a kind of brushstroke applied with a great deal of brutality to those things he
wanted to be most careful about, and with *borrones*, which are
somewhat vaguer streaks. All the beauty of Velásquez's *tachisme*
lay in the fact that these streaks were so separate as to appear
distant, one from another: that is, the way he set down his
taches made the object appear closer or farther away. In contemporary abstract painting, the brushstrokes are all laid out
on a surface in such a way that what results is only decoration;
whereas in Velásquez, all those *taches* were set down so rele-
vantly that they describe something."

Dali looked around the room, then riffled through his papers
on the table in front of him. "It is almost impossible to talk
about this without being able to show you his method with the

tip of a brush—what was called at that period *bravura di tocco*. That is what Mathieu does today, in his way of attacking the canvas. Picasso did the same thing constantly. And that, I discovered, is what Meissonier did, too. He had the same *bravura di tocco* as Velásquez. He was the slickest painter in the world; then suddenly he would add just what he needed to make a nose shine or two or three nails in a chair stand out with a maximum of luminosity. A painting by Meissonier is a sublime thing because everything in it is prepared in such a way as to lead up to those three brushstrokes—and they are the three strokes of genius, so perfect that they contain the whole cosmos. If there is only the head of a pin that interests him, *that* is what reaches out and grabs you.

"Things like that are completely neglected today. There are people like Arman and Roy Lichtenstein who seek to bring out the mystery of an object. Lichtenstein says, 'I don't want anyone to feel the intervention of the artist in any way,' and so he gets down on his knees before some anonymous machine-made object. That is the attitude of the absolute realist. Of course, when Vermeer painted his city of Delft, he didn't want to interfere in any way with things as they were. He wanted only to make a copy of what his eyes saw. He was in love with the city he was born in, and his act of love was to try to render exactly what he saw. The moral position of Roy Lichtenstein, although it's a caricature of that, is a true one and will have an elevating effect on others. The pure act of opening up his heart before reality, to fall in love with it—even if it is a Coca-Cola poster— is something."

I asked Dali what he felt this kind of "pure act" would elevate painting above.

"Above the cult of ugliness," he said. "The greatest disaster in art is the tendency toward Expressionism in all its forms. We should no longer put up with the slightest distortion in a painting. If one is painting a face, all the proportions should be absolutely correct, just as in a photograph. That's the way it is with the most immortal things in the history of art. Take Praxiteles' *Hermes*, for example. To achieve that kind of perfection the Greeks often used casts of parts of the human body. If you took color photographs of the city of Delft and compared them to Vermeer's paintings, you would find they were absolutely the same thing, the only difference being that the photograph would have been made by a rigidly inflexible camera, and the painting by a divine camera, the most sublime apparatus there is—the eye—and filtered through the sensitivity of the brain. The world's great masterpieces are always works in which the artist has not needed the slightest deformation in order to express his thought. As soon as Expressionism began— let's say with Goya—things started to fall apart. In the painting of character, which presupposes a certain measure of caricature, there is the beginning of weakness. The greatness of Velásquez lies in his not changing anything. His personages are exactly the way they looked. The proportions aren't arranged, any more than in Praxiteles or Vermeer. There is no deformation at all, and these artists are the ones who have most truly expressed something, whereas the Expressionists, by definition, are those who have nothing to express. They express nothing but try very hard to put across the idea that they are expressing all kinds of feelings. Modigliani, for example. Even El Greco is a disaster. Oh, he's more important than Cézanne, because his was a great period, but in comparison to Velásquez he expresses nothing. His work is caricature. That's why people understand him and like him. Instead of presenting his ideas in a sublime manner, he presented them like caricatures, and people adore caricatures. That's why they like Piero della Francesca better than Raphael. Piero has the ideas of Raphael but caricatured. Everything of Piero della Francesca is in Raphael but expressed, as in Mozart, with exquisite balance."

Dali looked at me piercingly. "Yes, I know what you're thinking: the avant-garde says Raphael is out, Piero is in. They know nothing. They say Dali is *pompier,* but I am the most avant-garde artist of our times because I am the only one who has truly scientific knowledge. A very brilliant young atomic scientist who studied with the Prince de Broglie and Niels Bohr has written a book on my painting. He says I am the only one to have found a valid cosmogony consistent with the advances of modern science. The so-called avant-garde will tell you anything. They will even tell you that Cézanne is the great French painter. For me he's one of the worst who ever lived. He was very honest, with admirable ambitions, although very reactionary. He wanted to do over Poussin according to nature. He wanted to do things in perspective, but since he didn't know how to paint, he got everything backwards. If he tried to make a flat table, it came out slanted. If he wanted to do something round, it came out square. He had high intentions, but after him painting went all to pieces."

The phone in the bedroom behind us started to ring. It rang faster and faster and Dali talked louder and louder. Finally the phone on the table beside us started in. Dali picked it up. *"Allô.* Yes. Yes. Yes. Ees not too much deefficulty? Ees my fault. Yes. For me ees okay. For me ees pairfect. Ees no necessary. Sank you. Sank you." He hung up, began whistling a drearily tuneless air, then stopped. "No, Cézanne is the worst," he said, then seemed to reconsider. "Oh, not quite. There are always the English painters. They're abominable. The worst one of all is Turner. Compared with him Cézanne is a genius. At least Cézanne had an idea of constructing things, and they do hold together, after a fashion; there is a kind of solidity. But Turner, he wanted to make things that were luminous, and when you look at them now—all smoke and nicotine, drab and dirty— they're a total disaster. On the other hand, the pre-Raphaelite group is splendid. Huntington Hartford has given over a whole room to them in his new gallery: Burne-Jones, Rossetti, Millais, and the others. They are the only English painters who will live, as documents of psychoanalytical types, a certain kind of neurotic, with qualities outside the pictorial. From a literary point of view it is amazing painting. Beautiful. They're the only interesting English painters. Of course, they aren't in a class with someone like Meissonier. They're English painters, and that means a very inferior strain."

Who are the interesting French painters? I asked. Other than Meissonier, that is. Dali pulled at his mustache.

"Not poor old Cézanne," he said. He hesitated. "Of course, there is Millet."

Millet of *The Angelus*? I asked him.

He nodded solemnly. "Of course. *The Angelus* is the most erotic picture ever painted."

The Angelus? A peasant couple standing in a field at dusk, facing each other, their heads bowed; the man holding his hat in front of him, waist-high; the woman with hands clasped under her chin in an attitude of prayer; beside them, a pitchfork, a basket, and a loaded wheelbarrow. That *Angelus*?

"The most erotic picture ever painted," Dali repeated quietly. "It is a masterpiece of disguised sexual repression. If Freud were here, he would back me up. That image has obsessed millions of people ever since Millet painted it. Why? It has obsessed me ever since the summer of 1932. Why? I'll tell you why. One day in June, 1932, without any visual reference or association of ideas or traceable memory, I suddenly saw that picture in my mind's eye, in full color, and I realized it was one of the most haunting, enigmatic pictures ever painted, with layer on layer of unconscious meaning. There is no easy explanation for the disturbing effect that vision had on me. I simply understood, all at once, just what that picture was about. The new mental image of it that I had constantly before me was a paranoiac vision: that is, it corresponded in its slightest detail to the picture as I knew it in the original and in reproduction, but at the same time it was charged with such *new* significance as to make it, simultaneously, a completely *different* object. At the surface level this is exceedingly curious. It is a relatively trivial and insignificant image and yet it is by far the most widely reproduced of all the stereotypes in mass circulation. This is true in almost every country of the western world. And it is bought, almost invariably, by people who have no conception of what they are buying.

"A few weeks after I had my vision of *The Angelus* in the summer of 1932, a visitor to the Louvre drove a hole through the original painting. They locked him up, of course. Later, he was visited by the psychoanalyst Dr. Jacques Lacan. He told Lacan he had planned to stave in the "most famous" painting in the Louvre, but at first he hadn't been able to make up his mind whether it should be the *Mona Lisa, The Embarkation for Cythera* of Watteau, or *The Angelus*. After much thought he had settled on *The Angelus*. His preoccupation with the *Mona Lisa* is very understandable—and significant. It, too, is a mysterious and obsessional painting. After all that Freud has taught us about Leonardo, it's only too obvious that the *Mona Lisa* has an incestuous fascination for all Oedipus types. The woman portrayed is the ideal type of maternal beauty, and that renowned enigmatic smile, what is it but the inscrutable Sphinx before whom every overdependent son lays his anxieties? So there is a close link—the Oedipus complex—between the *Mona Lisa* and *The Angelus*. I won't get involved with *The Embarkation for Cythera* here. It's a very long and complex matter and would take us too far afield. Let's get back to *The Angelus*. Don't forget that at the height of his madness, Van Gogh painted a number of copies of Millet's works from postcards. Now, how do you explain the effect—the appeal to violence—of this painting, which superficially seems a pretty conventional and banal affair? Just how could this placid old chromo induce such violent reactions—whatever form they may take—in almost everybody? First of all, it is a twilight setting, with all the atavistic connotations that implies—dreams, reverie, so-called poetic yearnings, the stillness that conjures up the aura of an earlier, happier day: in other words, back to the womb. Then, consider the position of the woman, standing head bowed, hands clasped under her chin, with all the erotic symbolism of mystical ecstasies. Both the male and the female figure are, of course, motionless. But whereas the man's immobility is passive, the woman's is definitely active. Below the waist her body projects an attitude of expectant exhibitionism—not very far from the stance of the praying mantis: in other words, the immobility that announces imminent sexual aggression. The female figure represents the mother; the male is the son, dominated and immobilized by the irresistible erotic attraction of the mother. The hat is a familiar sexual symbol in dreams. Here it shows clearly the son's desire to cover the all too evident symbol of sexual excitement and thus doubly symbolizes the act of coitus. You see?"

This was a new view of *The Angelus* for me. I asked Dali if he had other evidence to substantiate his thesis.

"Naturally," he said. "What is the most significant element of the composition beyond the two human figures?"

I suggested the wheelbarrow.

"Exactly. Now, you remember the wheelbarrow has two sacks in it, the smaller, thicker one backing heavily into the taller, thinner one. This, you see, represents the act of incest, the male holding the female by the waist and accomplishing the sexual act from the rear—the most animalistic and atavistic of all the positions. Beyond that, the wheelbarrow itself is one of the fantasies most richly endowed by farm laborers with erotically symbolic overtones." He paused. "What it all adds up to is this," he said. "The male and the female figure, facing each other, motionless, in that irresistible crepuscular solitude, goaded by the incestuous act in its most atavistic posture taking place in the wheelbarrow. And as a final savage touch, the sharp-tined fork sticking upright into the furrowed earth—another reference to the maternal element. It is inescapable."

He made out a very convincing case, I told him.

"I wrote a book about it," he said, "and then lost the manuscript just before leaving France at the time of the German occupation. I have found it again and it has just been published in France, in a small edition. But there I make out a much *more* convincing case. Here I have only been able to suggest a few of the key points."

I asked him if his thesis extended to all of Millet's work or applied only to *The Angelus.*

"Oh, no. Millet's entire work is impregnated with eroticism. Take the painting *Motherly Solicitude* in the Louvre: the mother, standing in the entrance to the farmhouse, bends over from behind to hold up the clothes of her little boy so he can make *pipi* out the door. There is surely a point to be made about penis envy, with the voyeurism of the little sister, who stands just outside the door peeking at him. And in *The Harvesters,* what a wealth of significant detail in the posture of the reclining mother with her head, in three-quarter profile, resting in the lap of the mysterious, shadowy, muscled male figure behind her, at the same time as her naked child, clutching her around the upper thighs, burrows deep into her lap. And *The Winnower,* with his basket, portrayed in the act of *throwing out his seed!* Technically, by the way, *The Winnower* is a perfect foretaste of Van Gogh. You might say that it's the beginning of Van Gogh. Of course it's very erotic. Van Gogh was obsessed with Millet, and he never really understood why, poor devil. And in *The Straw-Binders,* you remember how the men crouch down, their knees spread apart, pulling in to their loins the sheaves of hay?"

He shook his head. "The man was absolutely obsessed. And to think they used to talk about *The Angelus* as 'an expression of the noblest and most elevated religious sentiment.' Millet himself, when he finished it, said he wanted to give an impression of music and he wanted the noises of the country and even church bells to be heard. They may be there, but they're drowned into silence by the roar of the blood coursing through his veins. He didn't have the faintest idea of what he was doing, of course. But who does?"

Dali reached down into his mass of papers and drew out a folded sheet. "Here is a nineteenth-century American document I found. It is extraordinary. It has an erotic significance, obviously, but behind that there is a religious meaning." He opened up the paper. It was captioned "Hard Times on the Farm" and showed an American farm wife wearing a checkered shirtwaist, a long skirt, an apron, and heavy brogans, her face hidden behind a poke bonnet. She was propelling her husband —a typical hayseed Uncle Sam caricature with chin whiskers, a corncob pipe and a ten-gallon hat—across a field. The husband's body was suspended horizontally about a foot above the ground, supported in front by a single small wheel with crossbar which he grasped underneath his chest. In the rear his wife held him by the boots, one on each side of her sturdy frame, like the handles of a wheelbarrow, as she trundled him along to plow the field, the blade of the "plow" being the husband's rigid penis furrowing the earth but now up against an impenetrable subterranean obstruction ("By golly Sally I gess yer hit something").

"People talk about women's rights," Dali said. "It all boils down to this. In the matriarchy of America, woman wants to put herself in the man's place, reducing him to the status of a simple tool of productivity—even to the point of castrating him. There are countless references to this symbolic function of man in astrological and mystical texts that speak of the work of the father as being nothing more than 'the passage of the divine plow.' That is the divine plow—fecundation. Here it is at the most popular iconographic level: the man completely dehumanized. Stylistically, all this derives from Millet. And as you know, Van Gogh does, too. And Seurat." Dali reached into his papers once more and finally found a sheet that reproduced a conté crayon drawing known as *The Potato Harvest,* by Millet, showing a man and a woman loading sacks onto a wheelbarrow. "It is obvious that Seurat couldn't have existed without Millet. Again, it's a question of caricature. Seurat simply stylizes to the point of caricature the volumes in a drawing like this one. Never did Seurat make anything more monumental and enveloped in light and astonishing in the layout of its composition than that."

I told Dali it was obvious that the art historian in him was in danger of getting the better of the painter.

He replaced his documents in their folder. "What nobody understands today—painter *or* art historian—is that the most important thing about any picture is its subject," he said. "Throughout the history of art the subject has been what counts; yet it is what everyone today overlooks. Every painting of importance has an important subject. This is true even in the case of those who thought the subject didn't matter. Cézanne painted apples. Does that prove me wrong? Not at all: the apple is one of the most important subjects in history. It begins with Adam and Eve, then the Judgment of Paris, then William Tell, then Newton. It's one of the outstanding archetypes, as full of significance as today's atom, ready to burst open. Cézanne didn't paint carrots; it had to be apples. So the subject does have importance, even for Cézanne. Why, that's as much of a subject as Velásquez had in the *Surrender of Breda,* or Raphael in *The Marriage of the Virgin,* or Millet in *The Angelus.* From among a thousand things he might paint the painter chooses one. The choice is enormous. In abstract painting, too, the choice is wide: from the trajectory of a proton to the explosion of an antiparticle—the subject is the essential thing. And we will again have great painting when we have, once more, painting centered on great subjects which have been modified by the times we are living in and expressed with a realist technique strengthened by the discoveries of modern science. That will be the contribution of abstract painting. After all, the new painters will emerge from things that are going on today; there's no disputing that. What is lamentable is when you have a young painter who pays no attention to what is going on around him and considers that everything in modern painting is worthless and just sits down in front of a boat to paint the usual old realistic things that have no interest. The abstract painters, at least, have lived through an authentic drama of our times, whereas the old-line realist painters haven't understood anything of what has been taking place. They're just imbeciles. The new painter is the one who has understood all that terrible catastrophe that has happened to modern art, very similar to the sort of thing that has been happening politically, like the Russian Revolution, which demolished all the institutions, wiped out all the past, but still won't be able to prevent a reestablishment of the monarchy in Europe. There is no human effort that is not useful. Everything counts. And the intelligent painters are those who will be able to integrate into classicism even the wildest experiments, the most disordered and chaotic of our time."

I pointed out to him the apparent contradiction between his earlier statement that painting must be an exact rendering of the object seen and his indictment of realist painters.

"There's no contradiction," he said. "Realist painters like those have no technique at all. None. Take this man Annigoni, for instance, who paints the Queen of England. He has no technique. He just doesn't know his business."

I asked him about Balthus.

He looked very dubious, then, grudgingly, said, "Yes, he has certain qualities, but he hasn't taken part in any of that revolution, so he shows the lack of having passed through all those things. I have done every kind of experimental thing. I've even painted with a spray gun. I've exploded a hand grenade on my work to see the consequences of that. I've gone from one adventure to another, but I've made a careful distinction between the experimental side and my work itself. Some of the experiments are more interesting than my paintings. But my ambition is to incorporate, to sublimate, my experiments into the great classical tradition. My work from now on will be in the tradition of Spanish realist painting because I'm Spanish and I can't escape it. It's the greatest thing in the world." The phone began ringing insistently. Dali shouted at it to stop. It did. He picked up the receiver, said, *"Allô. Non,"* and hung up.

I said I thought that few would agree that the acquisition of a first-rate technique was enough to make a good painter, no matter how gifted he might be in that way.

Dali opened his eyes very wide. "In the present state of painting, that by itself would be very remarkable," he said, "but then, after that, it would be necessary for him to be a Meissonier or a Dali or someone like that. Technique in the hands of someone like Meissonier becomes something extraordinary. Of course, Meissonier is French, but when that same technique is at the disposal of someone like Fortuny—well, as I've said already, Fortuny will one day be looked on as *the* great painter of modern times. But he was Spanish and had the Spanish genius behind him. Of course, he lived in a time that was already decadent. After Velásquez everything began to decline. Necessarily. Occasionally there is a thrust up from that decline. Fortuny is one of those: a great *petit maître*. Of course, you can't place him beside the great masters of all time: in Italy, Raphael; in Holland, Vermeer; and then, perhaps the greatest genius of all, Velásquez. Not long ago I showed some enlargements of details from a painting by Velásquez to De Kooning. He said, 'That's Action Painting raised to the sublime.' I suppose by that he meant that it was by someone who really knew how to paint."

Again the phone began to ring in the bedroom. Finally Dali ran in to it. By the time he got there it had stopped. The one beside me started, even more insistently. Dali came back into the sitting room. I handed him the phone. *"Allô. Non. Non. Non."* He hung up.

I saw it was nearly train time. I got up and picked up my hat and coat.

"When do you go back to Paris?" Dali asked me.

At the end of the month, I told him.

"Good. I will be there two weeks after that. At the Meurice. Come see me. We have to finish this conversation. It's very important."

I told him I would and reminded him not to let Field forget to send me the paper.

Dali nodded. "Very soon," he said. He picked up the telephone and began leafing through a small black address book.

I walked out to the elevator and pressed the button. Almost at once the red light flashed and the doors opened. I stepped inside. There was one other passenger. I saw that it was Foret, the publisher of the five-hundred-pound book. He looked gloomier than ever. I greeted him. He seemed surprised that someone should be addressing him. I sensed that he hadn't recognized me. I told him I had just left Dali. The elevator doors opened and we walked out into the lobby. He appeared not to have understood.

"I don't know where Dali is," he said, absently. "We had an appointment. I've been calling him from my room all morning but he can't be found."

PART TWO

When I reached Paris two weeks later, Dali—past and present—was everywhere in evidence. The largest retrospective exhibition of the Surrealist movement ever held had just been installed in the Galerie Charpentier, across the street from the Élysée Palace, the home, as one commentator put it, of "the most surreal of our Presidents of the Republic." Long lines of the nostalgic were forming daily up and down the Faubourg St.-Honoré to file past the more than five hundred exhibits collected from ten different countries.

Surrealism as a literary, artistic, or quasi-philosophical movement had been born officially in 1924 after five years' gestation, with the poets André Breton, Louis Aragon, Paul Éluard, and Benjamin Péret as founding fathers. The four of them had broken away from the Dada movement in 1922 in the hope of establishing, out of the nihilism of Dada, a brave new world of wonder and beauty, still antilogical but not anarchical. Dada had been founded in Zurich in 1916 by a group that included Hugo Ball, Tristan Tzara, Richard Huelsenbeck, and Hans Arp. Its name had been taken from a dictionary opened at random. Dada's program was clear-cut: to wipe out all the old standards of value. Art, aesthetic attitudes, the family, the class system, politics, religion, established order (the police, the army), and hand-me-down concepts of morality were prime targets. Surrealism inherited these targets but aimed more specifically at social improvement—up to a point—and Breton and some of the other Surrealists eventually joined the Communist Party. But later on, when Aragon tried to turn the Surrealist movement into a political-action subdivision of the Party, Breton called a halt and *that* honeymoon was over. The revolution Breton was working for was not one that could be ruled by the commissars; it was the triumph of desire over constraint, and the elimination of all conventional modes of thought. The world was obviously in bad shape. Something new had to be tried. For Breton, the simplest Surrealist act consisted in "going out into the street, revolver in hand, and shooting wildly into the crowd." Breton never did that, nor did any of his disciples, but talking about it was all part of what Breton called their "passionate quest for liberty."

The central figure in Surrealism's pantheon, enshrined among such notables as Lautréamont, Baudelaire, Rimbaud, Alfred Jarry, Raymond Roussel, and the Marquis de Sade, was Freud. Breton's definition of Surrealism reflects Freud's importance to the group. Surrealism, for him, was "pure psychic automatism by means of which we propose to express, in speech, writing, or any other manner, the true function of thought. The dictation of thought, in the absence of any control exercised by reason, outside of all aesthetic or moral considerations. . . . Surrealism is founded on the belief in the higher reality of certain forms of association neglected until now, on the all-power of dream, on the undirected free play of thought . . ."

The path through this metaphysical maze was largely uncharted, and in their progress toward its high-sounding but ill-defined objectives, Breton and his group quarreled more and more frequently. Aragon's continuing and devious involvement with dialectical materialism provoked one of many such clashes. Breton ruled with a firm hand and seemed to acquire a taste for excommunication. In the exercise of his papal function he managed to dispossess his movement of its most illustrious exemplars. Aragon was not the first to go, nor was Max Ernst the last—Ernst was expelled by Breton in 1954 for accepting the Venice Biennale painting prize (for "compromising with the Finance Pump," as Breton put it). Weaving in and around their departures were those of a number of poets and painters who, all by themselves, very nearly form a *Who's Who* of the literary and artistic avant-garde. Among them were Marinetti, Cocteau, Antonin Artaud, Robert Desnos, André Masson, Philippe Soupault, Michel Leiris, Jacques Prévert, Raymond Queneau, Buñuel, René Char, Giacometti, Georges Hugnet, Arp, Hans Bellmer, Man Ray, Domínguez, Matta, Miró, Séligmann, Yves Tanguy, and a number of others including—after a series of unheeded warnings in the mid-thirties—Dali.

Following two earlier exploratory forays, Dali had come to live in Paris in 1929. Late that year, preceded by a small group of his newest paintings, he arrived in Paris for his first French exhibition, at the Goemans gallery in the Rue de Seine. In that group were such well-known paintings as *The Lugubrious Game, Illumined Pleasures, Accommodations of Desire, The Face of the Great Masturbator,* and the *Portrait of Paul Éluard,* the Surrealist poet whom Dali had met on one of his earlier visits, and whose Russian wife, Gala, was soon to leave him for Dali. Dali had painted most of those pictures that summer. They reflected in some measure the influence of Giorgio de Chirico, with a haunting perspective of infinitely receding planes and hallucinatory handling of light and shadow which emphasized the bizarre nature of their subject matter. But that subject matter, along with a marked technical brilliance, was Dali's own: a new and particularized pictorial expression of the unconscious and of the world of dreams. It was a world of terror, with a gamut that ran from foreboding to frenzy.

In his foreword to the exhibition catalog, Breton wrote that this was perhaps "the first time that the mental windows have been opened wide. . . . We feel ourselves sliding toward the trap door of an evil sky." The lions' heads, the profiled lips mating with the praying mantis, and the other haunting and incongruous symbols which filled Dali's canvases frightened and excited Breton. His fright may well have been largely literary, but his excitement was undoubtedly very real. There was something both ominous and promising in all these pictures, and the world, for Breton, was a very ominous place, with evil and beauty alternately hiding behind and covering up each other.

Dali's art, Breton realized, was "the most hallucinatory we have yet seen." It was a "veritable menace. Completely new beings, visibly ill-intentioned, have started on the march." With "somber joy" he noted that this invading army of new imagery could hardly be resisted by the tattered remnants of what up until then had passed for reality. That old-time reality had been Breton's main target; now, with the full Freudian arsenal in the hands of a man who could put paint onto canvas as skillfully and as imaginatively as Dali, it was surely doomed. Although Krafft-Ebing was soon to appear on the Surrealists' "don't-read" list, his case histories were already beginning to reappear, in even more startling form, among Dali's dream imagery. Breton adopted Dali.

In his book *La Femme Visible,* published the following year, Dali set out a target of his own: "to systematize confusion and to contribute to the total discredit of the world of reality." In launching the book, Breton and Éluard declared that it was up to Dali more than to anyone else to liberate man from that "cavern of lies," that "miserable expedient that calls itself reality." The instrument of liberation was to be what Dali called his "paranoiac-critical method." Basically, it involved setting down an obsessional idea suggested by the unconscious and then elaborating and reinforcing it by a perverse association of ideas and a seemingly irrefutable logic until it took on the conviction of inescapable truth. It corresponded exactly to Dali's pictorial technique of giving to the most incongruous or unbelievable material such detail and precision that it acquired, in the process, a life of its own and became almost plausible.

Dali brought new life and directions to the Surrealist movement. The films, highly subversive by intent and in effect, on which he collaborated with his countryman Luis Buñuel—*Un Chien andalou* (1929) and *L'Age d'or* (1930)—caused riots and quickly became classics. His Surrealist objects were in the tradition of Picasso and Marcel Duchamp but with an added dimension: the "marvelous" as filtered through the method of paranoiac obsession. One of the primal qualities of many Surrealist objects was an insistent eroticism. Formed or found by chance, subject to "continuous transformation," these objects could be considered as a "precipitate of our desire," Breton wrote in presenting the first exhibition of Surrealist objects in May, 1936, at the Charles Ratton gallery in the Rue de Marignan. There were natural objects from the mineral, vegetable and animal kingdoms, some of which had been "interpreted" (i.e., worked over) and others "incorporated" into other agglomerations; "disturbed" objects—such as household utensils found after the eruption of Mont Pelée on the island of Martinique in 1902; found objects which had appealed, for reasons often unknown, to members of the group; Eskimo and Indian objects, masks from Oceania, now-historic "ready-mades" such as Marcel Duchamp's bottle rack of 1914, a Calder mobile, Picasso's celebrated sculpture *Glass of Absinth,* Meret Oppenheim's fur-covered cup, saucer, and spoon, and two objects by Dali: *The Aphrodisiac Jacket* and *Monument to Kant.*

But whether it was language, object, or action, it was the unexpected, the incongruous, the disturbingly fascinating, which labeled itself Surrealist. "The chocolate umbrella has lost its gilding. Dip it in the door and plait" was one of the *papillons* that Surrealist activists pasted up in likely spots. The call for a spiritualizing alchemy went out in the form of "You who have lead in your head, melt it down into Surrealist gold." The world had to be waked up at any cost, and the mildest of the battle cries were such slogans as "If you like love, you'll love Surrealism," and "If you're not a priest, a general, or an ass, you'll be a Surrealist," and the stern "Unbutton your brain as often as your fly."

From the very beginning the unity of the Surrealist movement had been almost continuously shaken by the divergent aims and motivations of its stronger members. Dali's collaboration compensated for some of the vagueness of the "revolutionary phrase-makers," but his greatest strength—his unpredictable independence—soon got him into trouble. Even before he became a member of the group, they were trying to modify, if not dictate, the content of his painting. And as early as 1934 he had been called to account for what seemed to some members an unacceptably ambivalent attitude toward Hitler. In his explanation Dali went to great pains to separate the aesthetic from the political in his feeling for the Führer. What fascinated *him,* he claimed, was the soft, plump flesh he felt every time he began to paint Hitler in his tight-fitting military tunic.

A few years later Dali was accused of racism, for Latin-supremacy theories which may have been nothing more than a combination of his paranoiac-critical method and Spanish pride. But his enormous commercial success in the United States and his well-publicized obeisance to Franco (whose forces had earlier executed Dali's best friend, the poet Federico García Lorca) finally forced Breton's hand and he expelled him from the Surrealist movement. But that didn't interfere with Dali's commercial success, and the anagram of his name with which Breton labeled him—Avida Dollars—seemed each year more appropriate.

It wasn't only the Galerie Charpentier that was bursting with renewed Surrealist activity when I reached Paris in the spring of 1964. All the Paris newspapers were, too. Even before the exhibition opened, André Breton had denounced it in the pages of *Le Monde*. Two earlier important exhibitions devoted to Surrealism—one held in 1938 at Wildenstein's Paris gallery, the other in 1947 at the Galerie Maeght—had been organized by Breton. In them he and his collaborators had tried to create an atmosphere that would make people think of Surrealism as a state of mind rather than a period in the history of painting or literature. The newest and biggest exhibition had been organized by Patrick Waldberg, an art critic who had broken with the movement in 1951, and Breton—whose official communiqué referred to Waldberg as the author of "a little work quite elegantly perfidious enough to please"—could hardly be expected to like the way *he* had arranged matters. He even went on the air and said he didn't. For one thing, Breton didn't care for the use, in speaking of the exhibition, of the word *bilan*—balance sheet. It smacked too much of the bookkeeper's ledger and made Surrealism seem a thing of the past. Surrealism had existed before him, Breton said, and he expected it to survive him. A really dynamic exhibition, he wrote in the Paris weekly *Arts*, would show what Surrealism was up to at this very moment, rather than limit its scope to some dusty relics of a bygone, no matter how glorious, past. He accused the Galerie Charpentier "enterprise" of aiming at the liquidation of Surrealism, whereas Surrealism was still very much alive, and to prove it he spoke of projects, planned and under way, that included an exhibition, a film, several books, and a magazine.

Raymond Nacenta, director of the Galerie Charpentier, applauded politely these evidences of Surrealism's continuing vigor but made the point, in rebuttal, that this was no reason for depriving the public of a view of some of the major works of Surrealism's greatest artists, many of which had never been shown in Paris. Furthermore, he pointed out, the official Surrealist group couldn't possibly assemble such an exhibition itself. Since Breton had excommunicated all of its great men at one time or another, he could hardly readopt them now. Nacenta suggested that the main thing wrong with this exhibition, in Breton's eyes, was the fact that it had been assembled by still another ex-Surrealist: a heretic, hence eternally damned.

But the heretic, Mr. Patrick Waldberg, had done a very thorough job, I saw when I visited the Galerie Charpentier. Almost nothing had been omitted. One section of the premises had been given over to works by some of the artists of earlier periods whom the Surrealists considered their precursors: Hieronymus Bosch, Brueghel, Arcimboldo, Delacroix, Grandville, Bresdin, Odilon Redon, Gustave Moreau, and Méryon. The smaller rooms were filled with Surrealist objects, books, magazines, tracts, manifestos, catalogs, prospectuses, bulletins, invitations, primitive masks, dolls, fetishes, and a fair number of taxidermist's specimens, including one of the great anteater. One critic called the show "a kind of museum of horrors for overgrown children." That was unnecessarily harsh, I thought, as I made my way through the crowds that filled the small center rooms between the two main galleries. And yet the darker, more crowded corners did resemble somewhat an overstuffed attic in a Charles Addams Victorian Gothic mansion whose trunks and storage boxes had spilled out an incredible profusion of mementos of one's more eccentric ancestors.

Along both sides of the main hall, fronting on the Faubourg St.-Honoré, alcoves had been set up, each of them given over to one of the major painters of the Surrealist movement: Dali's alcove contained four oil paintings including the celebrated *The Lugubrious Game,* which had been shown in his first Paris exhibition, at the Galerie Goemans, and one version of the "soft" watches that, in the minds of many, stand as his trademark. There were drawings, also, and the catalog listed, in addition, several Surrealist objects attributed to Dali, including the well-known *Venus with Drawers* and an entry entitled *Homage to Kant.* These two objects were not visible from the alcove where his paintings and drawings had been hung. I asked one of the gallery attendants where I might find them.

He pointed over the heads of the crowd in the direction of two long glass cases behind us, across the front wall of the gallery. Many of the smaller objects were there, he said, but the *Venus* hadn't shown up; he wasn't sure just why. When I had finally squeezed my way through the crowds to reach the glass cases, which were about seven feet high, I saw that they had three interior shelves containing at least forty assorted Surrealist objects. The *Homage to Kant,* which was listed as an object found by Dali in 1936, was a squarish pile about eight inches high, somewhat smaller at the top than at the bottom, carved out of a greenish-yellow, veined, translucent stone and bearing a bronze plaque with an inscription in German headed "Immanuel Kant (1724–1804)"—all in all, an unexpectedly restrained and sober piece. The light was bad, the crowd made it impossible to stand in one spot for very long, and so I left, planning to return for another look some morning, when, I assumed, attendance would be lighter.

A few days after my visit to the Galerie Charpentier I read in *Le Figaro* that Dali had arrived in Paris, that he would be spending his spare time making a sculpture of the Venus de Milo, and that he would send "it, too," to Tokyo. Like most newspaper articles this one was somewhat incomplete and didn't specify why, for what, or—particularly annoying in the light of the "it, too,"—in addition to what. The idea for the sculpture had come to him, I read, as he looked out at the Louvre from his hotel windows. The reporter quoted Dali as saying that twenty-five years ago he had already restyled "the Greek masterpiece" by adding drawers all over its body to show that *his* Venus was of Freud's century, and that her psychic nature flowed from hidden springs. I learned, also, that the first volume of Dali's *Le Journal d'un génie* was to be published in a few days.

Dali's archivist, Albert Field, had told me, that Sunday evening in the King Cole Bar several weeks earlier, that Dali was a "very interesting man—more interesting than anyone realizes." I had come away from the long session I had had with

Dali the following morning on the seventeenth floor of the St. Regis convinced that Field had not exaggerated. Before I left the States, I had decided to write a long piece—perhaps even a book—about Dali. I was planning to call him within the week but I had not yet got around to it when I read, five or six days later, another article in *Le Figaro* headlined "Dali Will Say Tomorrow Whether There Is a Forgery at the Galerie Charpentier." The first part of the article was concerned with the launching of *Le Journal d'un génie* but the last two paragraphs explained that in reading the catalog of the Surrealism exhibition, Dali had noted "with . . . stupefaction" that No. 95—*Hommage à Kant*—was attributed to him. He had no recollection of having "painted" that work, the article said, and he was to go to the Galerie Charpentier the next day to see whether it was actually his.

The next morning *Le Figaro* devoted nearly a quarter of a page to the forgery story. "Dali Has Lost His Memory Before This Found Object" was the headline, and a large photograph showed Dali peering into a microscope that seemed to be perched on top of the *Homage to Kant* that I had seen in the glass showcase at the exhibition a week or so earlier.

"This is the first time I have seen that object," Dali was quoted as saying. It did have Dalinian elements, he conceded—the "amber," the reference to Kant—but he had no recollection of ever having touched it before. He would guess, he said, that the object had been found by a friend of its present proprietor, who, according to my copy of the exhibition catalog, was M. Charles Ratton, a dealer in African sculpture. But he would remedy that, he said, by going to the Galerie Charpentier, signing it, and making it, henceforth and forevermore, a genuine Dali "found object."

I decided to reestablish communication with Dali, and the next day I called him at the Hotel Meurice, where he had told me he would be staying. I reminded him of our unfinished conversation in New York and told him I would need to see a lot more of him, now that I was planning to write about him.

"*Parfait*," he said. "Come tomorrow at twelve sharp."

A few minutes before noon the next day, I presented myself at the desk of the Meurice's concierge and told him I'd like to see Mr. Dali.

"There are several others who would like to see him, too," he said, "but we have just received a call from upstairs that Mr. Dali is not to be disturbed. If you will be patient, I can call back and check in a little while."

I sat down in a high-backed chair across from his desk and tried to pick out, from among the rest of the lobby population, the ones who might be waiting for Dali. Just then an exceedingly tall young woman, her blond hair piled mountainously high, came into the lobby from the front of the building and walked over to the concierge. For some obscure reason I thought of Dali's Venus de Milo with its secret drawers. This girl was a bit too slender and far too tall for a Venus—easily six feet in her high heels—and the conformation of her features was too fine to be classical. Her long and graceful body blocked the view I had had of the concierge and so I wasn't aware of what he might be doing about her, but in a minute or two she quickly swept back across the lobby in the direction of the elevator.

In about twenty minutes I saw the concierge leave his desk and go over, first, to a tall young man with a briefcase; then, to two short dark men—one carrying a camera; the other, a flat package that might have held a small painting—and, finally, to a man in his early fifties who had been pacing back and forth across the lobby. The four of them left the lobby, headed in the same direction. He next came over to me and told me to follow them up to No. 110 on the second floor. The route took us through several wide connecting halls, past a bar and a restaurant, into the large mosaic-tiled outer lobby, and finally, with a turn to the right, into the Meurice's historic elevator, a dimly lighted luxury cage in green and gold with a cushioned banquette and three small windows, which had once been used as a sedan chair by Marie Antoinette. Last in, I was first out. I let the others, led by one of the short, dark men, who was obviously on familiar ground, find their way to Dali's suite. About thirty yards down a wide corridor they stopped in front of a black-cushioned door and the leader knocked. There was no answer. He opened one side of the padded door and knocked on a paneled wooden door behind it. In a moment Dali opened the door. He was wearing the same clothes he had worn each time I had seen him in New York. This time, though, he wore no necktie. We all filed in. Dali gave us each a nod and a very Spanish *"Bonjour"* as we passed into the salon. It was a pleasant, high-ceilinged, sun-filled room about thirty-five feet square, facing on the Rue de Rivoli, with two pairs of double windows to the floor overlooking the Tuileries gardens. Between the windows stood an oversize Chinese cabinet. In the center of the wall at the left was a large fireplace with a tall mirror and a recessed clock above it. Facing it, on the opposite wall, was another mirror and under that a long, deep crimson divan. At the right end of the divan sat the tall blonde who had preceded us upstairs by about twenty minutes. The tall young man with the briefcase began talking quietly to Dali. Midway in his third or fourth sentence, Dali cut him off.

"I have no sympathy for modern art," he said. "Cézanne and all that." The young man quickly left. Dali bowed as he shut the door, then pointed in the direction of the blonde. "I present to you Mademoiselle Yvonne," he said, addressing all of us. "She is a model." The short man with the camera walked over to one of the windows and looked into his camera from three or four positions. Dali busied himself with the man with the package.

Mlle. Yvonne might have been twenty-five. She had certainly the longest and perhaps the shapeliest legs I had seen since a childhood visit to New York during the heyday of the Paradise

Restaurant. As she sat there, well back in the deep and downy divan, crossing and uncrossing her legs with a studied indifference, they grew longer and longer under my gaze until finally they seemed to stretch all the way up to her mauve eye shadow. It occurred to me that this was the essence of the Dalinian paranoiac-critical activity, which Dali has defined as a spontaneous method of irrational knowledge based on the interpretative and critical association of delirium phenomena. I decided to focus my attention on Dali. He was standing with the visitor who had brought the flat package. The man had unwrapped his package. It was, indeed, a painting, to all appearances a characteristic Dali landscape, about seven by ten inches, with vast, solitary distances and a pale sky. Dali put on his glasses and studied it.

"It's good," he said. "Very good. I'll sign it. You can pick it up tomorrow. Then be sure to varnish it." The man with the camera came over to them and looked at the picture. "You'd better photograph that, Descharnes," Dali said. "I think it's perhaps 1941."

Dali introduced me to the man with the camera—Robert Descharnes—and then moved along to the pacer. Descharnes, I realized, was the photographer whose book *The World of Salvador Dali* I had seen in New York.

I told Descharnes that Dali seemed a little gloomier to me now than when I had last seen him. Descharnes looked surprised. "Gloomy? Well, he's had another birthday. He was sixty just three days ago." He pointed to several baskets of fruit and flowers scattered about the room. "Perhaps it's that." He picked a grape from one of the baskets and popped it into his mouth.

Prints marked *épreuve d'artiste* in Dali's handwriting and representing Versailles, the Place de la Concorde, and other familiar monuments were propped up on tables, commodes, and mantelpieces around the room. They made an odd contrast, in their free and splashy watercolor technique, with the daintily tinted, coy but somehow sedate *galanterie* of the gilt-framed eighteenth-century color prints by Moreau le jeune, Lavreince, and others that hung on the walls. The furnishings were comfortable but almost outsize and highly colorful. I asked Descharnes if these were the accommodations Dali always had when he stayed in Paris.

He nodded. "This used to be the apartment of the King of Spain, Alphonse the Thirteenth." He hesitated a moment and then smiled broadly. "Ah, yes," he said slowly. "Maybe that would account for the gloom. One of the things Dali always prized most about this apartment was the toilet seat. It was a very solid one in varnished wood with a gold lamé cover. You can imagine—for a monarchist like him—the comfort and satisfaction he used to derive, every spring and fall when he came back to Paris, from the fact that that toilet seat was the very one that had been warmed and polished, over the years, by the royal buttocks of his king. When he arrived this year, he found they had replaced his royal throne by a brand-new one in white plastic." Descharnes shook his head. "What an outcry! He made them dig out the old one, but after they had brought it back he said it wasn't the same: they couldn't fool him about *that*. The real one had a certain pattern of markings—digs and cracks that were missing from the one they had brought back. Finally they found another one that satisfied him more, but now he won't leave it here any longer. He's going to take it back to Spain with him and install it there. That way he'll be sure that nobody will tamper with it, and when he gets to Port Lligat each year he'll feel more than ever at home."

Across the room Dali jumped up from his chair. "I have just the thing," he said. "This girl is beautiful. We'll take off her clothes and dress her in this." He left the determined pacer, to whom he had been quietly talking in the far corner of the salon, and walked over to a Louis XVI-style *bergère*. He reached behind it and picked up a man's black dinner jacket which had been hanging from a molding in the *boiserie* behind the armchair. It was, apparently, a replica of his celebrated *Aphrodisiac*

Jacket, of the mid-1930's. About forty liqueur glasses had been glued onto the front of the jacket and onto its sleeves. "I'm going to put a dead fly into each one of these, fill it with peppermint, and then stick in a yellow straw. But it's very difficult to get real straws and I don't want the plastic kind. And they must be just the right shade of yellow. Then it's very aphrodisiac."

Yellow straws, all right. The flies, too, I could understand; they are an old ingredient in Dali's work. But what role did the peppermint play? I asked him.

"I read in the *Scientific American* a paper on the molecular structure of odors," he said. "Peppermint has a special odor which corresponds to that form." Dali hung up the jacket and turned to me. "You should see this," he said. He beckoned to me. As I went over to him, he took me by the arm and pointed to a microscope on a table in the corner. "Look in there," he said. I looked but saw only a blur. Finally, after setting the lenses to fit my vision, I saw some kind of three-dimensional crystalline forms. I asked Dali what they were.

"Those are the eyes of two dead flies I've been studying. Now look at this." He picked up two sheets of translucent plastic from the table and, holding them flat against each other, moved them in different directions. They formed perspectives that advanced and receded around the same kind of forms I had seen under the microscope, much like the shifting of colored glass in a child's kaleidoscope. "That's the principle of moiré," he said, "and my painting is going to become three-dimensional just like that. And just like the eyes of the fly, which are made up of little mirrored facets that work in just that way." He tossed the plastic sheets onto the table. "I've got another idea," he said, turning to the pacer. He walked over to Mlle. Yvonne, still sitting quietly at the end of the divan. "She has such long, slender legs—wonderful for the film." He took her by the right arm and she stood up. He looked up at her spiraling mound of blond hair. "Your hair goes all the way down to there, doesn't it?" He pointed to the spot he had in mind. It did, she assured him. "Are you English?" he asked.

"Swedish," she said, smiling.

"That's all right," Dali said. "No matter." He went back to his corner with the pacer. Mlle. Yvonne sat down. Descharnes and I drifted back to our corner. I asked Descharnes how many photographs he had taken of Dali.

"Between the man and his work, maybe ten thousand, twelve thousand, fifteen thousand—I'm not sure. That includes a few of her in the jacket." He nodded in the direction of Mlle. Yvonne. "But I don't consider her a beautiful girl. The body isn't bad but the face hasn't enough character. Maybe it's because she's Swedish. I'd rather see him use an actress named Mylène Demongeot that I've photographed a lot." He picked up a banana and studied it. It was a little overripe. He set it down again carefully in its basket. I asked him how long he had spent on those ten to fifteen thousand photographs of Dali and his work.

"About a dozen years or so," he said. "I don't take so many now. In fact, Dali calls me the photographer who doesn't photograph."

What did he do, in place of photography?

"Right now, I'm assembling the big retrospective of Dali's work that opens in Tokyo this fall. Dali and Gala have turned it all over to me. They're not even going to the exhibition. They don't want to fly to Japan—they're afraid to fly—and they wouldn't take the time to go by boat. So it's all mine from start to finish. It hasn't been easy rounding up all those pictures, either."

I asked Descharnes if he had been to America in the process.

He nodded. "That's where I've had most of my trouble. The collector who has the most Dalis—eighty of them—a man named Reynolds Morse in Cleveland, won't lend us any of them for the show. And some of those who *are* lending have wild ideas about what their pictures are worth. The Winston Guests, for example, want a painting of theirs insured for two hundred thousand dollars when we have others far better than theirs insured for much less. Oh, no, my problems are not Japanese, or even Catalan, at the moment; they're very American."

One of the double doors in the far corner of the salon opened, and a small dark-haired woman looked in. "Dali, are you there?" she called out in a flat, Slavic tone. I recognized her as Gala, although all the photographs of her I had seen were from a much earlier period. Dali straightened up and went over to her. He took her arm and, pointing toward the girl at the end of the divan, said, "That is Mademoiselle Yvonne." Gala didn't seem interested. Dali guided her over to Descharnes and me. More than forty years ago, Paul Éluard, whose wife she had been, described her as having eyes that would pierce walls. They were still very bright and sharp. She looked very well-preserved for a woman in her seventies, but it was hard to imagine where she might "pass for forty-five," as Albert Field had put it during his conversation with me at the St. Regis. She extended her hand. Descharnes kissed it, and I shook it.

"Robert Descharnes is my friend," she said to me, and as they began to talk and Dali had gone to sit in the large, regal-looking armchair near the fireplace and was dialing a telephone number, I went over to the other side of the room where Mlle. Yvonne was still sitting alone in the corner of the divan. She had a cigarette in her mouth and was looking in her purse for something to light it with. I lighted it for her and sat down in her shadow. I asked her how she had come to work for Dali.

She laughed. "By a kind of accident, I guess. I happened to be in Paris. A friend of mine who works here for the Italian television told me Dali was looking for someone to model the jacket and she said I had to do it. That's why I'm here. But it's not work for me. I do it for the fun of it. He's been very nice to me. I like to be with him."

On a low table in front of us were five or six neckties from Pierre Cardin, woven with varying quantities and patterns of

gold threads and individually wrapped in cellophane. The man
to whom Dali had been selling Mlle. Yvonne came over and
looked at the ties. He selected one and held it up to Mlle.
Yvonne's neck. "I think this would work better than the
jacket," he said. He introduced himself to me as Gilbert Prouteau, a film director. I asked him if Dali was going to play in a
film of his.

"He's promised to," he said. "Picasso, Aragon, and a number
of other old friends of his are in it. It's called *Dieu a choisi
Paris*. It's a panorama of what has gone on in Paris over the past
fifty years or so. And no film of that kind can afford to overlook
Dali."

"No, no, no, no," Dali shouted into the telephone. "I want
a *real* sculptor—someone like Pomodoro. Not just a decorator—
a good artist. I have no use for those *maquettistes*. But"—and
he shook his finger in admonishment—"it must be someone who
will understand that he must efface himself completely to make
the work conform exactly to my ideas. Wait," Dali said. He
moved the phone away from his face. "Any ideas?" he called
over to us.

"How about De Gaulle?" Prouteau said. "He knows how to
work on masses." Dali smiled—his first since my arrival—and
transmitted the suggestion.

I asked Prouteau if the telephone conversation had something to do with his film. He shook his head. "Not as far as I
know. This must be another of his projects."

"Descharnes," Dali called out. "Pick me out a necktie to wear
to lunch." Gala was talking with a small, dark girl in her early
twenties, whose black hair was piled high in the approved Dalinian spiral. Coiffure excepted, she was under five feet and one
hundred pounds. Descharnes came over to the table to look at
the Cardin gold-thread ties.

"No, there aren't any sculptures in the film—not as far as Dali
is concerned," Prouteau said. "We are having a little trouble
with a painting, though. Not one of his; one by his idol, Meis-

sonier. There's a big Meissonier at the Hotel Raphaël—it's called *Vive l'Empereur*—and Dali wanted to use it as a backdrop for his scene. I went to see the managing director of the hotel to ask if we could borrow it. He was a tight-lipped, constipated-looking type and he didn't like the idea at all. 'If Dali wants to appear in front of my painting,' he said, 'it's probably to make an ass of us both'—he meant of Meissonier and him, I gathered—'and I'm not interested in *that*,' he told me primly. So I didn't get the painting. But he did at least tell me that there's another big Meissonier coming up at auction in a few weeks in a sale conducted by Maître Rheims. Dali's going to have a look at that one and see if it will do."

Dali came over to the divan to put on the tie Descharnes had picked out for him. He looked down at me. "Now it's lunchtime," he said.

What about Kant? I asked. I told him I was very much interested in learning more about that situation.

"That's a good idea," he said. "Come tomorrow. We'll get it all straightened out then." He escorted me to the door. He was perspiring lightly. "I'm glad you mentioned Kant," he said. "That's very important if you're going to write about me. You'll see, Kant was even crazier than I am." He opened the door, bowed, shook my hand, and I was outside.

As I started toward the stairway, I saw the small, dark girl with the spiral hairdo standing against the right-hand wall near the end of the corridor. She gave me a bit of a start because if anyone had asked me, I would have said she was still talking with Gala in the Dalis' salon when I left. In fact I would have sworn it. For a second I thought that this girl might be a twin, but then I decided that even if there *were* two of her, they just wouldn't be that identical. I wondered briefly if it could be a double image induced by looking at too many Dali paintings in recent weeks. I had already had one optical trick played on me by Mlle. Yvonne's legs. But this wasn't a mirage because when I came alongside, she was smiling and very real.

"*Bonjour, mademoiselle,*" I said.

"How are you?" she answered in a French-accented English. Ordinarily I would have walked down the one flight, but since she was waiting for the elevator, I decided to keep her company. It came almost at once. I followed her in.

"I like this elevator," she said. "It's almost worth coming here just to ride in it. It's very Dalinian, don't you think so?"

I looked around us. It was dark, warm, soft, and oval. Like a womb, only dry.

When I knocked at Dali's door the next morning, he called out, *"Entrez."* I turned the knob but the door was locked. I waited a moment, knocked again, and finally the door was opened by an unobtrusive-looking gray-haired man I had not seen before. Dali, dressed in the usual uniform and without tie, was seated in his thronelike *bergère* near the fireplace. A tall, good-looking young woman stood beside him. I shook hands with him.

"You'll excuse me for not getting up," he said. "I'm having trouble with my leg." Seated across from him was a pleasant-appearing fellow in his mid-thirties, with a round, ruddy, Slavic-looking face and a prominent square jaw. Dali pointed to him. "Monsieur Rutsch," he said. "A sculptor." Rutsch acknowledged the introduction in a very ornate Germanic-accented French. Weaving around them between the armchairs and backing toward the window was a photographer, not Descharnes this time but a tall, thin, black-haired fellow in his thirties, wearing a brown suede jacket. Dali waved toward the photographer. "Monsieur Richard," he said. The photographer kept his nose in the box. Dali looked up at the girl. "And Mademoiselle is a Belgian journalist." Mademoiselle smiled.

Dali was holding a pair of round stones, the size of walnuts. He rolled them across the patch of rug alongside his chair. Then, from the table at his left he picked up a billiard ball, a little deeper than café-au-lait, not quite ocher in color, bearing the number 7.

"*Alors,*" he said to Rutsch, "this is the color of the slipper. And the ball itself must figure in the object right next to the slipper so that everybody will see we have based the color of the slipper on that billiard ball." He rolled the ball around between the first two fingers and thumb of his right hand until he had the number facing him. "Ah, number seven. *C'est pas beau.* It would be much better if it were number nine." He began to whistle the tuneless, lugubrious air I remembered from New York. "Anyway, the color is good," he said. "It would be just about right for *le Caca Dauphin.*" The sculptor looked startled.

"You don't know about *le Caca Dauphin*?" Dali asked him. He didn't.

"Very interesting and by no means irrelevant. You see, if I take infinite pains with the most infinitesimal details of these matters, there is a long tradition for that, and three hundred years ago the *grands couturiers* of Paris were just as exacting. They planted their *modellistes* in strategic locations so that when the *dauphin,* the son of Louis the Fourteenth, made *caca,* they could take notes and make watercolor sketches, and on that *exact* shade, design their latest creations. But it had to be *exact.* And so this is the color of the slipper—but *exactly* this."

Rutsch giggled. At first I thought he was embarrassed. His ruddy face grew redder, but then he smiled beatifically. "The divine Dali must always be taken seriously," he said, addressing us all. "No matter what he says, when we decide it is frivolous— *we* are the frivolous ones for not taking the divine Dali seriously enough."

Dali picked up the telephone. "Will you get me the Vicomtesse de Noailles," he said. "Please, the Vicomtesse de Noailles,
Eleven Place des Etats-Unis. I'll wait for you to call me back."
He hung up. He beckoned to the gray-haired man who had let
me in. "Put on the tape of my last radio interview," he said.
"I want Mr. Lake to hear it." The man set in operation a tape
recorder on the other side of the room, and I could hear Dali's
voice giving out some of the views on money, moiré, flies' eyes,
and other subjects with which I was becoming daily more familiar, while directly in front of me Dali himself continued,
contrapuntally, his dialogue with Rutsch. After a few minutes
he turned to the Belgian girl. "When Mr. Lake finishes listen-
ing to that," he said, "I'll put on something more interesting
for you. A tape recorded by a woman who sleeps with two
men." The girl looked at him in amusement, half-raised her
eyebrows, then laughed. "How banal," she said.

Dali looked surprised. "*Non, non, non.* It's an amazing thing.
Étonnant. She comes six times, seven times." The telephone
rang. "*Allô.* I'd like to talk with the Vicomtesse de Noailles. It
is Monsieur Salvador Dali. Very well, in any case tell her I
called." Dali replaced the phone in its carriage, leaned over,
and picked up the two round stones he had tossed onto the rug.
He rolled them around in his hands. "Try this," he said, and
handed them to the girl. "Just feel." She took them from him.
"It's like gooseflesh," he explained, "as sensitive as a woman's
breast. You can feel the tiny nipples stand right up, can't you?"

"What are they?" she asked him, noncommittally.

"Fossilized sea urchins," he said, "given to me by Monsieur
Rutsch."

The girl handed back the stones to Dali and said she'd return
in a day or two. He seemed surprised. "You don't want to hear
that tape?" he asked.

"It's too near lunchtime," she said ambiguously. "Perhaps
another day." She left. Rutsch soon followed. "I have much to
do," he told Dali and beamed at him knowingly. The photog-

rapher followed along with him. Dali and I were alone, except for the guardian of the tapes, seated, not quite so decoratively as Mlle. Yvonne had been the day before, at the end of the crimson divan on the other side of the room. I suggested we get on with Kant.

"A wonderful idea," Dali said, almost cheerfully. "You can't imagine how beautifully everything is falling into place. Even this man Rutsch—it's incredible."

Just who *was* Rutsch? I asked.

"He's a sculptor," Dali said, "half-Austrian, half-Russian." He pointed to a book on the Chinese cabinet. "Would you hand me that book?" he asked. I went over and got it for him. It was the Gallimard edition of the French translation of Thomas De Quincey's *On Murder as One of the Fine Arts*. He flipped through it quickly until he reached page 179. By then it had become "The Last Days of Immanuel Kant." The margins of that page were heavily slashed in red crayon. "Read that," Dali said. Following his markings I read the French translation of the following passage:

On this occasion, whilst illustrating Kant's notions of the animal economy, it may be as well to add one other particular, which is, that, for fear of obstructing the circulation of the blood, he never would wear garters; yet, as he found it difficult to keep up his stockings without them, he had invented for himself a most elaborate substitute, which I will describe. In a little pocket, somewhat smaller than a watch-pocket, but occupying pretty nearly the same situation as a watch-pocket on each thigh, there was placed a small box, something like a watch-case, but smaller; into this box was introduced a watch-spring in a wheel, round about which wheel was wound an elastic cord, for regulating the force of which there was a separate contrivance. To the two ends of this cord were attached hooks, which hooks were carried through a small aperture in the pockets, and so, passing down the inner and the outer side of the thigh, caught hold of two loops which were fixed on the off side and the near side of each stocking . . .

"You see?" Dali said excitedly. "When I read that the other day, I thought the best thing would be to make a *real* monument to Kant, built around that idea. That object in the Galerie Charpentier exhibition wasn't really my *Homage to Kant*. It's not authentic. And that story in the book is the most fantastic, the most irrational of all. Imagine anyone having such a phobia! I decided to demonstrate that some of the most serious people who ever lived are even crazier than I am. To think that a man like Kant would go through all that business of rigging up pulleys to hold up his stockings! I've done some weird things in my time, but I'm not *that* crazy. So that was what started my thought processes vibrating around the monument to Kant. Then, almost the very next day, I ran across this sculptor. He came up to me on the street and said, 'I admire you tremendously.' So I asked him, 'What gift can you give me?' 'I have some extraordinary stones,' he said. I went to call on him in his studio and the stones he showed me *were* extraordinary. They were fossils. He made me a present of one of them—this fossilized sea urchin." Dali held up one of the stones he had been rolling on the rug a few minutes earlier. The other was gone; I assumed Rutsch had taken it away with him. "While I was there, I looked at his sculpture—mostly things made out of old iron. I told him what I had in mind about Kant and asked him if he wanted to make it. He was delighted. He'll turn out something good. He knows just what I want."

The phone rang. Dali picked it up. "*Allô.*" He listened for a moment and then said to me, "La Vicomtesse de Noailles." He waited. "Yes," he said finally, "I've found a magnificent slave who is helping us in his atelier with everything. The monument will have two helicopter wings. That's right. Oh, he'll keep at it. We've been able to find a slipper that's very close to the kind Kant wore. At the Musée du Costume. I wanted Cardin to make all those things, but since he's not here at the moment, it would be too complicated. We'll do it ourselves. It's all based on a document I found. I think it would be a good idea to follow that very closely. I'll tell you more about it on Thursday. *Parfait.* Maybe Friday we'll go get the object, after lunch. That's right. After coffee we'll go to the Galerie Charpentier. And then Saturday night our little ceremony will run off right on schedule. The television will be there, *Le Figaro* will be there. *Non, non, non.* I don't want to talk about it with Patrick Waldberg. The best thing is for him to be at your luncheon. We'll talk about it then. I think everything is falling into place with an almost alarming harmony. *C'est ça.* I'll see you on Friday. I'll make note to be there at one o'clock sharp. I know it's sacred for you—everyone must sit down to eat, right on the dot. I'll bring someone, I don't know whom. Perhaps someone very close to our—to Kant but, in any case, someone who will add a little zest to the gathering. *Je vous embrasse.*" He set down the receiver, muttering, "Friday, one o'clock," and humming as he wrote it into a small black notebook.

I told Dali I wasn't entirely clear on a point he had made about his plans for using in his painting the parabolic lenses of flies' eyes and I wanted to go over it with him in more detail. He shook his head. "No. The important thing is to *spread* confusion, not to eliminate it."

"In that case, perhaps I should show you what I've written about it, to make sure it's sufficiently confusing," I suggested.

He shook his head again. "No," he said firmly. "I'll read it when you publish it. I like to be surprised." He walked over to the mantelpiece and thumbed through a book that was lying on it. Then he turned to me. "I have an optician coming here in a few days to consult with me about flies' eyes in connection with a painting I am working on which will be in relief. It's called *Gala with Bees.* Perhaps you'd like to be on hand." I told him I would. Dali picked up the book. It was a copy of the French limited edition of his *Le Mythe tragique de l'Angélus de Millet.* He put on his glasses, borrowed my pen, and began to sketch rapidly, on the page opposite the half title, the two principal figures of Millet's painting of *The Angelus:* the man and woman facing each other, behind them the last rays of the setting sun. He completed each figure quickly in one continuous spiraling stroke. Both figures had their head bowed. The woman, at the right, had her hands raised in an attitude of prayer. In Millet's painting, the man's hands are waist-high, holding his hat in front of him. Dali, I noticed, was drawing *his* man's hands in the same prayerful position as the woman's. I asked him how he felt about the matter of faith. I had read and heard many ambiguous accounts of his conversion to Roman Catholicism and his devotion to the church. He stopped drawing and looked up.

"Faith? That comes only by the grace of God," he said. "We cannot do anything about it."

But in New York he had told me he had found faith through science, I reminded him. How about *his* faith? I insisted. He looked at me over the rims of his glasses. "I feel it's going to come in a more certain form. It's *going* to come, but I don't know just when. It comes and it goes. Sometimes it comes near and then it recedes. It oscillates," he said and went back to his drawing. Almost as if he were illustrating his point, he drew in, just below the male figure's waist, in place of the hat of Millet's painting, what must have been the man's penis, but he drew it with such a frenzied circular movement of the pen and repeated it so many times that the penis itself was swallowed up in the dynamics of its centrifugal movement.

"It oscillates," Dali muttered between clenched teeth. "It oscillates."

"Dali, it's time to eat." It was Gala calling from the door on the other side of the salon. Dali set down his book, returned my pen, and went over to the table that held his selection of Cardin gold-thread neckties. He made his choice, put on the tie, adjusted his gold lamé waistcoat, reached into an inside pocket, and took out a rectangular gold purse. On one side was a triangular button-down flap that was torn and crumpled. He held it up with glee.

"Look at this," he said. "On the outside everything about me is normal. But as soon as you start fishing around inside, you come up with something like this." He put the purse back into his inside jacket pocket. "I wouldn't part with it for anything," he said. "It's old and torn, but the worse shape it gets into, the better I like it. And the better it works."

"You are an American? How interesting! Do you know where I can get some bubble gum?"

I looked down at the small, dark-haired woman standing beside me in the salon of Dali's Hotel Meurice apartment, the next afternoon. Mafalda Davis, Dali had called her. Her age and accent were questions I would have found hard to guess. Her eyes were large and dark and heavy-lidded, and her lashes swept the smoke from her cigarette over to me. Still, she didn't look like a bubble gum chewer.

"It's for an experiment Dali wants to try," she explained. I told her my ten-year-old son might know the answer. "I'll send a *chasseur* to your place to pick it up. What's your address?" she asked.

I said I doubted that he had any on hand but he just might be able to get some from a little place around the corner.

"French bubble gum?" she asked. I supposed it was. She lost interest. "It's no good. We've tried that already—four or five lots. It doesn't work. We need the American kind."

I suggested Le Drug-Store on the Champs-Elysées. Since they

sold hamburgers and hot dogs, milk shakes and banana splits, why not American bubble gum? "Very good idea," she said. "I'll run up there now and see if I can get some so Dali can go to work on it right away." Dali came alongside. "I've never seen you looking better," Mrs. Davis told him. "Of course," he said and moved on.

I asked her what the bubble gum was for. "It's for a sculpture," she said.

I recalled Westbrook Pegler's description of Frank Crowninshield's pet sculptor, Mike Hogan, the Kansas City ashman, who worked in chewing gum, matchsticks, and hair combings—a great artist, long before anyone talked about Pop. Did he fit into this picture somewhere?

Mrs. Davis wasn't familiar with Hogan's work. "But Dali doesn't work *on* the bubble gum," she explained. "He just chews it into shape and uses it as an adhesive in assembling the *maquette*. It's a sculpture he's doing for me. I'm commissioning it. When it's done we'll have it cast, maybe in gold, and send it to the big Dali show next fall. There's the girl who's working with Dali on it—Christine Forani." She pointed to a woman in her forties who stood talking with a small group behind me. Madame Forani was Belgian, she told me: a wiry, tanned blonde with high cheekbones, a bowl haircut, and a husky voice. "The two men next to her have come from Sweden just to see Dali," Mrs. Davis went on. "They want him to paint seven pictures for them. He says he'll do two—if he has time. He's maddening." Dali came by again, shook hands, and deposited in our midst the pretty little dark girl with a high spiral of black hair with whom I had shared a ride in the Meurice's elevator a few days earlier. Dali introduced her as Mlle. Lussato.

"She's very Dalinian," he told me with a meaningful glance. He kissed Mlle. Lussato on the forehead.

"We are going now out onto the banks of the Seine to conduct an experiment for a new style I am creating," he announced.

A new style of what? I asked.

"A new style of decoration. It can be applied to furniture, to architecture—anything at all. Like Louis Seize or Louis Quatorze. But French architecture—French style in general—is ruined by French preoccupation with good taste. The French need someone to help them get rid of their compulsive sense of moderation." He caressed the upswept curves of his mustache.

I asked him what his style would be based on.

"It is based on the coefficient of plasticity of tar," he said. "It is also based on the parabola, on curvilinear surfaces, and also— since he has always been a strong influence on me—on the ideas of the Catalan architect Gaudí. The tar must flow in various geometric forms and then be subjected to a certain torsion." He looked around the room. "Let's go," he said, with all the terse vigor of a military commander jumping off for the assault. He picked up a gold-pommeled walking stick which he had told me once belonged to Victor Hugo, grasped Mlle. Lussato firmly by the arm, and we trooped after him out into the hall. As we passed a small coffee table near the door, I noticed that the bananas in one of the birthday baskets were approaching a stage of decomposition that called to mind some of Dali's Surrealist paintings of thirty years ago.

We were too many for Marie Antoinette's sedan chair, so we walked down the curving staircase that led to the front lobby. As we reached the ground floor, the elevator started its slow, majestic climb upward. One of the women asked Dali what he thought of the elevator. "It's very Dalinian," he answered, confirming Mlle. Lussato's verdict of a few days earlier, "but I don't like the lights in the corners. I'd like to see them replaced by a pair of quarreling lovebirds."

We walked through the reception rooms to the rear lobby. At the door stood Dali's chauffeur; behind him, Dali's black Cadillac convertible with New York license plates. Dali allotted the seats available in his car and assigned the overflow—Richard, the tall, black-haired photographer—to me. I asked Dali where we were going and how to get there.

"Do you know the way, Baroness?" he called over to Christine Forani.

"It's the Société de Pavage et des Asphaltes de Paris et l'Asphalte," she said. "Eight, Rue de Javel in the fifteenth *arrondissement*. You go past the Eiffel Tower and it's just off the Quai de Javel. Why don't you follow us?" she suggested to me.

It wasn't easy to follow them, bucking the usual late-afternoon logjam in the Place de la Concorde, but once we had got beyond that, the route was clear. When I reached the Rue de Javel, Dali's car was already parked opposite No. 8, and his party was streaming in, through two wide-open metal gates, to a large workyard where everything was labeled S.P.A.P.A.— steamrollers, road menders, boilers coughing up billows of acrid yellow smoke, and everywhere the lung-searing smell of tar. Dali and Christine Forani bypassed a group of five or six workmen in blue denim and went over to talk to a tall man, who seemed to be the boss. In a minute or two they all started back out to the street, along the Rue de Javel. I followed them across the *quai* and down a flight of steps onto the bank of the Seine. Dali strode on purposefully, his long, black hair curling in the wind, a team of television cameras picking him up at appropriate angles. He paced back and forth across the cobblestones until he had selected a background that could not have been improved. Behind him was a barge-loading hoist to frame the entire composition. In the middle distance, on the Pont de Grenelle, the small version of Bartholdi's Statue of Liberty left over from the exposition of 1878—*La Liberté éclairant le monde* —and behind that, the Eiffel Tower.

"Very good. Right here," Dali said. Christine Forani put on a blue smock and stepped out of her dark-blue high-heeled pumps and into a pair of broad, flat, brown walking shoes. She was wearing a complicated silver necklace formed of sugges-

tively phallic components. She removed that and put on a pair
of rubber gloves. The tall head man from S.P.A.P.A. and two
of his co-workers came down the steps from the *quai*. One of
them carried an iron pail with a large circular hole in the bottom and three metal inserts to fit over the hole: one with a
smaller circular hole, another with a square hole, and the third
with a triangular hole. A workman brought over a bucket of
steaming tar.

"Try pouring it through the small circle," Dali said. "As it
comes out, the Baroness will mold it into the proper form under my direction." Another workman held the empty bucket at
arm's length and the man with the full bucket poured in some
of the steaming tar. It came coursing through the bottom hole
hardly less liquid than it went in. Mme. Forani stuck in a finger or two gingerly and yelped.

"How hot is that stuff, anyway?" she hollered, pulling off her
rubber gloves.

"About four hundred degrees," the director said.

"It's much too runny—and hot as hell," she said. "We'll let
it cool awhile. That will slow it down."

The head man looked doubtful. "Once it goes below a certain temperature, you won't be able to spin it out very thin," he
said. "It will grow brittle and you won't be able to mold it."

"I'll work on it before it reaches that stage," she said. She
turned to another of the workmen. "Get me a bucket of water."

Dali continued pacing back and forth. "Not enough body to
that tar," he said. "It won't work."

"It will when it's cooler," Mme. Forani said. "Be patient."

"I didn't come here to be patient," Dali said.

"Perhaps we should try asphalt," the head man suggested. "It
will be about four hundred and sixty-five degrees, but it has a
heavier consistency." He sent one of his workmen back to the
yard to get some. When he returned with a pailful, the asphalt
was not only steaming but bubbling.

"This should have been done in the atelier," Dali said, "so the temperature could be controlled."

"Look," Mme. Forani said, "I've got a better idea. We'll suspend the pail from the hoist. That will give the asphalt more time to cool as it runs down." She climbed up onto the metal framework.

"Find something about seven feet above the ground," Dali called out. One of the cameramen came running over.

"The light is bad at this angle," he said. "How about trying to hang it at the head of the stairway leading down from the *quai?*" Mme. Forani climbed down from her perch. By now a dozen or more workmen from the yard were hanging over the railing above the stairway.

"Well, is it for today or tomorrow?" one of them shouted. Mme. Forani turned to the man with the asphalt.

"Pour some out onto the ground," she said. He emptied half of his pailful onto the cobblestones. Without bothering to put on her rubber gloves, she scooped up half of that in her pail with the small round hole and held it, with both hands, as high as she could. The cooling, thicker asphalt started to ooze out of the hole, more slowly than the tar, and broke off periodically into small, thick blobs.

"That's disgusting," Dali said. "It's of no use at all. I need one long continuous piece. How do you expect me to twist that into any kind of decorative form?"

"We'll try the tar again," Mme. Forani said. She emptied out her bucket onto the ground and fitted into it the bottom with the square hole. One of the workmen poured in tar from the first bucket. Lacking the body of the asphalt it streamed through thinly onto the cobblestones. Dali looked as though he had suffered the ultimate indignity.

"It's finished," he said. "I'm through." He took Mlle. Lussato by the arm and strode off toward the parapet. Mme. Forani poured some tar into the bucket of water the workman had brought her. It streamed out of her bucket, but as soon as it hit the water it solidified. She scooped up a handful of it and kneaded it vigorously. It seemed pliant and workable. She looked around for Dali. He and Mlle. Lussato had just reached the top of the stairs.

"Dali," she shouted, "come back. Come back. It's going to work."

Dali kept on walking and crossed the *quai,* still clutching Mlle. Lussato's arm. The television cameras followed him as he started down the Rue de Javel toward the black Cadillac convertible. Mme. Forani pulled at her wet tar. It was hard, almost brittle.

"Merde, alors," she muttered, and shook it out of her fingers.

I didn't want to miss any of the preparations for the Kant celebration, so in spite of the asphalt fiasco I returned the next morning to the Meurice. I had to pick my way among heavy television cables that were strung along the second-floor corridor. They were visible only as far as the royal suite; there they disappeared behind the black padded doors leading to Dali's apartment. I followed them in. The paneled inner door was wide open. Inside, Dali was enthroned on his customary *bergère* near the fireplace, with three batteries of heavy projectors throwing light onto a face that looked like insufficiently cooked veal glistening with oil. Even off to the side, where I stood, the light was dazzling and the heat rippled across the salon in shimmering, visible waves held in by the tightly closed double windows that overlooked the Tuileries.

Next to Dali sat a cherubic little man dressed in black and wearing horn-rimmed spectacles—a journalist named Jean-Pierre Lannes, who was interviewing him for the French national television service. In front of them sat a group that appeared to include the producer, director, and script girl. Scattered around the room were sundry props and the usual quota of technicians.

The cherub spoke: "What image of you would you like posterity to have, Salvador Dali?"

"I won't answer that," Dali said, "but I'll quote the distinguished academician Eugenio Montes, who said that if Dali is to be compared with anyone, it should be with the great Mallorcan mathematician Ramón Lull. But my entire effort, every day, is designed to help me succeed in being Dali."

The interviewer nodded gravely. "Do you consider the bulk of humanity to be made up of imbeciles?" he asked.

"Not entirely," Dali said. "I have the same point of view on that as Teilhard de Chardin: that is, *'Chez Dupont, tout est bon.'* Even with all the stupid women in the world, even those so horribly stupid that they might be compared to—oh, not to the ones Picasso paints; his women are always redeemed by their color, nor even to the ones my friend William De Kooning paints—but even among the stupidest of them there is hardly one who at some moment or other—at the height of an orgasm—is not capable of a tone of voice or a sigh that is worthy of the best work of the divine." And here, given the construction of Dali's French sentence and his fondness for referring to himself as *le Divin*, it was not entirely clear whether he was referring to God or to Dali. The interviewer must have felt the same confusion. "Tell me, Salvador Dali, are you God?" he asked.

Dali shook his head. "Not at all. Dali is, above all, intelligent, and God is not. God is the Supreme Creator, who invented everything. Intelligence is always the contrary of creation. That is why I am a very bad painter and a very bad artist —I am too intelligent. If that is a paradox, it is also a vicious circle. Since God created everything, He created also man, who has that unique faculty which He Himself does not possess— intelligence. And with that intelligence expressing itself through nuclear physics and biology, man will be able, more and more, to approach the idea of the reality of God. You see?" The phone rang. Dali picked it up. "Yes, any time," he said and hung up. "Cut," the director yelled. He went up to Dali's armchair and spoke quietly to him and the interviewer and then returned to his seat. "Sound, when you're ready," he called out. "*Ça tourne*," the sound man answered. A man with a clapper board walked up to Dali and held it in front of his face. "Dali, one, eighth time," he called, and snapped the two pieces together. Dali covered his face briefly and smoothed the curves of his mustache.

"Finally, Salvador Dali," the interviewer said, "how do you envisage the new television?"

Dali reflected. "It will certainly be liquid," he said. "I am working on it at the moment. It is based on what is called *la pourlèche*. That is, if you drool at the corners of the mouth and don't wipe away the moisture, you get a crystalline formation, like a tiny pebble, with an acid base. If you superimpose one of those tiny pebbles onto another, as I discovered when I examined two of them under the microscope recently, you produce the phenomenon of moiré. In my research on gooseflesh, I discovered that human skin is the perfect ground for a moiré pattern. And so it works out very simply: the application of my liquid on the layer of flesh taken at the moment of a shiver, combined with the moiré-producing biological concretion in the form of the tiny pebbles produced by drooling, and you receive the image: in color, even, as the result of the crystalline irisation. It's the modern, scientific extension of the magic mirror of the Middle Ages. When a knight went away on a Crusade, simply by breathing on the magic mirror his lady was able to see him in the Holy Land."

There was a knock at the door behind me. I opened it and let in Marina Lussato, followed by Mafalda Davis with a Chihuahua under one arm and six packs of American chewing gum in the other hand. The telephone rang. Dali interrupted his monologue to answer it and the director yelled, "Cut." The technicians began to move some of their equipment around and turned off the spotlights. Mrs. Davis nearly tripped over one of the cables, parked her chewing gum on a corner of the mantelpiece, and made signs to Dali: I'll be back later, she seemed to be telling him. She scurried out, bumping into the film director Gilbert Prouteau as he came in.

Dali went over to Prouteau. "What's the news on Meissonier?" he asked.

"I've talked to Rheims," Prouteau said. "He'll go along with whatever you want. The trouble is, the painting will be at the photoengraver's until tomorrow and it's a little hard to move around. It measures over five feet by eight and a half, you know."

Dali looked pleased. "I think my friend Huntington Hartford will be very interested in it. He has a museum of academic art. But we ought to find out the date of the sale. Why don't you call Rheims now?"

Prouteau started for the telephone. "By the way," he said, "when is the investiture of Immanuel Kant?"

"In two days," Dali said.

Prouteau called the office of Maître Rheims. After a brief conversation he passed the telephone to Dali.

"I've already alerted Huntington Hartford," Dali told Rheims, "but I'd like to talk with you about the details. Perhaps you could come see me tomorrow—at noon. *Parfait. Bonjour.*" He hung up.

"Monsieur Dali," the television director called out, "could we have another take on the end of that question about God? Just before the end, will you lift up your head, come forward a little, and put your hands out—like this?" He demonstrated the position, palms outstretched. "And then wait for two or three seconds before finishing up," he added.

Dali went back to his seat. He rubbed his eyes, blinked at the lights, and smoothed his mustache. The sound turned, the clapper clapped.

"Furthermore," Dali said, "according to Teilhard de Chardin, since the full complexity of life reaches its apex in man"— here Dali raised his head higher, looked fiercely at the camera, and threw out his arms in what came close to being a gesture of supplication—"man is the only being capable of understanding the supreme sublimity of God." The phone rang insistently. Dali picked it up. "Cut," the director called, wearily. "It's me, yes," Dali said. "Perfect. Perfect. In New York. Perfect. Good-bye."

The director made another attempt to get on with his taping. "We have just one more sequence," he said to Dali. "The part that shows you making the original cover of your book." *Le Journal d'un génie,* excerpts from Dali's diary of the years 1952–1963, had just been published. There were several copies of it on the mantelpiece. Its front cover carried an enlarged photographic reproduction of a Spanish news agency report, datelined London, of the Christine Keeler case. In place of the usual dust jacket, the book had a transparent plastic wraparound carrying the profiled head of a bearded classical figure, printed in red.

One of the assistants brought over and set up next to Dali's chair a cardboard blowup of the book's cover, without the classical profile. Dali settled himself into his chair. The crew set in motion "Dali, two, first time."

"All last summer," Dali said, pointing to the blowup, "each night before going to sleep, I used to study this press cutting. And each night, without my doing anything whatever to it, I would see a different head begin to take shape on it—Socrates, Homer, Lorenzo dei Medici—all formed by the droppings of the flies. From time to time I would sprinkle on a little sugar here and there to make the flies shit more abundantly. As a result, all summer long the flies executed for me portraits like the one I am now going to execute for you in one minute by a different method. This picture, incidentally, I consider one of the most important of my life, from the paranoiac-critical point of view."

From the table beside him, Dali picked up a bottle of hair spray, a copy of the book minus its transparent plastic jacket, and a stencil cut out in the form of the red-bearded profile reproduced on the plastic jacket. He placed the stencil over the book and pushed the blowup gently onto the floor in front of him. Then, bending toward the camera, he aimed the atomizer top of the bottle of hair spray at the stencil and pressed the plunger. He began to whistle, pressing faster and faster. "Cut," he said. No one paid any attention. "Cut, cut now," he repeated. "I'm out of fluid." He sat back in his chair and held up the bottle of spray and the book without the stencil. Only the faintest suggestion of a profiled head was visible against the typography of the cover. "Cut," the director called out.

"The bottle is empty," Dali said. He tossed it down, ran over near the window, and tried two other bottles that were sitting on top of the Chinese cabinet. Nothing came out but air. He picked up what looked like a salt shaker and started to shake some of the crystals onto the book's cover. "No point in that," he said. "There's just not enough liquid." He turned to Marina Lussato. "Run out and get me a dozen more bottles. The gray."

As soon as she had left, Dali picked up another copy of the book from the mantel. "I've already given this copy the treatment," he said. "We'll fake the beginning with an empty can of spray, stop the camera, and then run in this copy for the last shot." The director perked up at once. "That's marvelous," he said. "And then, since this is the final sequence, when you get through, say 'Bonsoir.' "

"I never say 'Bonsoir,' " Dali said. "Only 'Bonjour.' "

The director conceded. "All right. Say 'Bonjour.' Just explain why you're saying it, though."

They ran through the scene again—right through the point where Dali had called "Cut" on the previous take. This time he kept on squirting air from the empty bottle. Finally the camera was stopped, Dali substituted the previously prepared copy of the book for the unfinished one, and then, with the camera again turning, he held up the finished product. Across the typographical cover, in silver-gray, was the same head, hand-sprayed by the Master, that was printed in red on the transparent plastic jacket.

"That is the result that the flies will obtain for you in a much more direct and realistic manner," Dali said. "The portrait of Homer on the cover of my book, *Le Journal d'un génie*. And with that I say to you, instead of *Bonsoir, Bonjour*—because I'm in the habit of it."

The technicians began to dismantle the lights and the sound equipment. Dali laid his hand reflectively on the telephone. Richard, the American photographer, quickly came over to him with a book and asked him to sign it. Dali borrowed my pen and wrote in the book, ending with a small squiggle resembling a snail and his swashbuckling signature. As Dali wrote and drew, the photographer walked around him, recording the process. One of the sound men came over with the carton of his tape. Dali signed it for him with an immense flourish. Then he picked up the half-treated copy of *Le Journal d'un génie*, replaced the stencil on its cover, and began to wander around the salon, picking up and testing, one by one, the six or seven plastic bottles of hair spray that were lying about. The photographer reminded him that they were all empty and that he had sent Marina Lussato out for replacements.

"Oh, I know," Dali said. "It's just that I'm very economical and I want to make sure there's nothing left in any of these." Rummaging around on one of the tables, Dali came across the billiard ball numbered 7 and colored in the shade he had referred to as *le Caca Dauphin*. He held it up to me.

"Don't forget Saturday night, Galerie Charpentier," he said. "Very important."

The visit of the optician whom Dali had called in to
consult with him in the matter of flies' eyes as a prep-
aration for his painting in relief had been scheduled for
the next morning—a Friday. When I reached Dali's suite at the
Meurice, I found *le Divin* deep in one of the large crimson-
velvet armchairs in his salon, his glasses low on the bridge of
his nose. He was holding a piece of composition board about a
foot square on which he had drawn in pastel crayons a vague
outline sketch. It was so vague it resembled nothing so much
as one of the mistier passages in the work of the painter who
tops the list of his *bêtes noires:* the Englishman J. M. W. Turner. He kept picking away at it industriously with the corner
of a razor blade. Finally he looked up at one of the three visitors seated opposite him.

"What did you come about?" he asked and went back to his
scraping.

"I wanted to ask you how much direct influence Dr. Jacques
Lacan had on your paranoiac-critical system," the man said
quietly.

Dali looked up at him questioningly. "None," he said. "Oh, at first Lacan seemed brilliant and showed signs of promise." He hesitated a moment.

"In Paris he passes for the great master of analysis," the man said.

Dali looked unimpressed. "Yes, yes, I know." He applied his razor more vigorously.

"I say he *passes* for," the man emphasized with a conciliatory smile.

Dali set down his picture. "I have seen nothing original by him since the Surrealist period. He never followed through. He must know all about the madman who tried to destroy *The Angelus* of Millet in the Louvre. I believe he even questioned him. Why doesn't he communicate with me about that?"

"I think he wrote about that—in part, at least—in an issue of *La Révolution Surréaliste.*"

"No, no," Dali said. "I cite that point in *Le Mythe tragique de l'Angélus de Millet,* but I'd like to know the details of Lacan's interrogation of the man. Besides that, I think Lacan was the one who found a letter by Millet in which he said that originally there had been a casket in that painting, between the two standing figures. That casket is central to my interpretation of the painting. I should be in contact with Lacan."

"Shall I tell him that interests you?" the man asked.

"It interests me a great deal," Dali said. "The most practical thing, since Lacan comes each year to Spain, near Cadaqués, would be for him to come see me there about it."

A slender, pink-cheeked boy of about twenty, wearing a blue suit, sat opposite me at the end of the coffee table in front of the divan. His long, blond hair had been teased out to nearly wiglike proportions. Dali looked over at him.

"Do you know eleven boys—young, good-looking like you? I need twelve—eleven more, that is—to carry the monument to Immanuel Kant on their shoulders. Could you find them for me?"

The boy shook his head. "I don't know eleven boys," he said. "You're a student?"

"For the moment, yes," the boy said evasively. Dali looked puzzled. The phone rang. He went across to the other side of the room to answer it.

"*Allô. Oui, oui, c'est moi. Ah, bonjour, Monsieur Rutsch. Très bien.* You're back in Paris. Good." He sat down in the large *bergère* and stretched his legs out comfortably in front of him. "Good. I'm sure you're going to make some great discoveries. Yes, I'm having lunch at the Vicomtesse de Noailles' house today. Perhaps you could drop in for coffee and we could talk about it. No, I'm afraid it couldn't be for lunch because the arrangements are all made. The Vicomtesse isn't expecting you, you see. But telephone me there at two o'clock. Yes, Eleven Place des Etats-Unis. Perhaps, if there's time, we could all get together later on. You'll have to ring up at two. Ask them to call Monsieur Dali to the phone. By then I'll have spoken to her; everything will be prepared. It might be diplomatic—even useful—for us to see each other during the course of the afternoon. Because the thing must be ready for . . . let's see, today is Friday. I leave on Monday. So I think the affair at the Galerie Charpentier—I prefer to have it tomorrow. Tomorrow evening. Ah, well, you'll have to do that yourself. You'll have to take a look at the object, see about the ceiling height, but that's no great problem." There was a long pause, then Dali said, "Ah, no, that won't be possible. We decided that it wouldn't be a Dali show. I must stay out of the limelight as much as possible. The only ceremony attached to all this is the use of two—I mean twelve—or maybe sixty—young men who will carry the object. Anything else would give it the appearance of something theatrical, too carefully arranged. I don't want to go beyond carrying the object and placing it—that's all. No speeches, no manifestations—nothing. The only problem is the twelve young men. Perhaps we won't find twelve, maybe only five, but five is a good number. The important thing is to get the leg right away

and the stocking and all those things. And for that there is
Mademoiselle Lussato, who will keep in contact with you.
She'll run your errands, pick up whatever equipment you need
at the Bazar de l'Hotel de Ville, and so on. No, I don't have the
Vicomtesse de Noailles' telephone number. But you can get it;
the address is Eleven Place des Etats-Unis. Just ask the Hotel
Meurice operator. Say it's for me. They get it for me whenever
I call. I never carry telephone numbers around with me. I have
yours, though, so you'd better let me call you at your place
around two. Oh, yes, I have it. Right here in my pocket." He
reached into a pocket and pulled out his little black notebook.
"I'll read it to you, just to make sure there's no mistake. It
is . . . Fontenoy 74-63. Very good. It will be in the pocket of
the jacket I wear to lunch. *C'est ça.* Don't bother to call me;
I'll call you. You just follow a completely normal rhythm. *Parfait. Bonjour.*"

Dali hung up and went over to a small commode near the
entrance door, where his third visitor, a toothy, florid man in
a mustard-colored suit, was examining a twelve-inch-square
copperplate propped up against the wall. I joined them. Dali
pointed to the copperplate, on which had been photoengraved
a portrait of himself as Mercury, wearing only sandals and
carrying the symbolic caduceus.

"I'm going to make a painting of that in relief," he announced. "The crosslines are already there." He picked up two
sheets of engraved transparent plastic and moved them back
and forth over the surface of the plate. Dali-as-Mercury moved
correspondingly through three dimensions behind the plastic.
"It jumps around, doesn't it?" he said proudly.

Next to the copperplate was a collage under glass, a rectangular composition about eighteen by twenty-four inches signed
with the name Salvador Dali formed of printed letters of varying sizes, apparently cut from a magazine. The predominant
tones were gold and crimson, and the head of a ram, at lower
left, was balanced at upper right by the bust of Thomas A.

Edison, which topped a pair of lips above a nose set within a room that looked out across a balcony onto a vast open space. In the center of the composition was a bulbously perpendicular strip of the red paper with the fuzzy, textured surface that Dali had shown me in New York. When I had touched it that morning at the St. Regis, my finger had appeared to sink beneath its surface as the result of an optical illusion created by its moiré patterning. Dali pointed now to that pattern.

"You see the lights these throw off. This part comes forward more than that, right beside it. Are you an engraver?"

The man seemed puzzled. "I'm the one who did those things for *Les Heures Claires*—the suites in black and white."

"You're an engraver, then," Dali said.

"Yes, I am. I made your plates for *The Divine Comedy.*"

Dali looked surprised. "Ah, yes. Well . . . good. Now, what I need is someone to make on the copperplate the kind of effect you get from this red paper in the collage. I want those hollowed-out areas to sparkle just like mirrors—perfect glistening parabolic mirrors. There is some mechanical process which takes care of the hollowing and burnishing at the same time. Then, after that, I need to find someone who is capable of making a screen formed of tiny parabolic mirrors. That's the complicated part. But that's the only kind of thing that interests me—the really prodigious." The phone sputtered. Dali picked it up. "And on that I paint," he said to the man in the mustard-colored suit. *"Allô. Parfait. Parfait.* Send them up." He hung up. "I want you to use a special kind of varnish. There's one that's used for both wood and metal and it's better than the one that's especially concocted for engravers."

"I know," the engraver said, "it's called dog's-head varnish."

Dali nodded. "That's it. Use it."

There was a knock at the door. Dali pulled it open. "Aha," he said. Marina Lussato, Christine Forani, and a fat, bald, middle-aged man in a dark-blue suit, carrying several small boxes, trooped in.

"Here's your eye specialist," Mme. Forani said, presenting the fat, bald man.

"Very good," Dali said. "Let's make this a collective intro-duction: I hereby present all the pretty women and all the handsome men—*Bonjour.*" Mme. Forani unloosened a boister-ous guffaw, then coughed apologetically as Dali looked at her questioningly.

"Do you have the flies' eyes?" he asked.

"Yes," she said, "and the ox eyes, too." She pointed to one of the small containers.

"*Parfait.*" Dali looked over her shoulder at Marina Lussato. "Ah, Mademoiselle Lussato, we need sixty young men for the homage to Kant, to carry the object. Can you find them?"

Marina looked perplexed. "Why sixty?" she asked. "It's so many."

"It's a very good number," Dali said. He took one of the small boxes from the eye specialist, opened it, and poked around inside.

"There are flies' eyes and all kinds of bugs' eyes—even the praying mantis," Mme. Forani said. "Those are fantastic. They have the most sharply cut facets of all. I've studied them under a microscope." She picked them out and handed them to Dali. He ran over to his microscope and focused on them. In a min-ute he was back.

"I'll keep these and study them later," he said.

"And there's a whole box of human eyes," Mme. Forani said. The fat man handed him another box. Dali poked around in-side but looked unsatisfied.

"What I want are things that look like contact lenses," he said. "I've seen them in beauty parlors like Helena Rubin-stein's. Mannequins wear them sometimes. The colors are very pretty but in bad taste."

"What you want don't come ready-made," the fat man said. "Those you saw were probably samples."

"That's what I want," Dali said. "Get me some."

"I can make you up some. What width do you want?"

"Normal width," Dali said. "I want them realistic, very life-like, but with colors that are not normal."

Two more men came into the group. The first, of medium height with brown, wavy hair and wearing tortoiseshell glasses, was carrying a book. He was followed by a tall, thin, younger man. He introduced himself as Maurice Rheims, the tall man as Philippe Rheims, his cousin and associate. He handed Dali the book he was carrying.

"A little thing I've done recently," he said. "I believe it's a subject that interests you." It was entitled *L'Objet 1900*. Dali thanked him and flipped through the pages, pausing briefly at a few of the color plates reproducing *art nouveau* decorative objects. "Very fine," he said and returned to the eye specialist.

"Now, I want to have the eyes engraved like this." He borrowed my pen and sketched two eyes on the cover of Rheims' book. The fat man looked at the sketches and then at Dali.

"You mean you want a projection of relief sticking out on the eyes like that?"

"Exactly," Dali said firmly and handed him the book.

Gilbert Prouteau walked in, shook hands with Dali, then went over to speak with Rheims and his cousin. Dali followed him. "What was it you wanted?" Dali asked Maurice Rheims. Prouteau explained that Maître Rheims had come, at Dali's request, to talk about the Meissonier painting that was soon to be auctioned off in one of his sales.

Suddenly all the pieces fitted together. "*Ah, oui,*" Dali said with more enthusiasm. He seated Rheims and his cousin and Prouteau on a sofa near the fireplace and drew up a chair for himself. "My friend Huntington Hartford is very interested in that Meissonier," I heard him say. "He has a museum for *art pompier*. Now what I want to know is . . ." At that moment Mafalda Davis walked in. She was carrying her Chihuahua. The dog was shivering. Dali jumped up. "Get that dog out of here," he said and ran to the telephone, which had been ringing almost continuously. As Mrs. Davis opened the door to leave, Richard, the American photographer, came in, followed by four young Frenchmen.

"We brought the editor with us today," one of them said. Dali set the phone down and came over and shook hands with all of them. The editor presented him with a copy of the latest issue of his magazine—called *Hara Kiri*. Dali told him to sit down; he'd be right back. He handed me the copy of *Hara Kiri* and ran over to Gala, who had just come in from the bedroom, a blue coat thrown over her shoulders. He introduced her to the two Rheimses, then went back to the eye man, to forage in his box of human eyes. Suddenly he darted back to the telephone, which he had left five minutes earlier, hung up, looked into his little black book, picked up the receiver again, and read a number to the operator. In just a moment I heard him say, "Mademoiselle Yvonne? *Bonjour.* Everything will be ready for Saturday or at the latest, Sunday. I'll know this afternoon at five thirty. Call me then."

Mrs. Davis, minus her Chihuahua, came back into the salon, followed by three large Italians speaking all at once, and they by a young blond girl who looked as though she might be Dutch. Close behind them I heard people speaking German. The salon, which was about thirty-five feet square, seemed, for the first time, very small and airless. I noticed it was already past one o'clock, the hour at which Dali should have been sitting down to lunch at the Vicomtesse de Noailles'. Having heard their telephone conversation and learned the importance the Vicomtesse attached to punctuality in such matters, I wondered if I shouldn't try to extract Dali from his compulsive merry-go-round and push him in the direction of 11 Place des Etats-Unis. But he was obviously enjoying himself so thoroughly racing from one little island to the next that I decided not to break up his fun.

Just then, a tall, slender girl with long, blond hair cut in low bangs and wearing a form-fitting pale-pink coat came in. Dali saw her, dropped the human eyeballs he was playing with, and rushed over to where she stood, under the huge crystal chandelier in the center of the salon. He kissed her, then went over to the divan, where Gala was sitting, and kissed *her*. He returned to the blonde, who, presumably, was the "someone very close to Kant" that he had referred to in his telephone conversation with the Vicomtesse de Noailles a few days earlier. He nodded gravely to me and started for the door. Suddenly he stopped. "Ah, my cane," he said and went over to the corner commode, picked up his small cane, and started off again. As he passed me on the return trip, he motioned to Marina Lussato, who was standing near me. "Stay here," he said, then slipped out, blonde in hand.

I found a narrow empty spot in the corner where his cane had been, settled myself into a small side chair, and began to look through the pages of *Hara Kiri*. It was about the size and shape of *Look* but was more closely related, in its general intentions, to *Mad*. The national differences, however, were evident on every page. The humor was, to say the least, more sophisticated and, in spots, both black and blue. ("If Jesus Christ came back on earth, would you go right on pissing in the sink?") The artwork would never have passed the censor in Boston, with or without the help of the Watch and Ward Society. How it got by Mme. De Gaulle, I couldn't imagine.

Suddenly I became conscious of a marked shift in the noise pattern: no longer the burble of competitive conversations but the hurried shuffling of many feet. I looked up and saw the entire crowd—there must have been nearly fifty of them—pressing through the doors that led into the outside corridor. I got up and went over to Richard, the photographer, who was on the side nearer to me.

"Gala is sending everybody away," he said. I could hear her voice behind the herd, but it was hard to make out what she was saying.

"Why?" I asked him.

"Beats me," he said, "but she's obviously very unhappy about something."

In a minute or two more they were all outside. Gala looked over at me bitterly.

"That's the press for you," she muttered. "You're nice to them and look what happens."

The only person in the salon of Dali's apartment when I arrived the next morning was *le Divin* himself. He was standing at the mantelpiece studying an object which I took to be the sculpture Mafalda Davis had told me that Christine Forani was executing in collaboration with Dali. It was a slender piece about two feet high, not easily classifiable. The base was a turtle. Clutching the turtle's shell from above was what appeared to be the claw of an eagle, which was continued upward by a convulsively winding stem in which it was difficult not to see the influence of the Catalan architect Antoni Gaudí. At a height of about fifteen inches above the base, the stem flowered into a pair of lips. From each end of the lips emerged a kind of ear from which hung a circular earring. Above the lips the sculpture continued its ascent in the form of a neck for another four inches or so before reaching its climax—another turtle, this one smaller than the one at the base and upside down, held in place by a slender six-inch spear. The main body of the sculpture had been worked in a reddish-brown wax.

Dali picked up a whitened, V-shaped bone formation that strongly resembled the framework of a turkey wing. "I found this just the other day," he said. "I knew I'd have a use for it sooner or later. It will look good here. It makes a kind of nose." He pressed it into the wax above the lips, then hooked it around the back of the neck to give it a firmer hold. He stood back and studied it for a moment, then looked around the room. "Ah!" he exclaimed. He went over to a basket of fruit someone had sent him for his birthday a week or so earlier. A lone banana, blackened, shrunken, and now, at one end, covered with a thick greenish-white mold lay on top of the remains of a bunch of grapes. Dali picked up the banana and brought it back to the sculpture. He wrapped it around the stem, trying it in several positions until he found one that satisfied him. It oozed at one end like an overripe Camembert and began to sag. He picked up a piece of green string from the table and tied the banana into position, then stepped back for another look.

"That's the miracle," he said. "I want this to be more complicated than any known style—Louis Quatorze or anything else. This is the way it will be—just as you see it now. And these things come to me because I keep on the move. Like the turkey wing: I found it on the street the other day. Someone who sits around all day with his fist pressed against his jaw, like *The Thinker* of Rodin, is all fucked up from the start. That's fine for shitting, that posture, but not for thinking. As soon as you put yourself in that position, ideas stop coming. Whereas with me, one person comes, then another, and they all give me ideas. I go out into the street, from one place to another, and the ideas keep flowing. I have the philosophy of the man who works and plays at the same time; that is, who thinks but who acts, whose whole life is an elaboration of his thought and whose thought is constantly expressed in his play—in his whole way of life."

I told him I had never seen anyone work quite so hard at his play.

"Because when I play, I get results. After I've left Paris, the ideas bear fruit and the results come streaming in. The play is all part of my work. Everything is grist to my mill. Everything serves some purpose. Even the scraps that are left over find their way into my next book." He pointed to the sculpture. "There it is: my work and at the same time my play. Behind it are all those other people, all those meetings and chance encounters and all the little details that in themselves don't always seem to make sense, until you see the results. That is, unless you understand the way I function. For that reason I'm glad you were here yesterday. You had a good chance to see how I operate.

"You see now how important every one of those little details is. Like the flies' eyes." He took a quick glance into his microscope. "You've seen that already," he said. He picked up the two sheets of engraved transparent plastic with which he had demonstrated the three-dimensional moiré pattern on the copperplate the day before.

"These sheets are made up of parabolic lenses on a plastic film, to be used in my three-dimensional painting. The painting would be extraordinary, even using that. But when I use the eyes of a fly, it will be much better, because flies' eyes are smaller and more perfect. They were made by God with a precision a thousand times greater than any human hand could achieve. The man who engraved that strip of plastic did it bit by bit with great care, just as though he were working on a copperplate. He worked all day long with a magnifying glass just to turn out a piece an inch or two square. It's an exhausting job. But when I put real flies' eyes in my painting, they will already contain those lenses, the most perfectly constructed in the entire range of nature. The idea is pure genius. When I lay on my varnish, I'll plant the eyes of the fly on the canvas and then let it dry. And when I paint the fly, he'll already have his eyes—the very parabolic lenses that nature provided."

Was this for the painting he had mentioned before—*Gala with Bees?*

"That's right," Dali said. "And now that they've brought me all those other eyes, I'll be able to superimpose other things right out of nature." He held up an eyeball and squinted at it. "With this I'll make the pupil. I much prefer to do it with things made by the good Lord than to utilize those plastic sheets and the varnish. I'll have those patterns engraved on the part of the pupil that swells and you'll see the eyes pop right out of the canvas into another dimension—just like that moiré-treated paper I showed you."

The telephone rang. Dali answered it. It was Gilbert Prouteau. "Ah, yes, about Monday morning. Your assistant telephoned me," Dali said. "It was agreed that someone will come pick me up. But at nine fifteen I must be back here because I promised Madame Dali that we would leave for Spain at nine thirty. I take it seven thirty is too early for you. Well, you don't need me for the whole sequence, anyway, do you? Your assistant said fifteen minutes ought to suffice. *Bon*. Come at eight o'clock and physically pick me up here. You'll take me there, I'll make my little speech, which shouldn't last more than ten minutes, so that by nine thirty I can be ready to leave. Because after that it will be too late. Those are the conditions laid down by Madame Dali. *Merci. Bonjour.*" He hung up. He went back to the sculpture and adjusted the green string a bit more carefully around the precariously perched oozing banana.

"We'll get this cast in bronze right away," he said. "Descharnes is preparing the exhibition for Japan and this will go along with the rest."

There was a timid knock at the door. Dali had picked up the telephone and was giving a number to the operator, so I went over to the door. It was the tall blond girl from a Brussels newspaper whom I had met the morning of my second visit, the girl Dali had tried—and failed—to impress by offering to play for her a tape recording of a woman in bed with two men.

"*Allô*," Dali said into the phone and then looked up at the girl. "*Bonjour*," he said without much enthusiasm. He contin-

ued to look as she walked toward him and then said, *"Ah, non.*
I thought you were someone else. I'll say *Bonjour* again, with
more feeling this time." They both laughed. He went back to
his phone conversation with a woman he had called to say good-
bye to, then, after a moment, hung up.

"Excuse me," he said to the girl. "We had an appointment?"
She shook her head.

"Ah, very good. Very good," Dali said sarcastically.

The girl laughed. "Dear God, preserve me from my friends.
I'll take care of my enemies."

Dali walked over to the sculpture and began pinching the
wax here and there. He began to talk to me about the girl as
though she were not there. "Another Dalinian by spontaneous
combustion," he said. "Along with a thousand others. Perhaps
she's not fully blown yet, but she's going to become one." He
turned to the girl, then nodded in the direction of the American photographer, Richard, trailing the maid out of the bedroom, each of them carrying an armful of old papers and empty
boxes. "That photographer who is helping the maid clean up
the bedroom right now has to do that job in order to placate
Madame Dali because he came here twice without notifying us
in advance, without telephoning—like you. The other times you
always called." The girl hung her head in mock shame.

"Suppose I was busy," Dali said. "Let's say I had my finger
in a young virgin when you came along. That's all right with
me; you could complete the circle. That would make it more
amusing. But when I'm with Madame Dali, there should be less
confusion." He turned back to the sculpture. "Oh, this is a
marvel," he said admiringly.

The photographer came into the salon and stopped to watch
Dali give a few finishing touches to the wax model. Dali looked
at him in the mirror. "Is your job finished?" he asked, without
turning around.

"Yes, everything's fine," Richard said.

"All right. Just make sure there are no old boxes or tubes

lying around. That way, Madame Dali *may* forgive you for showing up without telephoning." Dali turned to the girl. "I'll figure out something for you later on. You'll do your penance but not right away. You have to be worthy of it first."

"Shall I tell you a story instead?" she asked with great politeness.

"What's your story?"

"It's about a man who went to see his doctor. The doctor asked him what was wrong. He said, 'I have a penis the size of a three-year-old boy.' The doctor held up two fingers about half an inch apart. 'Like that?' he asked. The man held out his hand about two feet above the floor. 'No, like that,' he said."

"*Ah, oui,*" Dali said slowly. "Well, have you heard any of the stories going around about black balls?" The phone spluttered. Dali picked it up.

"*Allô. Oui. Ah, bravo, bravo.*" He looked over at me. "Mademoiselle Yvonne," he said, then returned to the phone. "Did they telephone to you about this evening at the Galerie Charpentier—eight o'clock? Yes, I know you know, but your television lady should know, too, because they're supposed to come here, she and her husband. They've got to pick up the jacket. You can't put it on here and wear it. It will have to be carried over and she will have to pick it up—I can't remember her name—and you'll put it on over there. So have her call me right away. I'll be here until one. Then maybe Monday at eight o'clock you'll have to take part in a film. No, eight in the morning. You see how it is: for Dali you must suffer. A lot. *Bonjour.*" He hung up. I asked him if everything was all set for this evening.

"Oh, yes," he said. "The sculptor has been away in Brussels, but he's back now and working feverishly to get the job done. He's trying to slip in a few ideas of his own, and I telephone him from time to time because I can see his imagination is trying to run away with him. It's a very ticklish situation. Anyway, the ceremony will take place at eight this evening at the Galerie

Charpentier. We've decided it should be completely secret: just the Vicomtesse de Noailles, myself, the sculptor, and maybe sixty bearers. But no friends. If I invite *some* friends, I'll have to invite others and then it would get out of hand. This way it will be a kind of Masonic rite, all very private."

And the film? I asked.

"That's for Monday. We've got the Meissonier that Rheims is going to sell. It's a marvelous one, better than the one at the Hotel Raphaël. I'm going to make a speech which will last about ten minutes, Mademoiselle Yvonne will make a dream appearance, and that's all, because at nine thirty I must be ready to leave here; otherwise I'll be late for lunch."

Someone knocked. The Belgian girl opened the door and Descharnes came in. He shook hands with us. "There's another number for your catalog," Dali said, pointing in the direction of the sculpture. Descharnes went over to look at it. "Is it ready for casting now?" he asked.

Dali nodded. "It's a marvelous thing," he said. "I think I'll send two—one in bronze, one in gold." The phone rang. Dali picked it up.

"Ah, yes," he said. "The situation is as follows: the ceremony takes place this evening at eight o'clock at the Galerie Charpentier. You or your husband should come here at seven to pick up the jacket she will wear. Perfect. Thank you very much. Yes, that's possible, but that is for a film on the history of painting—nothing to do with television; there'll be no conflict, therefore. We'll talk about that this evening. Thank you. Good-bye."

There was a knock at the door. *"Entrez,"* Dali called out.

Marina Lussato came in with a young man, short, dark, with bright, dark eyes. Her brother Bruno, Descharnes told me. Dali kissed her on the forehead and held out his hand to her brother. He kissed it. Marina handed a paper bag to Dali. He opened it and took out a sheer pink negligee. He held it up to his face. "It's perfumed," he said.

"Will it do?" she asked.

"It's perfect," he said. He stepped back and sat down on his *bergère.* "What's the latest news?" he asked. Speaking very fast, Bruno Lussato started in on a recital of his relations with the sculptor Rutsch. Dali cut him short. "Just tell me this—in your opinion is the news good or bad? Then I'll give you my version."

"I think it's rather bad," Bruno said.

"You mean the object won't be ready, or it's only so-so, or what?"

"I don't know whether Rutsch will get it done or not," Bruno said excitedly. "I keep calling him but I don't get any answer—all last night and this morning."

"That's good," Dali said. "That means he's in his studio working."

"But I did get the leg," Bruno said. "And the stocking."

"Good. Bring the leg. And she'll need a piece of gauze. So go back to the Bazar de l'Hotel de Ville and get a yard—no, better make it two—of tulle. White tulle. And have some red roses sewn on."

"How many?" Marina asked.

"Enough to cover the face and the back of the neck."

"Live roses?" Bruno asked.

"No, no, no, no. Artificial. The most artificial you can find. She'll have the most extravagant coiffure and she'll be carrying Kant's leg in her arms. What would she be doing with *live* roses?"

Christine Forani and Mafalda Davis came in, followed by two men I hadn't seen before.

"Come here, Baroness," Dali said. "I want to show you something about the mouth." He took Mme. Forani over to the sculpture. "I want that mouth more natural-looking. Follow the same contour but make it more natural. Wider, too."

"The mouth on the Venus de Milo is two and a half inches wide. Would that be wide enough for this?" Mme. Forani asked.

Mrs. Davis moved into the circle. "Make it more sexy," she said.

"No, no," Dali said. "I don't want any sex in that mouth."

Mme. Forani shrugged. "All right. I'll do it over. I'll make it larger, but I don't like the idea." She seemed to be looking at the banana for the first time. "What's that? A rotten banana? What's the point of that?"

"The point of that is a rotten banana," Dali said. "You leave everything just the way it is."

"But if you send that to Tokyo, it will run all over everything."

"Once it's cast, it won't run anywhere," Dali said. "Then it will be a rotten banana in dark bronze. Besides, it's going to be done in gold." His eyes glistened. "And when the Japanese see that thing in gold quivering away inside its glass case, that *will* be something."

"Oh, wait, I almost forgot," Mrs. Davis called out. She picked up one of the packages of American chewing gum, stuck a piece in her mouth, and passed out the others to Marina and her brother, Mme. Forani, and the photographer. "This ought to work better than the French bubble gum," she said. They all chewed vigorously for a minute or two, then passed back the results to Mrs. Davis. She wadded them together and stuck the ball onto the statue. In spite of her efforts it kept falling off. She looked crestfallen. "That's no better than the French bubble gum," she said. "In fact, not as good."

"It's the sugar," Mme. Forani said. "I've found a gum manufacturer who's going to get me some without the sugar."

Dali looked over at her with raised eyebrows. "Good. Good. That's what I like to see—people who function."

Mme. Forani smiled broadly. "In that domain all things are possible."

Dali took a sharp look at the upside-down turtle. "That's too small," he said. Mrs. Davis fingered it. "Yes. You want a better-looking turtle than that," she said.

"A bigger one, too," Dali said. "And it should be darker."

"But there aren't any bigger ones anywhere in Paris," she said. "I've called every taxidermist in town."

"Then we'll get one in Barcelona," Dali said. "Just like the one I have at home. A beauty."

"Oh, good," Mrs. Davis said. "That will make a nice trip for somebody."

Descharnes took a closer look at the turtle. "That looks a lot like the one you have in Cadaqués."

Dali shook his head. "No, it's much smaller. And it doesn't have the same shape, either."

"I think there's a place at the Flea Market where we can get one," Marina said.

"I've seen a huge turtle, with beautiful markings, in a shop in Montmartre," Richard said. "Just what you need."

"Bravo," Dali said. "But find it by five o'clock this afternoon and bring it to me here before six. There's a lot to be done before I leave on Monday, and I don't want anything to hold up the ceremony at the Galerie Charpentier tonight."

"But if all this takes too long," Mrs. Davis said, "Susse may tell us they can't finish the casting by the end of August. They're pretty busy."

"Then we'll tell them, 'If it's too much for you—good-bye,' " Dali said.

"That's right," Mrs. Davis said. "And we'll tell them we'll send someone to pick it up. They'll change their tune. They'll find a way to finish it within a week."

"But that's not the problem now," Dali said. "What we need first is the big turtle."

"But if it's very big, it will make the sculpture top-heavy," Marina said.

"I'll take care of that," Dali said. "It will be screwed to the top with a golden ball." He turned to Mme. Forani. "I'll give you the *bon à tirer* on that tomorrow."

"Are you going to keep it here till then?" she asked.

"Of course. I want to be thinking about it. Already I've had the inspiration for the banana. Something else good may come along." Mme. Forani looked unconvinced. "You let me worry about that," Dali said. "We'll do this systematically. Now go look for the big turtle—all of you."

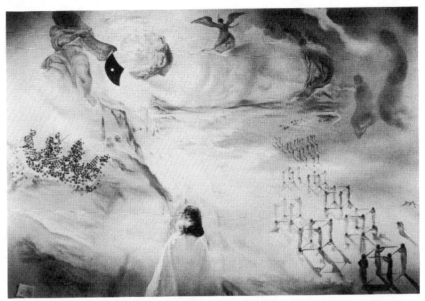

Salvador Dali. *Galacidalacidesoxiribunucleicacid (Homage to Crick and Watson).* Oil on canvas. "...my longest title in one word." Photograph courtesy M. Knoedler & Co., Inc., New York.

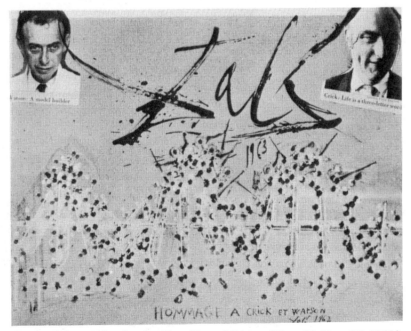

Cover of the catalog for the Knoedler exhibition (Nov. 26–Dec. 26, 1963) that featured Dali's painting *Galacidalacidesoxiribunucleicacid (Homage to Crick and Watson).* "...its vertical axis was now horizontal." Courtesy M. Knoedler & Co., Inc., New York. Photograph by Barney Burstein.

Salvador Dali. *The Persistence of Memory*, 1931. Oil on canvas. "... I foresaw the whole idea, and now they are getting around to proving it scientifically." Collection, The Museum of Modern Art, New York.

J.-F. Millet. *The Angelus*. Louvre. "... the most erotic picture ever painted." Photograph by Roger-Viollet.

Salvador Dali. *Illumined Pleasures*, 1929. Oil and collage on composition board. Sidney and Harriet Janis Collection. Gift to The Museum of Modern Art, New York. One of the paintings shown at Dali's first Paris exhibition, at the Galerie Goemans. Photograph by Geoffrey Clements.

à l'assurer contre la transpiration, s'il était occupé à quelque exercice actif, il avait un singulier remède en réserve. Il se retirait alors dans un endroit ombragé et demeurait immobile avec l'air et l'attitude d'une personne qui écoute ou qui attend, jusqu'à ce que son *aridité* coutumière lui eût été rendue. Même par les nuits d'été les plus étouffantes, si la plus légère trace de transpiration avait souillé ses vêtements de nuit, il en parlait avec emphase comme d'un accident qui l'avait choqué au plus haut point.

Et, puisque nous sommes en train d'exposer les notions qu'entretenait Kant sur l'économie animale, il pourra être bon d'ajouter un autre détail, qui est que, par crainte d'entraver la circulation du sang, il ne portait jamais de jarretières. Cependant, comme il avait trouvé difficile de garder ses bas tirés sans leur aide, il avait inventé à son usage un appareil extrêmement élaboré que je vais décrire. Dans un petit gousset, un peu plus petit qu'un gousset de montre, mais occupant assez exactement la même place qu'un gousset de montre au-dessus de chaque cuisse, était placée une petite boîte assez semblable à un boîtier de montre, mais plus petite. Dans cette boîte avait été introduit un ressort de montre roulé en spirale, et autour de cette spirale était placée une cordelette élastique dont la force était réglée par un mécanisme spécial. Aux deux extrémités de cette cordelette étaient attachés des crochets : ces crochets passaient à travers une petite ouverture des goussets, descendaient ainsi tout le long du côté interne et externe de la cuisse et allaient saisir deux œillères fixées à la partie extérieure et intérieure de chaque bas. Ainsi qu'on peut bien le supposer, une machinerie si compliquée était soumise, comme le système céleste de Ptolémée, à des dérangements occasionnels. Mais, par bonne fortune, j'étais alors capable de remédier facilement à ces désordres qui autrement

Dali's text for the Homage to Kant ceremony at the Galerie Charpentier: from the French translation of De Quincey's "The Last Days of Immanuel Kant." Photograph by Barney Burstein.

Marcel Duchamp. *The Large Glass*, 1915–23, or *The Bride Stripped Bare by Her Bachelors, Even*. A "delay in glass, just like a poem in prose or a spittoon in silver." Louise and Walter Arensberg Collection, Philadelphia Museum of Art. Photograph by A. J. Wyatt, staff photographer.

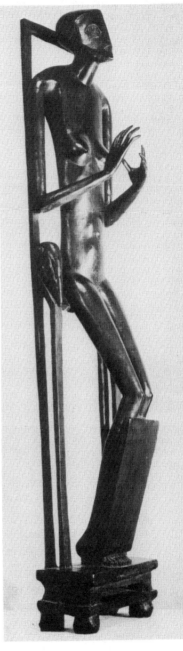

Alberto Giacometti. *Woman*, 1926. "...a
highly abstract bronze...four feet
high..." Photograph Galerie Maeght.

Alberto Giacometti. *Invisible Object*,
1934–35. Bronze. "...both mysterious
and mystified." Photograph by Claude
Gaspari, courtesy Galerie Maeght.

Alexandre Rutsch. Sculpture in welded iron. One element of the Monument to Immanuel Kant. "It might have been a tree form hugging its branches or an abstraction of a human figure."

Alexandre Rutsch. Metal sculpture.

Alexandre Rutsch. Detail of the Monument to Immanuel Kant at the Galerie Charpentier. Photograph by Pierre Joly—Véra Cardot.

An early sketch by Alexandre Rutsch for his Monument to Kant sculpture. Photograph by Barney Burstein.

Alexandre Rutsch's final design for his Monument to Kant sculpture. Photograph by Barney Burstein.

Salvador Dali himself. Photograph courtesy of Brown Brothers.

I arrived at the Place Beauvau at about twenty minutes before eight Saturday evening. That stretch of the Faubourg St.-Honoré was deserted except for the usual *gardes républicains* in front of the Élysée Palace. Across the street, at the Galerie Charpentier, there were no signs of life, but the glass doors leading from the sidewalk to the lobby were ajar. As I entered, a watchman came out into the lobby from a small room at the left. I told him I had an appointment with M. Dali.

"He's not here yet, but you can go in," he said and opened the door into the gallery for me. The Surrealism retrospective was still on view, and since the gallery was otherwise almost empty, I had the impression I was seeing the exhibition for the first time. I could stand in one spot and see all around me groups of paintings and sculptures by Dali, Max Ernst, Miró, and others that seemed to be parts of a cohesive whole. My earlier visit had seemed more like a trip through dense undergrowth with, here and there, an occasional stop before an isolated tree in an otherwise invisible forest.

The room was about seventy-five feet deep. What stood out most clearly now, halfway down, beyond a long refectory-type table that during visiting hours held books, posters, and catalogs sold by gallery attendants, was one of the great monuments of the modern movement in art: Marcel Duchamp's *The Bride Stripped Bare by Her Bachelors, Even.* It is a large, transparent glass, more than nine feet high and nearly six feet wide, set in a heavy steel framework. It would be considered a painting except for the fact that Duchamp didn't care for the idea of calling it one and named it a "delay in glass." "Just like a poem in prose or a spittoon in silver," he wrote. He was writing in French and his word for delay—*retard*—was not to be considered as meaning any one specific thing, he made clear; simply a vague collection of all possible meanings of the word.

Duchamp's oil on canvas *Nude Descending a Staircase* had been a *succès de scandale* at the New York Armory Show of 1913. Soon after that, Duchamp gave up painting, which he no longer considered an adequate means of expression. Even before the Armory Show, and for ten years after, he devoted most of his energies to *The Bride.* The kind of painting he executed on the glass was an extension of mechanical drawing put to philosophic and metaphorical purposes, because Duchamp had come to feel that conventional drawing and painting had reached a dead end and had to be unlearned; they were too manual and visual and not sufficiently cerebral. That criticism could not be leveled against *The Bride.* Its various formal elements, such as the chocolate-grinder, at lower right, the bachelor-machine (nine Malic molds), at lower left, the bride, or "hanging female," at upper left (a fuller version of which Duchamp had painted on canvas in 1912), resemble equipment that might be used in chemical or other scientific laboratories. But Duchamp's concept of the work, which he had elaborated in a series of notes and drawings between 1910 and 1915, endows them with an identity and function not immediately visible to the casual observer. For example:

The bachelors serving as an architectonic base for the Bride, she becomes a sort of apotheosis of virginity. Steam-engine with masonry foundations on this brick base. Solid course, the bachelor-machine, fat, lecherous (develop). At the point (still going up) where this eroticism (which must be one of the main cogs in the bachelor-machine) is revealed . . . this tormented cog gives birth to the desire-part of the machine. This desire-part then changes its power from steam to the internal-combustion engine. (Develop the desire motor, a consequence of the lecherous cog.) This desire motor is the last part of the bachelor-machine. Far from being in direct contact with the Bride, the desire motor is separated by an air- (or water-) cooler.

This cooler (graphically) in order to express the fact that the Bride, instead of being only an asensual icicle, refuses hotly (not chastely) the rough offer of the bachelors . . .

In general, if this Bride motor is to appear as an apotheosis of virginity, that is, ignorant, blank desire (with a touch of malice) . . . a white-metal bracket could simulate the virgin's attachment to her girl-friends and her parents (they corresponding graphically to a solid base on firm ground, just as the masonry base of the bachelor-machine, also, rests on firm ground.[)]

The Bride, at bottom, is a motor. But before being a motor which transmits its timid power—she is that timid power itself. This timid power is a sort of baby automobile fuel of love, which, distributed to the very weak cylinders, within range of the sparks of its ever-present life, helps bring about the opening-up of this virgin who has reached the end-point of her desire . . .

For five years, before he went to work on the glass, Duchamp explored in minute detail, along parallel paths of literal and symbolic suggestion, every aspect of the Bride's function. In his notes he gives the machine a life of its own and raises countless disturbing and unanswerable questions about its role in ours—questions that fifty years later seem just as relevant and no less disturbing. It seems eminently logical that after thirteen years of constant preoccupation with *The Bride,* Duchamp should have left it unfinished in 1923.

The Bride, even less finished than it is today, was first in the Arensberg Collection. In 1921 the Arensbergs sold it to Miss Katherine Dreier. Today, along with most of Duchamp's other works, it is in the Philadelphia Museum of Art. The Galerie Charpentier *Bride* was not the Philadelphia original but a copy executed by Ulf Linde in Stockholm in 1961. It was marked in French, "Certified an exact copy," and signed in white paint, "Marcel Duchamp, Stockholm, 1961." It had been loaned for the exhibition by the Stockholm Modern Museum.

As I looked through the glass—the greater part of its surface having no painting to obstruct the view—I caught a glimpse of the blond student whom Dali had commissioned to find eleven other young men to carry the *Homage to Kant* in tonight's ceremony. There was no sign of his eleven, but I did see three young bearded Spaniards, one very short, the other two very tall. The tallest carried some kind of walking stick with which he kept hitting himself on the hand or the leg. They had just finished moving into place, about twenty feet beyond *The Bride,* eight high-backed chairs covered in red velvet and divided into two separate clusters, each facing toward the marble steps that led up to the platform at the far end of the gallery. At the top of the steps, on a landing about eight feet deep, Rutsch and Bruno Lussato were arranging a sculpture group that could only have been the monument to Kant that Rutsch had been working on, under mandate from Dali, over the past five days.

At the far left and right ends of the platform, which stretched for thirty or more feet across much of the gallery's width, stood two of Giacometti's best-known older sculptures: at the right, a highly abstract bronze *Woman,* four feet high, of 1926; at the left, *Invisible Object,* of 1934–35, a more readily recognizable female figure in bronze, about five feet two inches high. This second figure, seated in a kind of chair frame, inclined slightly forward, her mouth agape and her hands reaching out toward the new sculpture group, seemed both mysterious and mystified.

At the center of the right-hand element of Rutsch's assemblage was a fifteen-foot pointed iron pole. At the top, flaring out on each side, was a pair of silver-painted metal winglike forms that had a familiar look to them. As I studied them, I realized they were the rear fenders from a Citroën *deux-chevaux,* the popular low-powered, low-cost French car sometimes referred to as "the sardine can."

Near the top of the pole, on the right, hung an iron form that suggested the outline of a leg. Over that was stretched a heavy nylon stocking. Nearer the center was a rusty chain from which hung a lady's gilded pump with a gilded paintbrush inserted into the vamp.

At the left of this group was another sculpture unit, about five feet high, broad and solid, with darkened bronze strips across the front and rising out of the top, that bore a vague resemblance to a Benin bronze.

From the foot of the steps Rutsch and Bruno now carried up and set down at the right of the other two pieces a third one, formed of thin rusty welded-iron bands that swirled upward to a height of about seven feet. It might have been a tree form hugging its branches or an abstraction of a human figure. It had a round metal coil-like arm that jutted out to the left toward the high central element of the group. Rutsch was wearing gray trousers and a high-necked blue knit jersey. He was sweating and his face was flushed. He picked up a squarish object bearing a small bronze plaque and set it down on the projecting arm. This, I realized, was the *Homage to Kant,* attributed to Dali, that I had seen in the glass case at the back of the gallery on my first trip to the Surrealism exhibition.

Rutsch stood off and surveyed his sculpture group, then pushed the seven-foot piece on the right nearer to the tall part in the center. He reached up to the iron leg form to adjust the stocking. As he moved it to one side, he brushed against the piece at the right and knocked the *Homage to Kant* off its projecting arm onto the platform. It rolled over to the steps and then bounced all the way down to the main floor, shedding chips as it went. Everybody groaned. Rutsch looked horror-stricken. He ran down the steps, picked up the *Homage,* and examined it carefully. He held it up.

"That makes no difference," he said. "The thought is intact. This demonstrates the utter worthlessness of materiality." He turned to Bruno. "Pick up the bits," he said. "We'll spread them around the base of the statue." He started up the steps toward his sculpture. Two steps before the top he tripped, lost his balance, and fell. The *Homage* slipped from his hands and came crashing to the floor. This time when he picked it up, cotton wadding was oozing out of the top. Without looking back he walked slowly up the steps and replaced the object on its coil.

Near the top of the pointed pole in the center was an upside-down horseshoe; a few inches beneath that, a rectangular metal box resembling the cover of an old-fashioned telephone box, full of used electric light bulbs and cheap plastic pens. Between the two was a small rectangular piece of metal with two holes. Into each one a green eye had been inserted. Rutsch stood up on a chair and attached a small pocket flashlight behind the metal rectangle. One of the eyes lighted up eerily; the other remained dull. He took another small flashlight from his pocket and attached it next to the first. The second eye glowed.

"It's like two universes," he said.

Bruno Lussato, standing below, called up to him. "I doubt that those batteries will last."

"How much time in them?" Rutsch asked him.

"Perhaps an hour. Perhaps not that much."

Rutsch jumped down off his chair. Another upside-down horseshoe had been fitted onto the pole, near its base. Rutsch tested its solidity. He began pushing and tugging at the two outside elements of the group, bringing them nearer the central pole, then pushing them away. He seemed unsure of just what relationship the three parts should have to one another.

"Leave it alone, Rutsch," Marina Lussato called up from the foot of the steps. "It's just right as it is." Rutsch beamed down at her and bowed.

"Can you see the stocking and the shoe clearly?" he asked.

"Yes, they're fine," she called back. "*Laissez donc.*"

Behind the platform, at intervals of about six feet, were three doors leading to the smaller rear rooms of the gallery. Wearing black tights and high-heeled black patent-leather pumps and a short dark-blue raincoat obviously not her own, Yvonne came through the right-hand door, down the steps to where I was standing. Her hair had gone from golden blond to pale taffy, and instead of the usual upswept coiffure, she was wearing it long and bouffant. Marina Lussato came over to her, carrying a white tulle veil, to which five very artificial red roses had been sewn. Yvonne tried it over her hair and let it drape down over her shoulders like a mantilla, then took it off. Marina handed her the dinner jacket with its attached crème de menthe glasses, and she returned, over the same route, to the back room.

Up on the platform, Rutsch and Bruno Lussato continued to tinker with the flashlights. The green eyes went on and off like the night lights on a distant airliner. Twice Rutsch dropped one of the small flashlights but without breaking the bulb.

I heard a noise behind me. I turned and saw Dali bearing down on us, hatless, clutching his enameled stick, followed by Gala, Christine Forani, Descharnes, and a few other friends.

"No, no, that's not it. Take it all away," he shouted. As he passed me, I could see his slender mustache quivering. He ran up the steps to where Rutsch and Bruno Lussato were standing. "Take it all away," he said, giving a shove to the Kant-bearing tree on the right. Miraculously Kant stayed on his coil. Dali lifted off the *Homage*. "Leave the wings high up like that," he

said. "Put the monument down low." He set it down on the
floor.

"But why down there?" Rutsch asked.

"Don't worry, I'm going to put it up again, but for the moment we'll leave it there," Dali said.

"But I don't understand why you have to rearrange all these
things," Rutsch protested. "Why can't you leave it to the laws
of chance?"

"The important thing is to get rid of your old scrap iron,"
Dali said. "The wings must be free. Then I'll put the monument on a small base, down low." Rutsch, crestfallen, began
to push the offending elements away. Two of the bearded
Spaniards came up the steps and helped him pull them out of
sight into the corridor behind the platform. Dali came down
the steps.

"Anyway, the wings are beautiful," he said to me. "A lot better than those." He pointed in the direction of an immense oil
fresco—*Petals and Garden of the Nymph Ancolie,* by Max
Ernst—painted on eighteen grouped movable panels, which
dominated everything on the right-hand wall. It was about
fourteen feet high and eighteen feet wide, with yellow, green,
blue, and red abstract floral motifs—some of which bore a certain resemblance to wings—against a gray background.

Bruno Lussato came over to Dali, carrying a department
store display mannequin's leg dressed with a red stocking, garnet up to the knee, sheer pale rose from there on. "We haven't
got the slipper for this," he said.

"Never mind. We'll finish it tomorrow," Dali said. "Pierre
Cardin will come and dress it." Bruno took the leg up to the
tall lone centerpiece and moved gingerly around it, trying to
attach it without disturbing the two green-eyed universes. He
pointed to the two horseshoes.

"That's the Omega and the Omega-minus," he said proudly.

"Perfect," Dali said. "They can stay. Then there's just the
shoe, but that can be taken care of afterward. The important

thing now is to take the photograph just the way it is. Later we'll photograph it in its definitive form."

Rutsch brought over a small chair and set it down in front of the pole. He carefully placed the battered *Homage* on it. One of the bearded Spaniards came over with a white boxlike pedestal, not over a foot high. Dali transferred the *Homage* from the chair to the pedestal and handed the chair to Rutsch. Then he bent over and attached to the white pedestal, just beneath the *Homage,* a small gilt-framed object. I walked up nearer to him and saw, from the marginal markings in red crayon, that it was the page he had shown me in the French edition of De Quincey's essay "The Last Days of Immanuel Kant" relating to the method Kant had developed of holding up his stockings without garters in order not to interfere with the circulation in his legs. Apparently Dali had torn the page out of the book and had it framed.

"*Voilà*," he said, straightening up. "*Ça va maintenant.*" Descharnes aimed his camera at the revision.

"That will be just right for Tokyo," he said. "One more number for the catalog." He looked pleased.

Dali picked up the tulle mantilla. "Not enough roses," he said. He handed it to Marina. Yvonne came out of the corridor and down the steps. She had shed the raincoat and replaced it with the dinner jacket. Since the dinner jacket was much shorter than the raincoat, her legs seemed to have grown at least a foot in the interval. An eager volunteer stepped forward with a handful of straws—all glisteningly plastic, only a few of them a dubious yellow—which he carefully set, one by one, into her crème de menthe glasses. Marina returned with the mantilla: seven roses now grew where five had grown before. Standing on the tips of her toes she placed it over Yvonne's head, again like a mantilla.

Back on the platform, Dali detached the mannequin's leg from the pole and held it about four inches vertically above the *Homage.* "That's the way it belongs," he said to Rutsch. He

looked down at Marina, adjusting the tulle mantilla. He ran
down the steps, took the tulle, wrapped it loosely over Yvonne's
face, and held it together at the back of her neck. I could barely
distinguish her features behind it.

"That's the way it should go," he said. "Attach it in that position."

A short, full-bosomed woman, fortyish, deeply tanned, with
close-cropped, silvered hair, came over to us. She was wearing
an exceptionally low-cut, tight-fitting black sweater. Between
her breasts she had planted a package of Gauloises cigarettes.
The gray-blue of the wrapper on the warm brown made a pleas-
ing combination. She looked a youthful, cool Gertrude Stein.

"Ah, here's the television lady," Dali said. His eyes focused
on the Gauloises package. "It's a pity I don't smoke." She
laughed richly and compounded the resemblance. Dali left us
and went over to Yvonne.

"No, no," he said. "Like this." He rearranged her headdress.
The television lights went on and the camera began to prowl.
Dali turned and rushed past me toward the back of the room.
I looked up and saw Marie-Laure de Noailles standing at the
long refectory-type table twenty feet or so behind Duchamp's
Bride. Dali kissed her hand. The television lights and camera
moved in their direction. Marie-Laure held up her hand in the
gesture of a policeman halting traffic. "No photographers, no
television," she said.

The Vicomte and the Vicomtesse de Noailles were among the
early supporters of the Surrealist revolt, and when Dali arrived
in Paris, they were his first patrons. The Vicomtesse de Noailles
is a painter and signs her canvases Marie-Laure. I hadn't seen
her in at least a dozen years. Time seemed to have given her
more serenity than she had the last time I saw her. Dressed simply in black and wearing glasses, she looked almost benign and
quite grandmotherly. The camera and lights withdrew. Dali explained to her that the ceremony was about to begin. He sent
the three Spanish beards to take up posts around the monu-

ment. The tallest one seemed uncertain where he should stand. *"Detrás,"* Dali hollered, and motioned him behind the sculpture. The next tallest sat down on the top step at the left, and the shortest at the right of the monument.

Yvonne was standing on the left, at the foot of the steps. Dali went over to her and gave her last-minute directions, then started up the steps toward the sculpture. Richard, the photographer, came rushing in with a box in his arms and showed it to Dali. Dali reached in and pulled out a large turtle with handsome markings.

"Bravo!" he said. "You were right. It *is* just what we need." He walked up the few remaining steps and put the turtle in front of the monument. Dali stood beside it, staring straight ahead, gripping his stick, Mercury-fashion. The television lights were in position and I could hear the camera turning. Dali began to speak, gesticulating with one hand. It was no language I was familiar with. It seemed to have no vowels. As he talked, Yvonne walked elegantly up the steps and entered the left-hand door, turned right along the corridor, showed herself briefly through the middle door and came out at the far right, then walked in the same stately manner across the platform and started down the steps. By now Dali was shouting his unintelligible gibberish and waving a clenched fist. His eyes darted wildly in every direction. His face was flushed and the veins in his neck stood out. Yvonne reached the floor and faced the camera. Dali ended his harangue with a final series of explosive dentals, came down off the platform, and shook hands with the select audience in the red velvet chairs. After a moment he walked back to Marie-Laure de Noailles, still standing at the long table. The sculptor César, looking like a younger Jerry Colonna, leaned beside her. As Dali approached, the television lights and camera followed him. Marie-Laure held up her hands.

"No television, no photographs," she said. The Steinian television lady waved the men away. The lights dimmed. She shook hands with Marie-Laure. They began to speak about televising a visit to the Noailles art collection. I gathered that Dali had already discussed the project with Marie-Laure.

"But I can't have you dragging all that equipment into my house," Marie-Laure said.

"This is all there would be," the television lady said, pointing to the hand camera held by her husband, a slender, dark, bald-headed Italian. "The lights"—she pointed to the high, movable spotlights—"are autonomous."

Marie-Laure looked puzzled. "What do you mean—autonomous?"

"Independent. All the power comes out of that." She pointed to a box about the size of a small tool kit on the floor near the steel framework of *The Bride*.

"Well, I want to know who will be there," Marie-Laure said.

"Just two," the television lady said. She nodded in the direction of her husband and his assistant.

"And what about you?"

"I'll be there, too, of course."

"Oh. Before it was two. Now it's three. I want to know exactly how many and who they are."

The woman pointed to her husband. "He"—and to his assistant—"and he"—and tapped herself on her billowing bosom—"and I."

"All right, then," Marie-Laure said, "but let it be understood: in my house I run things. I'll be present and you'll do exactly what I say and nothing I don't say."

Dali broke in. "That's what I've said from the beginning. The Vicomtesse gives the orders."

"I'll think it over," Marie-Laure said. "Call me on Monday morning."

Dali, Gala, and Marie-Laure moved around the long table toward the exit door. I heard someone call out, "Look here, please. Everybody—look here." I turned and, looking through the transparent upper reaches of *The Bride*, saw Rutsch standing on the platform beside his sculpture. A few of those nearer to him than I was were looking up at him. No one in the group around Dali seemed to be paying any attention.

"Dali. Salvador Dali," Rutsch cried. "Come here." Dali's party moved slowly out the front door onto the Faubourg St.-Honoré.

"Everybody—please—watch me," Rutsch pleaded. He pushed at the central pole of his sculpture. Slowly it rose up and tipped forward, then toppled over and crashed down onto the marble steps. The chain, the garnet-sheathed plaster leg, the gilded shoe, and the stretched nylon stocking splayed out on either side. Rutsch followed it down the steps, kicking it violently all the way to the floor, as the lights and camera closed in on him. Photographers darted in and out of the crowd, taking shot after shot. One green eye blinked up feebly out of the debris and then died. As Rutsch reached the foot of the steps, he walked over to the disembodied garnet leg and gave it a final, splintering kick. His face was beet-red, and as he came closer to me, I could see that he was sweating heavily. The veins stood out on his temple. The tallest Spaniard reached out and patted him on the shoulder as he passed.

"I don't like petty people," Rutsch said. He kept on walking toward the door. As he reached the long table, he looked back over his shoulder. "The materials are mine," he said defensively. He walked out the door.

I went up to the front of the gallery to look at the rubble. The *Homage to Kant* had been pretty well wrecked by its third tumble: the bronze plaque was hanging loose, the cotton wadding that trailed out of the hole at its center gave it the look of a decapitated jack-in-the-box, and the "amber" was badly chipped on all four sides. Next to it, the mannequin's leg lay grotesquely broken, its garnet stocking half torn off. The marble steps were scratched and chipped all the way down.

The bald-headed television cameraman called to Yvonne:

"Come pose next to this." Yvonne walked toward him slowly. "I don't know whether Dali will like it if I do," she said.

"Be brave, Yvonne," someone called out.

"I *am* brave," Yvonne said, "but I'm tired." She slumped into an armchair near the ruins. Her long legs reached out toward the silver wings. The camera turned and the photographers clicked.

I saw Rutsch come back into the gallery and go into a small room next to the front door. I followed him in. He was standing near the far corner. He looked confused and a little desperate. I told him I knew he had been working hard and must be very tired.

"Yes," he said, "I worked all night. I *am* very tired, and some things have been bothering me—things one takes lightly when one isn't tired." He spoke more rapidly than he had spoken the day I met him at the Meurice, but his ornate way of stressing certain words had not deserted him.

"I didn't sleep all night long—you see? And the details that I would have had the wisdom to pass over without rebelling— because wisdom never rebels, does it?—Lao-tzu said so, long before Kant, two or three thousand years before . . ." He wiped his brow with a dirty hand. "But now, I'm very tired and those little details, well, they no longer seemed like details; they piled up and became chapters."

Raymond Nacenta, the director of the Galerie Charpentier, came into the room. He has a bland, owl-like face, carefully slicked-down graying hair, and pop eyes which his thick-lensed tortoiseshell glasses accentuate: the model R. Taylor man.

"Dali had left before all that happened, hadn't he?" he asked.

"I don't know," Rutsch said absently. "I called to him two or three times but nobody found it necessary to listen to me." Patrick Waldberg, who had organized the Surrealism retrospective at Nacenta's gallery, walked in. Short and stocky, he looked tense.

"What happened, anyway?" he asked. Nacenta told him, very briefly, about Rutsch's knocking over his sculpture.

"And where is the object?" Waldberg asked.

"He knocked it down, along with the rest," Nacenta said.

"And where was Dali when this happened?" Waldberg asked. Nacenta looked over at Rutsch. "What do you plan to do?" he asked.

Rutsch looked puzzled. "Do? If Dali wants to discuss with me, nicely, I will discuss with him, on a friendly basis. He told me, 'This is your work. I give you *carte blanche.*' But when he got here tonight he said—"

Waldberg broke in. "The point of all this is the fact that there was an art object which belonged to one of our friends, Monsieur Ratton—and now it's broken. You remember? I consider that absolutely disgusting."

"But that was broken by chance," Rutsch said.

"I don't give a damn about chance," Waldberg said. "You're the man who took it out of that glass case in the exhibition, and for what—just to kick it to pieces?"

I told Waldberg the *Homage* had already been dropped— twice, in fact—before Rutsch knocked his sculpture down.

"Who dropped it?" he asked.

"I did," Rutsch said, "but that had nothing to do with what followed."

Waldberg looked disgusted. "What difference does that make? The result is the same. The object is ruined."

"Not at all, monsieur," Rutsch said. "I'll fix it for you. There's no need to be upset. In two days that object will be exactly as it was made in the beginning. Better than before, because there was nothing inside but all that cotton wadding. It was badly made, believe me."

"Who cares! I'd rather have it badly made than broken," Waldberg said.

"But I was very upset," Rutsch said. "I didn't mean to break it; I slipped because I was tired."

"In that case you'd have done better to leave it alone in the vitrine and not make a mess of it." He turned to leave.

"But, monsieur," Rutsch pleaded, "aren't you interested in hearing the explanation?"

"No, no, no," Waldberg said. At the door he turned and stared fixedly at Rutsch. "Aaaah," he snarled and walked out. Nacenta followed him.

Rutsch straightened up. "All right, don't listen to what I say. But either talk to me all the way or don't talk at all. If you do want to talk to me, then talk. But don't half-talk and then go out and hide behind the door." Rutsch looked at me blankly. "He put on the exhibition, didn't he? I think he did, but I don't know him." He wiped his brow again, sat down, and stared at the door.

I asked Rutsch how he had happened to get involved in this homage in the first place. He sat quietly for a moment, then looked up at me.

"I was out walking, one day," he said, "just strolling around the Faubourg St.-Honoré. I had turned down that side street near Lanvin's and was crossing over to the other side of the street when I saw Dali and Gala. I recognized them at once. Dali kept looking at me, staring deep into my eyes. We spoke. Just then a car turned off the Faubourg St.-Honoré into the street we were standing on. Gala cried, 'Look out! Look out!' and grabbed Dali by the hand and pulled him away so he wouldn't be run over. I didn't move because I wasn't afraid. I knew that a car couldn't strike down a god. Dali asked me for my address and telephone number. When I got home, I had some friends with me. The phone rang. It was the divine Dali. He asked if he could come to see me in five minutes. I said he could, of course. He liked my studio very much. He saw things that nobody had ever noticed before, like a large painting high up on a wall, almost to the ceiling. He asked me if I had painted it. I told him I had. 'There's something there,' he said. I knew he meant that it had a soul.

"Later, when I called on him, I brought him two little stones that had been formed by the architect of the seas, who hollows out stones and draws faces on them as he forms them and then penetrates inside the stone and lives in it. Dali took one of those stones and he handled it as though he had discovered something extraordinary. He caressed it just as though he wanted to take away from it what was inside. I could see he was hurting it. And if he was hurting the stone, he wasn't doing himself any good, either. So I took the stone back and told him I would give him another one almost exactly the same. I took the stone home and tried to bring back its color. It was just the way your fingers get sometimes, in cold weather, when they become very white. Because he had kept rubbing it hard with his thumb, you see. How can you explain things like that to someone who doesn't understand? I used to think those stones were sea urchins from millions of years ago that had become fossilized. But it's not so. Because that form which is round like that"—he drew with his finger on the palm of the other hand to show me—"with a kind of star centering about a white point —that isn't a fossil; it's something drawn by a living being which moves over the surface of that stone and makes that white point in the center, and then enters, through that point, into the stone and stays there. If you take a magnifying glass and look carefully, you can see there's a whole universe inside.

"A few days after that, I gave Dali another stone, very much like the one I took back from him. He was *very* grateful. He told me lots of stories. Oh, he was always telling me stories. He was with me often. He invited me everywhere. And when I was with him, he often took me by the hand to draw me nearer to him or to show me something. He was very affectionate and demonstrative.

"One day he took me with him to the studio of Christine Forani, across from the Montparnasse cemetery. She had been working on a mask for a bust of Dante for Dali. He looked over what she had prepared, made a few retouches to arrange something here or there, and then he said to her, 'It's perfect. You mustn't touch it again.' When he turned away, he knocked down a kind of laurel wreath she had fashioned for it. I picked it up and placed it on his head like a crown. He looked at me, wide-eyed, just the way a child would look at his father or his teacher, and he seemed to be saying, 'Thank you, Father. I accept.' But without speaking. You see? And I felt then just as though I *were* his father. Just as though I had created a child.

"In front of Gala and other people, too, he said that this was the beginning of a great friendship and that he was going to take me to Spain and that together we were going to create the greatest sculpture ever made—bigger than the Colossus of Rhodes. And he told me that he already had the factory and the workmen who would work on it under my direction."

"But were you already working on tonight's Kant project?" I asked him.

"Oh, yes. That we had decided on right from the start. When he came to my studio, he said, 'Make what you want. It will be your work of art. All I ask is that it be a homage to Kant.' He showed me a page from a book that told about it so I could see what it should mean. He sent me a few more details, after that, through Marina Lussato and her brother, but he told them, 'Monsieur Rutsch will know how to do it.' And so I went to work. I had an idea—the idea for this extraordinary solution. And when you act, the thing that seemed impossible becomes possible. You see, he told me that the stocking must not touch the leg. I worked in such a way that the stocking, which was in wrought iron, didn't at any point touch the leg, which was also in wrought iron. It surrounded the leg without touching it.

"When Bruno Lussato told Dali that I was ready to install the sculpture, Dali had him get those two small pocket flashlights and tell me to place them between the stocking and the leg so anyone could see from far off that the stocking didn't touch the leg, and I did. In front of Bruno I made the light shine between them. I had exactly one millimeter to spare for the beam to enter."

"But why did they bring the mannequin's leg?" I asked.

"It was Dali's lack of confidence," Rutsch said. "He didn't believe I would be able to do it. He had given me *carte blanche,* and I had created a piece of sculpture that was organic and expressed a proper homage to Kant and his thought: the idea that everything on this earth makes me aware of the heavens spread out over my head and their relation to the ethical feelings here in my breast. All that was worked out by means of my composition of three statues and those three statues cárried within their forms other statues. The one on the right bore up Kant himself in its hands, enclosed within its robot body. He cries out, raising his eyes up to the heavens, to those three antennae above him at the left, on the other statue, with the arm reaching out from his heart, and he's carried along by this thing which is unexplainable as though to say, 'What brings me here on this earth?' "

"Had Dali seen any of these things before tonight?" I asked.

"Yes. He came to my studio and saw the tall statue with the wings. I had taken the wings from the Panhard-Citroën factory where I worked. Then he brought me to the Galerie Charpentier and introduced me to Monsieur Nacenta and a few other people, as the artist who was going to make the statue. He showed me the object in the glass case and pointed out the inscription in German on the bronze plaque. Then I had to leave for Belgium to hang an exhibition of my painting. I got back to Paris only yesterday. I worked all last night, and all day today. Dali had promised to send me sixty handsome English boys to carry the sculptures to the gallery. When I saw that time was slipping away, I began calling him, but either there was no answer or the line was busy or Gala didn't know where to find him. Finally, at the last minute, I was able to get a truck and transport the three statues to the gallery. When I got here, there was no one to help me. I had to drag those heavy statues inside and set them up all by myself.

"When Dali came, he didn't even look at the way I had solved the problem. He just said, 'We don't need those statues on the left and the right,' and he had them taken away, and then he put the *Homage to Kant* on a little chair, and in the middle, hanging down over it, that leg from the Bazar de l'Hotel de Ville. But what made me heartsick was that he didn't even look at my solution of the problem, something I had been able to achieve almost by a miracle. It's only in the middle of the night that a solution like that comes to you. I tried to explain all this to him but he wouldn't listen. He cut off communication. I hadn't slept for two days. I was almost ready to collapse. I had been working with electrodes, welding. My nerves were all frayed. But I did what he asked me to do. He told me to twist the leg out of its place and I twisted it, even though it was like twisting my own heart, and then he had that horrible plaster leg hung up. And I saw he was transforming a work of art into a department store window display. I suppose, in the eyes of the mass of people, it would look more elegant, and the single statue was more concentrated so the sheep could follow it more clearly since there was only one spot for the eye to go and in my arrangement there were three. Then I realized that I had been working for an idea and Dali works for the sheep. He had betrayed me. My idea was dismantled, my ideal violated and my interpretation destroyed. I said to him, 'But that's not the way it should be.' He said, 'See me later. We'll talk about it afterward.' And then he went up on the steps and began shouting that abracadabra, like all the forces of evil. Nothing was left of the original idea but a kind of ridiculous backdrop for that act of his. And then he started to walk out. I called him and he didn't pay any attention. Everything just welled up inside me and overflowed. I felt he had soiled and cheapened that object that I had made with a desire to create something pure and high, so I pushed it over to finish the job.

When I walked down the steps and saw that mannequin's leg lying there, symbolizing all the cheap trashiness of his treatment, I gave it the *coup de grâce*."

Rutsch fell silent, then looked up at me again. "I don't see what else I could have done. Do you?"

"Whenever catastrophe strikes, I'm never around. But this morning, when I heard what happened last night, I could see it all, just as though I had been there. You know, I have always asked sculptors who have made anything of that kind for me to destroy their work, but through pride or vanity they always refuse. And last night, without my having the slightest thing to do with it, that's exactly what happened. Good God, if you think over the development of that affair from the beginning right up to the climax, it's a masterpiece."

Dali's eyes were glistening. He sat on the edge of the crimson-velvet armchair facing the group he had convoked on Sunday morning for a discussion of Saturday night's homage to Immanuel Kant. Curled up at my left on the long crimson divan in the salon of his suite at the Meurice was Marina Lussato. Descharnes, another photographer whom I had seen at the Galerie Charpentier the previous evening, Christine Forani, and the Dutch boy with the fluffy blond hair were standing around Dali's chair. Gala stood off to one side, talking with Léonor Fini the painter. Fini was dressed all in black leather:

high-heeled boots, tight trousers, belted jacket to the knees, and a sombrero-type hat. Her face had an unreal, nocturnal look under layers of white powder.

Descharnes asked Dali where he had dug up the star of last night's performance—the sculptor Rutsch.

"In the street," Dali said. "He came up to me on the street and greeted me. I asked him, 'Do you have a present for me?' He said, 'I have a marvelous stone.' I told him I'd take a look at it. When he brought it to me, I saw that it *was* marvelous— a fossilized sea urchin—a wonderful thing." The phone rang. Dali crossed the room to answer it. "Richard? Bravo. Send him up." He came back to his chair. "Oh, it was a magnificent success," he said. "I couldn't have arranged a more beautiful ending."

"But Rutsch is wild with rage," Marina said. "You didn't see how he kicked that plaster leg to pieces at the end."

Dali shook his head. "Wild, maybe, but not against *me*. You'll see. When he cools off, he's going to become the wildest Dalinian there ever was. I've got him like a dog on a leash now."

I asked Dali if he had given Rutsch definite instructions about what he was to do.

"Absolutely everything. But you see, he had made up his mind he was going to turn the situation to his own advantage, so he brought in everything he had in his studio—all that junk— to show it off."

"He wanted to hold an exhibition of his work," Marina said.

"Exactly," Dali said. "And he couldn't hold one out in the middle of the street, could he? What better place than the Galerie Charpentier? But there's not much advantage to him in showing a department store leg and a costume museum slipper, so he had to bring in all his old scrap iron."

I told Dali that Rutsch said he had been give *carte blanche.*

Dali waggled his finger. "No. Originally he was supposed to make it all himself—the stocking, the slipper, the pulleys—and see to it that it all worked. I explained to him that the essential point was for the stocking not to touch the leg. He only had to follow instructions. I did tell him he could choose the materials and decide on the dimensions. And then there was a very interesting Pop Art side to it. I gave him the idea of utilizing those wings, which he had already made from automobile fenders. My idea at first had been to have the monument suspended from a helicopter which would be attached to the ceiling, but that was too difficult, so I suggested the wings instead. But the fact is, I told him exactly what needed to be done. Within the limits of what I *wanted* done, he had *carte blanche* —yes. That is, he could do it in lead, make it abstract, and so on. But he didn't have *carte blanche* to bring all those sculptures of his and group them around the monument. He just had his heart set on holding an exhibition. He even said to me, 'I want to be photographed at the gallery with you.' I told him not then but the day after—if he behaved himself. I would have invited people for a private showing and had Pierre Cardin there to dress the leg. But Rutsch lost his head. He's crazy."

"Completely crazy," Marina said.

Dali looked over at her. "But you're all crazy—all of you who make up my court." He pointed his finger at her. "You and all the others. Everybody except me." Everybody laughed. "But you are—all of you. You're all crazier than I am," Dali insisted.

Marina nodded. "No doubt of it."

Dali's eyes bulged out. "But it's absolutely certain. The proof is, I put you all through your paces like a bunch of well-trained fleas. Look at the way things went off yesterday. It was extraordinary."

Richard joined the group, very glum. Dali looked up at him questioningly. "I've got a headache," Richard said. "I was hit."

Dali looked pleased. "Bravo! I knew blood would run. Did you get a picture of it?"

"How could I? I was the victim. Besides, I wasn't in the mood to take pictures."

Dali rubbed his hands. "Sit down," he said. "Tell us the whole story. I heard the noise and I said to Gala, 'Something is going on around that monument to Kant,' but I had no idea things would go that far. That was exactly what I wanted to happen: I wanted that object destroyed and Rutsch had already started things moving in that direction, because the monument was already broken before the climax came."

"It was broken twice," Marina said.

"Then the rest was unavoidable. If a thing like that happens twice, you just know you've got to expect a third one, of much greater consequence. It was sublime!"

I told Dali that Patrick Waldberg hadn't seen it that way; he had been too concerned about the problem of explaining away the damage to M. Charles Ratton, who had loaned the Kant object to him for the exhibition.

Dali looked surprised. "But it's just as though I had made Monsieur Ratton a gift of it. It was a fake. And now that it's been broken in my service, nothing could be more authentic. It was authenticated by its destruction. Oh, no, he's being absurd. Something that wasn't by Dali now *is* by Dali—even if it's somewhat pulverized. Doesn't he understand the glory and the value that are wrapped up in that object now? Before, it was a piece of shit. Now it's something sublime."

I told Dali I had found a list of the contents of that first exhibition of Surrealist objects held at Ratton's gallery in May, 1936, and it had included something by him entitled *Monument à Kant*.

"That's incredible," he said. "When I first heard there was a Surrealist object called *Homage to Kant*, by Salvador Dali, in the Galerie Charpentier's exhibition, I said it was certainly a fake because I had no recollection of having made it. And when it was shown to me, I knew I'd never seen it before. Then later on I remembered that years ago I had made a Surrealist object called *Hypnagogic Clock*. It was a long loaf of bread with a dozen inkwells set into the top crust and a dozen small photographs hanging by threads from each end of the loaf, each one bearing an image of the loaf of bread and the inkwells and reproducing it to infinity. Anyway, it was shown at Ratton's gallery in 1936. They asked me what I wanted it to be placed on. I told them to get a plain, simple wooden base, the kind they would use for an African Negro sculpture. Then the Vicomtesse de Noailles went to the Flea Market and found that amber object with the bronze plaque. They told me about it over the telephone and I said, 'If the Vicomtesse de Noailles thinks it's all right, use it.' But I didn't see it at the time. Then the war came, and after that I forgot about it. Now, twenty years later, it turns up again, without the real Dali Surrealist object for which it served as a base, and all of a sudden it's an object by Dali belonging to Monsieur Ratton. And now that it's been destroyed, Ratton wants to make trouble for Rutsch on account of it. But he hasn't got much of a claim because if it belongs to anybody, it belongs to me."

He rubbed his hands again. "And Monsieur Rutsch is going to be the world's most devoted Dalinian—with no help from me. He'll be at my orders for the rest of his life, because he has committed the purest, the finest, the noblest act of his entire existence. He'll be attached to me like a watchdog. A one hundred percent Dalinian." Richard shook his head.

"You doubt it?" Dali asked.

"I do."

"Expose your reasoning, then. Tell your story."

Richard sighed. "All right. After you left, Rutsch was out on the sidewalk and the director of the gallery came out and started to bawl hell out of him."

Dali looked incredulous. "Coming from a man who is sponsoring an exhibition of Surrealism, that just isn't believable. What are you talking about! *Allons!*" The phone rang. Dali went to answer it. "If that's Rutsch, I'll tell him I'm preparing a new monument." They all laughed except Richard. "Oh, my head," he groaned.

Dali returned to the group and sat down. "All right. Get on with it."

"He was bawling him out," Richard continued, "so I began to take pity on poor Rutsch."

"Ah—that was a mistake," Dali said. "In the first place, never take pity on anybody. In the second place, you have to realize that this was the most glorious day of Rutsch's life. It's just as though he had taken his first Communion. Remember—never pity. Now go ahead with your story."

"Anyway," Richard said, "I stuck my nose in. I said to the man, 'Listen—Rutsch can do what he wants with his sculpture.' "

"What you should have pointed out," Dali said, "is that it was a perfect Surrealist act within the framework of a Surrealist exhibition. It was the most completely Surrealist action possible in the circumstances. Those people have no idea of what Surrealism is all about. Go on."

"Then the director asked me, 'Who was the bastard who carried away the leg?' I told him I supposed it was the one who brought it, since it belonged to him. 'What's his name?' he asked me. 'I don't know,' I told him. 'That's none of my business.' 'Then why are you butting into something that's none of your business?' he wanted to know. 'Because it concerns Dali, and *that's* my business,' I said. 'In fact I came here tonight for the express purpose of making this whole affair my business.' 'And you think it's all right to knock things around, chip the marble steps on my stairway, and destroy a valuable *objet d'art?*' he said. 'Look,' I told him, 'I'm getting a little tired of this.' When I said that, he hauled off and cracked me on the side of the head."

Dali sat up straighter. "That's too bad. But it's nice you took a blow like that. You'll be all the more attached to me, as a result. As for those Galerie Charpentier people, they should rub their hands with glee and say, 'This is the greatest piece of luck—the highest honor—that could have befallen us.' They just have no imagination." Dali sighed. "Yesterday I was all set—I was supposed to have sixty English boys—the most handsome imaginable. What a fuss that would have created!" He stopped and looked over at the blond Dutch boy. "You. I thought you were okay. But you didn't produce."

The boy seemed embarrassed. "I looked around at the Alliance Française, but I couldn't find the right ones."

"Looking doesn't get you anywhere," Dali said. "Picasso said, 'You don't go around looking for a watch but that doesn't stop you from finding one.' You shouldn't waste your time looking; the thing is to find. You didn't find. Bad point for you. You brought me a book to sign. So I signed it and gave it to someone else. But except for your falling down on the job, everything went off to perfection."

"There was one marvelous scene after we got out onto the sidewalk and heard the crash," Descharnes said. "Marie-Laure calling out, 'Salvador, they've broken everything! Run! Run!'"

Dali laughed. "And by the time everything *was* broken, I was sitting down to dinner at L'Escargot d'Or with the richest people I have ever met, receiving a magnificent commission. It's magic: while one thing is breaking up, another is beginning to be organized around me." He hesitated. "I must get that sculptor's name."

Marina prompted him: "It's Rutsch—Alexandre Rutsch."

"Ah, yes, Rutsch. That's it. It wasn't bad, what he did, as long as he limited himself to carrying out the job I set for him."

"But he was very unhappy at the way you walked out," Marina said. "He said to me, 'Why couldn't Dali have been there? I wanted him to see that.'"

Dali shook his head. "I don't feel I *should* be there for things like that. I originate the ideas and tell people how things should be done, but when they *are* done, I'm somewhere else. It's much cleaner that way. Especially when, like last night, things are done in a way that goes beyond what I had outlined." He looked over at me. "That's the way it was in New

York when that girl you saw with me last winter"—which one? I wondered—"one of the prettiest girls in New York, took off her clothes and rolled around with four pigs. She put her whole heart and soul into the thing, but I had a luncheon date at Le Pavillon with Charles de Besteguí, and when the ceremony dragged on and on, finally I had to leave in order not to be late for lunch. So when they were throwing the blood and the dead fish and all the rest at her, I was sitting down to lunch at Le Pavillon. Afterward she said, 'Dali is so cruel. While I was going through all that for him, covered with rotting fish and all those other things, he wasn't even there to watch my sacrifice. He had already left.' But I don't think I *should* be there at those moments. That's the way I feel about it. Some understand it; some don't." He looked up at Richard. "You've been around long enough to understand, especially since I put you to work the other day cleaning up the bathroom. We'll see whether it lasts or not. The ones who understand continue. The ones who don't—the dopes—get pushed out."

"But what do you think about my story?" Richard insisted. "Do you think I could sue?"

"Sue whom?" Dali said. "What an idea! I think you should consider getting slapped for Dali a very great honor and let it go at that. You've had enormous good fortune. To be a true Dalinian you have to become a total masochist. You went to a lot of trouble to find that turtle and bring it to the gallery and you got slapped. Good for you. Masochism is a very fine thing. Keep on suffering as long as your physiology and your psychic equipment allow you to."

Richard looked even glummer. *"Bon,"* he said.

"Cheer up," Dali said. "Thanks to you, I've got the turtle of my dreams. I'm going to make an object for Tokyo out of it and have it parade back and forth in a glass case with a mirror underneath. It will be colossal. Now I'll give you something in exchange—an idea. Photograph all your subjects as

though they were in the process of becoming turtles. Max
Ernst and all the others. You'll make a fortune with that."

Richard looked surprised. "With turtles? Old turtles?"

Dali slapped his knee in excitement. "You've hit the nail on
the head: we'll call them the old turtles of modern art. All the
old dummies of modern art—Monsieur Ernst, Monsieur Villon,
Stravinsky, the whole gang—everybody gotten up to look like
a turtle." Dali looked up at Gala and Léonor Fini. "The other
day he came and said, 'I'll bring you the most beautiful turtle
in all Paris,' and it turned out to be true. Now I'm paying him
off." He turned back to Richard. "You'll take pictures of them
all—not satirical; just the way they are. You'll make a fortune.
It will be a sensation. You'll call it *The Cuckolded Turtles of
Old Modern Art*. Everybody will buy it. People are fed up
with all these books buttering up the great modern masters,
so-called." Richard was visibly cheered by the prospect of sudden wealth. He looked up expectantly, but Dali had changed
his course.

"I can sense that Rutsch is reflecting on the role he played in
last night's dream," he said. "He's feeling very exalted by his
act; he thinks he's done something quite marvelous. He's gilding it all with favorable interpretations. His state of pain will
be purely ephemeral."

"Do you think he'll try to get in touch with you?" Marina
asked.

"He'll show up in the form of a letter," Dali said. "Where
is that thing he gave me?" He got up, walked over to the high
Chinese chest, and rummaged through its pigeonholes until he
found a card about eight inches by four, with a reproduction
of a sculpture that looked like the seven-foot-high treelike
statue Rutsch had dragged up on the right flank of the monument to Kant. The verso was filled with a group of about ten
maxims, in French, signed "Rutsch." His telephone number
was there, too.

"They're all bad," Dali said, "but there's one I can patch up and use." He pointed to one that said, "In daring the impossible, one creates the possible." Dali borrowed my pen and reversed the order of the adjectives. "Now, that's better," he said. " 'In daring the possible, one creates the impossible.' That's what happened last night." He signed the new version, "Thanks for everything. The Divine Dali." He held the card up to me. "You see, I even send him back his own words." He handed it to Marina. "Get it back to Rutsch. I return everything—even his telephone number." Dali sighed. "It's too bad. Just an excess of zeal. If only he had been satisfied to do the piece with the wings and stop there. I told him it was handsome—much more handsome than that giant-sized Max Ernst thing with the wing shapes. But judging from the way he acted, I guess that didn't satisfy him. By the way, did they film the debacle?"

I told him they did and that when the sculpture was all in a heap at the foot of the steps they had asked Yvonne to pose over it but she hadn't wanted to because she wasn't sure Dali would like it.

"Ah, that's nice," he said. "Very nice. Very Dalinian. And did you see César? He came over to me and said, 'I adore you.' Very Dalinian."

Marina nodded approvingly. "Indeed he is."

Dali began to hum, then stopped. "That was very thoughtful of Mademoiselle Yvonne," he said. "I must tell her so when I see her tomorrow."

I asked him what time in the morning we were to leave for the sequence involving Meissonier and Mlle. Yvonne in Prouteau's film *Dieu a choisi Paris.*

He looked at me skeptically. "I don't know whether they'll let you come along or not," he said. "It's a little dangerous. It's really a private affair—just I and Prouteau and the nude, who will pass in front of the camera at eight thirty. I think we

·should keep it secret. I don't believe Prouteau will talk much about it, for fear of creating scandal. Madame de Gaulle doesn't like that sort of thing. But check with him, anyway. If he says yes, it's all right with me."

I discovered, back home at lunchtime, that the only telephone number Gilbert Prouteau had given me was the one for his office. Since it was Sunday, I couldn't call him there. His home telephone was not listed in the *Bottin* and the operator found nothing on her lists, either. There was only one solution: be at the Hotel Meurice when Prouteau arrived to pick up Dali in accordance with the arrangements I had heard them make over the telephone a few days earlier. Since I knew that Yvonne was due to pass before the camera at 8:30 in a schedule worked out to dovetail with Dali's plans for luncheon at L'Aigle Noir in Fontainebleau, I showed up at the Meurice a little before eight on Monday morning. The front lobby was deserted. I sat on a divan near the entrance to the dining room and directly opposite the elevator and stairway that Dali would have to use to come downstairs from his second-floor royal suite. Busboys scurried in and out of the dining room, and from time to time the headwaiter craned his neck around the corner.

I had been sitting there about fifteen minutes when I saw

Yvonne and the television woman come in from the Rue de Rivoli arcade. They stopped, the gazelle and the teddy bear, midway across the lobby, went through a pantomime of indecision, and then parted. The television woman strode on in the direction of the rear lobby and the concierge's desk, and Yvonne came over and flopped down on the divan beside me.

"What a dreadful hour! Have you had breakfast?" she asked.

I told her I had.

"I had no time," she said, "and I was up so late." The large green eyes were as clear as a child's. Even the mauve eye shadow somehow reinforced her air of freshness. She got up and went over to the headwaiter, who had been standing outside the dining room door, ogling her. She was back in a moment.

"I've ordered coffee for us," she said, then lay back on the divan, stretched her legs out, and yawned. Suddenly she sat up.

"Do you know if I'm going to wear the dinner jacket for this thing?" she asked.

I told her I didn't think so.

"What *am* I going to wear, then?"

Just the eye shadow, I guessed.

She frowned. "But I *can't* do that. And besides, it's so early in the morning."

A young busboy brought a tray with coffee. Yvonne was pouring a cup when the television woman came into sight across the lobby.

"He's on his way down," she called out to us. "Let's go."

Yvonne quickly took a few sips of the black coffee and we hurried out to the rear lobby. Prouteau, standing near the rear entrance, saw us and smiled. As we reached him, Dali arrived. He shook hands gravely with us all and we followed him outside. Yvonne moved over beside him.

"Tell me, Dali," she said, "what am I going to wear?"

"Nothing," he said.

"But I don't *want* to do that." Her voice was all pout.

"All right, all right. You can carry my coat over your arm. That way people won't know whether you're nude or not."

"And what about my breasts?"

"Ah!" Dali simultaneously raised his eyebrows and lowered his eyelids. "They absolutely *must* be seen. Now," he said, turning to Prouteau, "just where is this place?"

"It's the Cour de Rohan," Prouteau said. "Does your chauffeur know how to get there?" Dali beckoned to his chauffeur. With the help of a map of Paris the three of them tried to pinpoint our destination. There seemed to be two possibilities: one at the Louvre, the other across the Seine on the Left Bank, both clearly labeled "Cour de Rohan."

"We'll try them in order," Prouteau said. "Since the Louvre is on our way to the other place, there's nothing to lose. Now— how about transportation?"

"You and Mademoiselle Yvonne can ride with me," Dali said. "That will give us a chance to work out our arrangements."

The television woman and her husband took off for their own car, a Sunbeam, parked a bit farther down the street, beyond Dali's black Cadillac convertible.

"You might as well ride with Mademoiselle," Prouteau said to me. Mademoiselle, I saw from his gesture, was a slender girl about five feet five, apparently in her early twenties, with large, brown eyes and curly, light-brown hair, whom I had noticed standing off to one side while Prouteau, Dali, and the chauffeur were studying the map of Paris. She smiled, showing a full complement of dimples and some very white teeth, and I followed her to a baby-blue MG across the street. We got in. She kicked off her high-heeled black kid pumps and slipped her feet into a pair of gold-trimmed embroidered burgundy velvet ballerina slippers. On the shelf under the dashboard was a large transparent plastic bag filled with a very imaginative variety of American-style penny candy: gumdrops, candy kisses, mint balls, lollipops, bubble gum, bull's-eyes, and myriads more. She dipped in for a gumdrop and offered the bag to me. She started the motor and let it idle while Dali's chauffeur made another check of the map. In a low, throaty voice, she began to half-sing, half-hum a song I recognized as "Black Girl." The words didn't sound exactly English; on the other hand, they certainly weren't French, but the voice was more than adequate, even without a clue to the meaning. After a lull, I asked her how she fitted into the morning's business.

"I'm the script girl," she said.

I asked her where the script was.

She laughed and blushed a little. "I'm really not, I guess you know, but I wanted to come along, so that's my status, officially. Prouteau has taken me with him before on some of these junkets and each time he passes me off as his script girl. He's already done sketches with Cocteau, Picasso, and Aragon. Now it's Dali's turn and I don't want to miss him. He's certainly one of the ten outstanding personalities of our time."

If she wasn't the script girl, then what was she?

She laughed. "Oh, I'm lots of things—singer, songwriter, actress, for a start. I play opposite Jean-Paul Belmondo in one of the earlier sequences of this film. I play his sweetheart of the First World War period. The film is a kind of panorama of life in Paris from 1890 up to the present. *Dieu a choisi Paris,* it's called." I asked her what her name was.

"Maria Latour."

Was that her real name or a script girl kind of name?

"It's practically all mine," she said. I noticed she was wearing a wedding band. She saw me look at it. "Oh, no, I'm not married. I just wear that as a kind of shield. It works, too. No, that's my name, except that I wasn't born Maria. I'm Basque and my first name is really Maïtena—which is Maria in Basque."

Dali's car emerged slowly from the Meurice's covered driveway into the Rue du Mont-Thabor and started up the street. The Sunbeam followed along, and Maria moved out into the line and quickly closed the gap. At the Rue d'Alger, Dali's chauffeur turned left and then right into the Rue St.-Honoré. The traffic moved sluggishly along for three or four blocks, then came to a halt at the Place du Théâtre-Français. I asked Maria what kind of songs she wrote.

"I just write for my own pleasure mostly. I've cut one record for Pathé-Marconi and I'm going to do another one pretty soon. Meanwhile I keep on writing. I've made lots of adaptations of American songs. I don't translate them. I take the music and supply my own words. I love all kinds of American music—jazz, folk, even Broadway musical comedy. I grew up on Irving Berlin, Jerome Kern, Cole Porter, Gershwin, Rodgers, and Bernstein. I'd love to sing nothing but that in France, but it wouldn't work. People just don't like it all that much. But it will come, the same way American folk music has moved in. I'm crazy about that: I have all the records of Joan Baez, Peter, Paul, and Mary, and lots of others. I like it all but I like best the spirit of American light music. It's so rhythmic and witty— it moves. French songs are heavy as lead. They may be all right for some singer in a bar, but they bore *me*. I like music you can dance to, like the songs in *Kiss Me, Kate*."

I asked her if she had sung in nightclubs.

"I sang in cabarets for a few months, a couple of years ago, just before and after I cut my record."

I asked her what her record was called.

"Like me—*Maïtena*. But I'm tired of it already. It's kind of tuneless and choppy—very French. I'm working in another direction entirely now, mostly on adaptations of American folk music and some from Mexico and Peru. But it's a long haul. The French like French music. When I first heard 'Black Girl,' sung by the Journeymen, I knew it was for me and I wanted to do a French adaptation. They said, 'Oh, no, that won't go here.' So I said I'd be back in two years when it was all the rage and that's just what happened. Peter, Paul, and Mary's version of 'Five Hundred Miles' was what turned the tide. It was the biggest seller in years. Now everybody says, 'Oh, isn't American folk music wonderful!' "

The traffic started up again. We crossed the Rue de Rivoli and went through the arcade into the Place du Carrousel. I asked Maria what had brought her into this film.

"I was working out at the actors' studio run by Yves Furet, and Prouteau came in one day looking for a girl to play opposite Belmondo in *Dieu a choisi Paris.* He gave me a test and then the job. It's not a great part. I don't feel it did much for me as an actress, and it certainly didn't do much for me financially, either. But I've enjoyed going around with him while he's filmed the sequences involving the great painters and writers. That *has* done something for me, I know. Especially seeing Cocteau. He was by far the nicest of them all. He charmed me completely. He was still recovering from a serious coronary attack, but he took time out to talk to me about his work. I was very timid in his presence, but when I left I asked him to inscribe one of his books for me. He did, of course, and then he thanked me for asking him. What a delicious human being—very much aware of his own value and at the same time showing a real concern for others. I knew I had no importance for him, but he *gave* me one by the extreme delicacy of his manner with me—in everything he said and did."

Maria began to sing again, then broke off to ask, "Tell me, do you know that big girl who's going to figure in this sequence with Dali?"

I told her I'd seen her perform on other occasions.

"Oh, she must have a beautiful body. She's so tall. We'll see, anyway. I'm going to be the script girl again. The crew won't know the difference. Of course, if I *did* have to function as script girl, I wouldn't know what to do."

Wouldn't there be a script girl when we got there?

She shook her head. "Prouteau wouldn't need one today. He'll play it by ear. He has a prodigious memory when he needs it."

I suddenly realized we had been circling the Place du Carrousel—how many times: three, four?

"I don't think they know where they're going," Maria said.
As if to prove it, the Cadillac stopped, after the next turn, at a
gatehouse that closed off the entrance to a parking lot. Prouteau
and the chauffeur got out and, map in hand, consulted the gate-
keeper. Maria pulled up at the side, about fifty feet behind the
Cadillac and the Sunbeam. I asked her what it was that started
her thinking in terms of the theater.

"I just fell into it, I suppose. You see, I was born in the Midi
and brought up in the colonies. We went out there right after
the war, when I was just a kid, and stayed for ten years. When
we came back, I was fourteen and about two years behind in my
education because school had been a very hit-or-miss affair out
in the bush. I always wanted to be a writer but I decided it
would be more practical to be a lawyer. Then a friend of my
mother's told me I'd have to study six years after my *bacca-
lauréat*. 'It's a beautiful idea, *ma petite*,' he said, 'but after
your six years you'll have just begun to fool around with your
first case and then you'll meet some handsome young lawyer
who'll marry you and turn you into his secretary.' So I decided
it wasn't worth all the trouble just for that. I still wanted to be
a writer but not the little-girl kind of thing. I wanted to do
something that would grow naturally out of my maturing.
That's when I began to think about the theater. It seemed to
combine a little of everything I wanted to do. After all, a
lawyer is only a kind of actor. And in the theater the experi-
ences I would gain by living the roles I would be playing
would teach me something about people. I'd realized ever
since I began dreaming about being a writer that people had
very individual ways of reacting and if I didn't know them
intimately I wouldn't be able to write anything that was true.
I'd be describing false reactions and attaching them to strange,
unreal people. So, I told myself, I'll go into the theater and if
I can live my roles successfully I'll have people who are true—

and my own. The songs were always there, for my own amusement, but then I began to study acting—the Method, Stanislavsky, we had it all. I went on tour with repertory companies,
then Prouteau picked me to play opposite Belmondo and I
began making television films and here we are."

The chauffeur and Prouteau were now back in the car. I
could see Dali and Yvonne in the back seat, Dali talking with
his usual explosive vigor. The Cadillac turned once again
around the long island in the middle of the Place du Carrousel,
the Sunbeam tagging close behind. We followed them through
the arcade, across the *quai* and over the Pont du Carrousel, up
the Rue des Sts.-Pères, and turned left into the Boulevard
St.-Germain. When we reached the Carrefour de l'Odéon, the
Cadillac swung to the left, beyond the entrance to the Rue de
l'Ancienne-Comédie, and pulled up at the curb. The Sunbeam
parked just behind, and we drew up ahead of them both. Prouteau, Dali, and Yvonne got out and walked quickly down a
cobblestone passageway marked Cour du Commerce-St.-André.
The wrought-iron gates that flanked the entrance were open,
and since there was no place outside to leave the MG, Maria
drove down the narrow passageway and parked, at the left,
opposite a tiny garden courtyard marked Cour de Rohan.

We got out of the car and went into the garden. At the left
was a small, two-story building. Dali and Yvonne were standing
by the door. Maria squeezed my arm. "I'm going to find a book-
shop," she said. "I'll be right back." I followed Dali and
Yvonne into a room at the right, just off the entrance hall. It
was about twelve feet by twenty and filled with lights, camera
equipment, and technicians. Across the back was the Meissonier
painting that Dali had been talking about. It was about five
feet high and eight or nine feet wide and bore the title
Friédland 1807. It showed a squadron of Napoleon's cavalry
racing through a field of tall grass and poppies, past the Emperor and his massed Imperial guard, in what was apparently

a dry run for their definitive appearance in the Metropolitan Museum's oil of the same name.

Dali was standing close to the picture, moving back and forth across its width, examining it inch by inch. Philippe Rheims, the tall, thin auctioneer who had come to the Meurice to talk with him about using the picture as a backdrop for the morning's filming, followed him in a careful *pas de deux.*

"It's not exactly what I was expecting," Dali said. "It's a watercolor, not an oil."

"Watercolor and gouache, to be precise," Rheims said.

"That's all right. It makes no great difference. What counts is the movement. It's amazing the way the grass and the wild poppies sway in the breeze." He turned to me and indicated a particularly agitated patch. "Look at this: it might almost be a Pollock. And look at the chin on this fellow"—he tapped one of the cuirassiers on his jutting chin. "Magnify that a hundred times and you've got as fine an example of Action Painting as anyone ever saw. It's an amazing piece. Now," he said, turning to Prouteau, "here's how we'll do it. I'll stand here and point out these things. As I talk, the camera follows each point I make on the painting, and at the appropriate moment, you pick up her"—he nodded in the direction of Yvonne—"walking along beside me."

"Nude?" Prouteau asked.

"Nude."

Prouteau looked a little uncertain. "I just hope the censorship won't jump on that."

"Not a chance," Dali said. "I'll be shielding her to a certain extent with my body so nobody will see the sensitive parts, anyway. Besides, she's the key to the whole scene. On one hand we have a minutely detailed, realistic description of the painting, and on the other, a kind of apparition in the form of this long, slender, golden-blond body that seems to float across the canvas. There will be a superposition of one body over another and it will seem almost like a dream sequence, not at all like real people. The censorship can't complain about *that*."

Prouteau nodded. "I guess you're right."

Dali took Yvonne's right arm and folded it around his left. "This is the way it will go," he said. He walked her slowly the length of the canvas. When they reached the corner of the room, Yvonne turned around.

"I'm not going to do it," she said. "There are too many people in this little room."

"I'll clear them all out," Prouteau said. "There'll be nobody but the cameraman, the sound operator, and me." He turned to the crowd, which had grown big enough for a mob scene. "Clear out, all of you." They began, slowly, to move out into the garden.

"What's the difference?" Yvonne said. "Now they're all looking in the windows."

Prouteau looked grim. "We'll cover up the windows." He called to one of his assistants, who was dragging his heels on the way to the exit door, and told him to get some material for a quick blackout, then hollered for the makeup girl.

"Take her upstairs," he said, jerking his thumb toward Yvonne. "Give her what she needs. She's a little pale." The two women left the room, and Prouteau came back to the camera. "Let's have this set up right so we can get rolling," he said. He measured the distance from the camera to the wall with his eyes. "Let's see, now. That girl must be nearly six feet eight." He tugged at the camera to roll it back a bit nearer the windows.

I walked out into the garden. Dali was talking with Philippe Rheims. I looked over to the garden door and saw Maria Latour bearing down on us. She was carrying two books. Just as she reached us, Dali said to me, in a loud voice, "Here's a girl who *wants* to take her clothes off. I can see it."

Maria flushed, then smiled and held out the two books to him. "You'd make me very happy, Maître, if you'd sign these," she said.

"Ah! I knew you wanted *something*," Dali said, "but I wasn't sure just what. I thought perhaps you wanted to take your clothes off." Maria flushed a little deeper. Dali asked for my pen, then scrawled his name all the way across the half title of each of the books—*Le Journal d'un génie* and a copy of the French edition of *The Secret Life of Salvador Dali.* She thanked him and walked back toward the MG. Dali asked me what time it was. It was nearly quarter past nine. He frowned.

"Already? We'll have to move fast if I'm going to be back at the hotel by nine thirty." He went back inside. Prouteau was making last-minute adjustments to the camera and the lighting. The man he had sent for the blackout cloth was beginning to tack it up at one corner of the bank of windows.

"We can take you now, maître," Prouteau said. He placed Dali in front of the right center of the picture, then stood back near the camera. "Come up a little closer to me, please. That's it. Perfect. Quiet." The background noises died down. The sound man moved in: "Seven hundred forty-eight, first," and banged his clapper board. Dali seemed more tense than usual. His eyes looked strained and he bit his lips. Then he began to speak, biting off his syllables slowly and with exaggerated precision.

"When they asked what would follow the Surrealist movement, Dali had already, with clairvoyance, foretold that there would be a period of abstract art and that those painters would then commit suicide through their romantic excesses, but that there would be a survivor like Georges Mathieu who would still be recognized and accepted because of his monarchic classicism. After that—"

"Cut," Prouteau yelled. He juggled the equipment around, then nodded to Dali. "You can go on now," he said, "but first put your hand in your waistcoat." Dali obediently unbuttoned his jacket and inserted several fingers in a fold of the gold lamé vest. The sound man called out the numbers.

Dali smoothed his mustache with his free hand and began

again: "As soon as they asked what would follow abstract art, Dali had answered: the hyperesthetic return to maximum objectivity. The artist will totally efface himself before the object, and that is what has come to be called Pop Art." Dali spat out the last two words in a fine spray that emphasized the morbid sensibility of his own hyperesthesia. "Now they ask me, 'What follows Pop Art?' And so, without any hesitation I say, after Pop Art, *l'art pompier*—the frenetic reactualization of Meissonier, who, in my humble opinion, is the greatest French painter, just as I have always said of Paul Cézanne that he is the worst." Dali nodded, removed his hand from his vest. "That's it," he said.

"Cut," Prouteau hollered. Dali asked me the time. It was now 9:30. He beckoned to Prouteau.

"I don't think I need to be here for the rest," he said. "I should have left before now. You take a couple of miscellaneous shots of me, then close-ups of this patch of grass and the chin of the cuirassier"—he indicated again the areas he had earlier characterized as worthy of Jackson Pollock and the entire range of Action Painting—"and dub in a bit of explanatory comment. Perhaps you should bring in the head of one of the horses, too, tying it in with the technique of Pollock and Mathieu." He rubbed it with his finger. "Look at it—it's a tornado, all ready to explode. And then—right at that point—Mademoiselle Yvonne will pass by, nude. After the realistic details of the painting, the contrast of her poetic appearance will give it the unreal quality of a dream. That's the authentic Surrealist manner."

They quickly recorded the miscellaneous shots and Dali's commentary on the close-ups. Dali shook my hand. "Don't lose touch," he said and was gone.

Prouteau raised his eyes skyward. "There's a man who knows what he wants," he said.

Yvonne came down the narrow stairway into the room. She

was dressed in a heavy layer of orange makeup and a very short coat that she clutched at the neck and just below the waist.

"Where's Dali?" she asked me.

I explained that he had just left for the hotel, about a half hour overdue.

"Then I won't do it," she said. Prouteau tried to argue with her. She stood firm, all two meters of her (Prouteau's calculation). Finally he gave up and called in the assistant he had sent out for the blackout cloth.

"You go out and get me a girl who *will* take her clothes off," he said. He turned to me. "Lose one girl and you find ten others ready to take her place. Never forget that." He walked out of the room, swearing.

Yvonne looked at her arms. "Now I've got to take another bath and I've already had one this morning." She went upstairs to dress and I went back out into the garden. Through the grille I could see Maria Latour sitting in the MG, reading. I walked over to the car. She looked up from *Le Journal d'un génie*.

"This is a disgusting book," she said. "But then, why shouldn't it be—he's a disgusting man." She tossed it onto the rear seat. I got in beside her and we started back to the hotel.

"You know, I've always admired Dali's painting," she said, "but I was curious to see what kind of *bonhomme* there was behind it, because it always troubled me somehow; it whispers something that I can't quite hear because Dali, the ringmaster, is shouting so loud. That's why I told Prouteau I absolutely must enter into contact with this fabulous personage. Now that I've seen him operate on the human level, I must say the man is in no way equal to the painter."

I told her it seemed to me that Dali the man corresponded pretty closely to his painting, good and bad, with whatever strengths and weaknesses it had, but that in any case the total personality was of far more interest than the painting alone, which was just one of its forms of expression.

"You know him better than I do," she said. "I know only the painting. As for the personality, I know only the act he puts on for the world. The pains he constantly goes to in order to shock —that bothers me. I saw him on television the other night. The interviewer asked him why he carries on the way he does. 'In order to be forgiven for my painting,' was his reply. But that's not true. It's the painting that makes you willing to forgive him all the rest. At least that's the way *I* feel about it. Besides, he doesn't give a damn about us, whether we 'forgive' him or not.

"Prouteau suggested I buy *Le Journal d'un génie* and ask him to sign it. You saw how he acted. He made no distinction between me and that Swedish model. He said to himself: She's a starlet, so her clothes probably drop off like autumn leaves any time the wind blows. When I asked him to sign the book, you heard him: 'Don't you want to take your clothes off?' If he hadn't been the painter whose work I know and admire, I'd have let him have it. If . . ." She smiled. "You know, Stanislavsky talks about the 'magic if.' If I were he and I were in that situation, how would I react? One never is, but one has to do *as if.* If I'm playing the role of a woman who kills a man out of jealousy, I've never killed a man—for jealousy or any other reason—but I have to give the impression that it's really me, Maria Latour, who's killing that man. And I think that if I hadn't learned how to do that, I would have done something to Dali today." She laughed. "Oh, not killed him, for heaven's sake, but something he wouldn't have liked a bit. Instead, I smiled, just *as if* I thought he was amusing."

I told her that Dali's performance with her was only the characteristic shock tactics based on Surrealist principles that he would have brought to any such situation.

"But does he react sincerely?" she asked. "If so, I give him complete absolution: he's marvelous, a being apart. But doesn't he do it deliberately, just to be different?"

I said that was one of the hardest questions to answer about Dali: how much was calculated stunt, how much spontaneous.

However, he'd been acting just that way, apparently, for a long time, if one could believe the record. And he was very fond of saying that his entire effort each day was designed to help him succeed in being Dali. But I suggested she shouldn't give up so easily on the book: there were a few rather moving passages in it—the parts devoted to his childhood friend, the poet García Lorca, and to the Surrealist writer René Crevel, for example.

Maria looked confused. "Prouteau told me he visited Dali in Spain and Dali behaved like a person of real quality." She shrugged. "Oh, well, there's no reason why he has to have only one mask, is there?"

We were in front of the Meurice now. I pointed out my car and Maria pulled into an empty space behind it. She turned and faced me. "I think I see more clearly into Dali," she said, "now that I can look back at the painting through the glimpse I just had of the man. Obviously he's obsessed by an exaggerated form of eroticism and it dictates the nature of everything he does. I didn't need to meet him to realize that; it's all there in the painting, clearly enough. But when you come close to the man in that way, even briefly, there's something about him that makes that idea stand out in relief in a way that it never did before. You suddenly understand this is not just a literary device as it sometimes seems in the painting; it's an obsessive eroticism that tinges everything." She shook her head. "I know this sounds silly when I put it this way, but beauty is my god. When I was younger, I decided that I had to experience everything, and I accepted everything and everybody. If something seemed sordid, I told myself that deep within, no matter how well hidden, there was a tiny, redeeming touch of beauty and it was up to me to find it. But you know, when you're a woman and you're neither a hunchback nor a cripple, not one-eyed or one-legged, you soon discover that this is a very tough world we live in and you have to struggle hard not to be submerged by all the ugliness. So I finally had to build a kind of wall of resistance against everything that does not come from or lead to beauty—directly."

I said I was sure Dali, too, believed in beauty. After all, who were his ideals? Weren't they Raphael, Leonardo, Praxiteles?

"That may be," Maria said, "but if so, then he's not whole in that respect, is he? If he were, he wouldn't be able to divorce form from content quite so easily and separate the categories into such neat watertight compartments. I suppose I'm seeing this from the point of view of a girl of twenty-four and he from that of a man—a Spaniard, at that—of sixty, but if I find beauty wherever I go, it's because I carry it with me. I look for it wherever I go and I give it—that is, I try to give it—in everything I do. I don't seek it in art and trample on it in the other parts of life. Or is that irrelevant?"

"I think it's very relevant," I said. "But so is the distinction you just made between a twenty-four-year-old beginner and an old pro, sixty and Spanish. Do you remember," I asked, "how you felt when you first began to think of yourself as an artist?"

"Yes, I do. Very clearly. When I was a little girl I was already beginning to write, and I started to write the story of my life. I saw it all stretched out before me for an infinity—at least ten years. I was never the poor little girl who needed to be saved by her brother or a knight in shining armor. I was Joan of Arc, the warrior. But I could see that in everyone else's eyes I was just a little grain of dust. And that made me so unhappy I told myself this can't last; it's just not possible. I was absolutely certain that I was really an important personage. I felt even then that I had my place in the sun and that everyone else should know it. But I was only a little girl and they just *wouldn't* know it. They didn't *want* to know it. So I wrote stories about it and then burned them. I felt then—and I still do—that I could write forever about myself. In fact I believe that if one is really a writer, one could write two hundred pages about that knob." She pointed to the end of the cigarette lighter that stuck out from beneath the instrument panel. "With other things coming into it, of course, but always with the central idea wrapped up in the form and shape of that knob."

"And you kept on writing those stories?"

"I never stopped. I was determined to make the world pay attention. And my audience of one did. I believed implicitly in all I wrote. But I had no illusions about my motive. I simply wanted to be very famous. And now that people begin to recognize me in the street, you can't imagine the pleasure it gives me. Over the past few months I've been seeing my picture in the paper more and more often, and more and more articles about me in the magazines. When I see my photograph in *Le Figaro*, I say, 'I'm on my way. It won't be for tomorrow but maybe next year.' " She smiled and her eyes glistened.

"Was it as a writer that you wanted recognition, or as an actress, or how?" I asked.

"As *me*," she said. "Writer, painter—because I've painted a lot—actress in the theater and the cinema, in my songs and my singing, in all the channels open to me. Even with horses, training and riding them, because I love horses. I know it's impossible; I can't do everything all at once, but Montaigne said, when you bring up a child you let him walk along all by himself, as soon as he can, and you follow along behind in case you need to catch him. But you don't tell him in advance, go here or go there. You give him his liberty to go where he chooses and you follow along after. That's what I've done. I've followed myself where my fancy has led me. And I fell into the theater that way. And now the cinema. And so I've told myself I'm going to be a great actress. But the day I decide I'm ready to make my mark as a painter or as a writer or as anything else, I'll know it and I'll do it." She stopped and looked up at me. She looked more like fourteen than twenty-four. "Does that sound crazy?" she asked.

"Not at all," I assured her. "And if you'll just lift out of that story the things that are exclusively you and put in their place details that apply more specifically to a gifted, inordinately ambitious Spanish boy, you'll come closer to the young Dali than you think."

She looked shocked. "But there's a lot more to Dali than that," she said. "Even to the young Dali."

"There *is* more," I agreed. "And a great deal of it, I think, can be wrapped up in a phrase you used a little while ago—obsessive eroticism."

She thought for a moment. "It's certainly evident in the painting," she said finally. "And you see it even in such slight glimpses as I had of him this morning. The interesting thing would be to find out what lies behind it. We see the effect, but what's the cause?"

Once Dali was out of range, I turned my attention back to Picasso. The publication of *Life with Picasso*, which I had written in collaboration with Françoise Gilot, was scheduled for early November, and there were rounds of galley and page proof, illustrations, indexing, and all the usual details of putting a book to bed.

I was reading galleys one morning when I received a note from Marina Lussato from Palma de Mallorca. She was on her way to visit Dali, she wrote, and she enclosed two clippings with her letter. The shorter one, from *Le Figaro*, gave an account of an evening auction sale of paintings conducted by Maîtres Maurice and Philippe Rheims. The "surprise" of the session, it said, was the adjudication at 55,000 francs ($11,000), after being put on the block at 7,500 francs ($1,500), of a watercolor with gouache by Meissonier entitled *Friédland 1807*, measuring five feet two inches by eight feet six inches. "This vast heroic composition," *Le Figaro*'s auction news correspondent wrote, "will leave for foreign shores, if the Government allows. It was even whispered that a painter who gets himself much talked about when he isn't doing that himself is the lucky purchaser."

The other clipping was from *Paris-Presse*. It concerned the homage to Kant—or, as *Paris-Presse* headlined it, that "dalirious" night at the Galerie Charpentier. Except for a few small details, any resemblance between the event itself and *Paris-Presse*'s account of it was purely coincidental. The story read:

> They had never seen that at the Galerie Charpentier, and it will be a long time before they see it again: a plaster leg 13½ feet long, weighing 440 pounds, topped by two fenders from a *deux-chevaux* and bristling with enormous nails shaped like boils.
> The Leg—such was its title—was the work of a completely unknown forty-year-old Austrian sculptor named Rutsch, and was dedicated to Immanuel Kant, who, as everyone doesn't know, was never able to stand the contact of a silk stocking against his leg. [Rutsch had] glorified this painful allergy . . . at the instigation of Salvador Dali . . . who is currently exhibiting his own works [at the Galerie Charpentier]. Little did M. Nacenta, director of the most illustrious gallery in Paris, imagine the excitement this leg would bring him.

The *Tout-Paris*, including Marie-Laure de Noailles and the sculptor César, and the "usual band of enlightened critics" had turned out for the occasion, *Paris-Presse* revealed.

> Dali decreed that the boils were too much and at the top of his voice called upon Alexandre Rutsch to extirpate them. . . . Then Dali expressed astonishment that someone had had the idea of having a mannequin parade around "the thing": that was Rutsch's idea.
> "Did you ask M. Pierre Cardin to create a stocking and a shoe for your sculpture?" Dali then asked Rutsch before the horrified assembly.
> "Yes," he answered, blushing. "But he was not free until Monday."
> Salvador threw him a scornful glance and, turning toward the *Tout-Paris* assembled at the foot of "The Leg," launched into a sparkling account of the universality of his own genius. He was

coming to a brilliant conclusion when a dreadful crash was heard. Rutsch, seized by a sudden access of destructive madness, was knocking down his "Leg" with his fists. First he tore away the thigh —which almost crashed onto Marie-Laure de Noailles. Then the knee burst into bits and the foot fell crushed at the feet of Gala Dali, wife of the genius. Panic reigned. Rutsch screamed frightening imprecations against Dali. The debris from the leg shot up to the ceiling like bursts from a fireworks display. . . . Salvador took to his heels and rushed toward the exit. He had found someone crazier than he.

"Stop him!" shouted Rutsch. Too late: Dali found safety in flight, followed by Marie-Laure, who cried, "He has broken everything! He has broken everything! Everything, everything, everything!"

Nacenta, the director, who was covering his head with his hands, stammered gaily, "But don't leave. Why, it's madly Surrealist. It's marvelous."

Rutsch, wild with anger, continued to pulverize his "Leg." Suddenly there was a resounding slap, administered by a friend of Dali's, Patrick Valberg, to the photographer Gilbert de Gratz, an old friend of Léonor Fini, who was defending Rutsch.

"He slapped me," he said to the policeman whom this tumult had attracted.

"Why?"

"Because of 'The Leg.' "

"Whose leg?"

"Kant's leg."

Reduced by now to the level of total confusion, the policeman wandered away, the reporter petered off into pure whimsy, and I went back to my Picasso duties.

Soon after that I returned to America and *Life with Picasso* preempted most of my time. But toward midwinter I began to be troubled by the fact that in spite of Dali's repeated promises to send me—through his archivist, Albert Field—a written analysis of the bank's giant-sized painting, *Galacidalacidesoxiribunucleicacid,* he had not yet done so. I reminded my friend at the bank, and the bank prodded Knoedler's. Knoedler's must have jabbed Dali in a particularly sensitive area because in a few weeks I received a scroll of heavy, handmade nacreous Japanese paper about eighteen by twenty-three inches covered with an ornate and rambling Dalinian script. Its text started off briskly to disentangle the painting's arcane elements but soon meandered off into a maze of Gala, Crick and Watson, Teilhard de Chardin, God, Christ, the Cid Campeador, with glancing references to Dali's past, modern science, and a vague theology, all of it punctuated by occasional highly decorative splotches and inkblots. The only clear-cut statement I came away with, thanks to an undescended footnote elevated to interlinear obscurity by means of an invisible caret, was the categorical declaration—Dali has never made a secret of his addiction to onanism—"*Je m'envois* [sic] *ce soir.*"

The right-hand half of the scroll was taken up by an old Catalan nursery rhyme which, in some way not clear to me, Dali related to the genetic code. However, since he had told me in Paris, earlier on, that the important thing was to spread confusion, not to eliminate it, I decided to accept his explanation on its own terms and let the bank make its peace with the nursery rhyme.

I had long since realized it was not possible to give an adequate idea of Dali's mind and methods within the compass of a magazine article, and so I had told him, before leaving Paris, that there would be another book about him. He had seemed pleased. Early in March, Albert Field, who apparently had lost my address and must have assumed that since articles of mine had appeared in the *Atlantic Monthly,* its editors would know where to find me, wrote to the magazine that "Salvador Dali would like Mr. Lake to communicate with him as soon as convenient." But even before I had a chance to do so, Dr. Colin, Dali's scientific and literary collaborator, somehow managed to ferret out my telephone number and reached me by phone one afternoon. Dali was most eager to reestablish contact with me, he said. When would I be coming to New York? Within a few weeks, I told him. That seemed to satisfy him.

I assumed that Dali was eager to get on with our unfinished business and so I wrote him a reassuring note. A few days before leaving for New York, I wrote him again, telling him exactly when I would be there. The following Sunday morning, in my New York hotel room, I was wading through the *Times* when suddenly, on page 12, Dali popped out at me from the middle of a seven-column ad run by Abraham & Straus "inviting you to meet . . . the renowned Spanish master," who would be at their Brooklyn store from 11:30 to 1:30 on Monday. Had it been anyone but Dali, I would have felt it more normal to walk three blocks down Fifth Avenue to the St. Regis and meet him there, but the Dalinian doctrine of gratuitous complexity began to take over from my usual logic and I wondered if a reunion in Brooklyn might not be a better idea. As I sat there debating the question the telephone rang. A woman with a strong Slavic accent—it could only have been Gala, I soon realized—asked for me and then asked me to wait. Soon I heard the familiar *"Bonjour,"* and Dali was talking.

"I regret very much you have not been more assiduous in your attention to me this winter," he said. "A number of things of spectacular interest have happened to me which it would be impossible to reconstruct. They would have been of great interest for the book you are writing about me."

I told him I, too, regretted it but there had been other jobs that needed attention.

"That is no concern of mine," he said impatiently. "I am merely stating the facts—and my regrets. Now—a second thing. I have seen the book you wrote with Madame Gilot. It is full of inaccuracies and people of no consequence. I saw Madame Gilot when she was here for her exhibition a few weeks ago and I told her the same thing. There's no point in going into it now, over the telephone, but when I see you I'll give you all the details."

I said I'd like to hear more about that. When?

"I'll be in the King Cole Bar this afternoon from five o'clock on," he said. I told him I'd be there.

When I looked in at the King Cole Bar shortly after five that afternoon, Dali was nowhere in sight. As I walked back toward the front lobby of the hotel I saw a tall, slender, prematurely gray-haired fellow with rimless glasses striding toward me. As he drew nearer I recognized him as Dali's archivist, Albert Field. He seemed to be staring fixedly at a point above my head and behind me. I reached the end of the lobby and turned back toward the bar. Halfway down, I met Field again coming toward me, still looking high up and far away. I sat down opposite the lobby bookstore. In a few minutes a short, plump man with an astrakhan hat walked by in the direction of the bar. I was sure it was Dr. Colin, who had telephoned me in Boston to ask when I would be coming to New York to see Dali again. He seemed not to see me. I walked up to the front of the lobby again. Field was talking on one of the house phones. "Yes, I have a list of all he owes," he was saying. I returned to my seat. In a moment Colin reappeared, this time headed for the front lobby. He walked past me, looking neither to left nor to right. Soon the two of them returned, heading for the bar. I realized they were in an awkward spot. Since Dali had told me he was displeased with *Life with Picasso* and had implied that he was going to rap my knuckles, there was a better than even chance that he had told Field and Colin so, too—and in more detail and stronger language. I could understand that they might not be eager to be caught in friendly conversation with me when the Master made his entrance. Still, it did seem a little silly to go on pretending that nobody recognized anybody. I decided to break the ice.

"Mr. Field, where are you going?" I called out. Field stopped in his tracks. Colin scurried on.

"I thought I recognized you," Field said, almost without turning in my direction, "but I couldn't stop. I had to talk with Dali." I walked along the corridor with him as far as the bar. I checked my hat and coat and then we joined Colin, who was hovering around the entrance, looking first inside, then back toward the lobby. Field presented me to Colin, who seemed a bit unsure about remembering me, and then said, "Well, we might as well sit down while we're waiting."

The captain led us to a large empty round table in the far corner of the bar. Field and Colin set down the dossiers they were carrying and began to look through their papers. A short, dark man with a sharp nose and a pleasant face came over to the table.

"Are you waiting for Dali, and if so, may I join you?" he asked.

Colin looked up from his papers. "If you introduce yourself," he said.

"I'm Dr. Foz," the man answered.

"From where?" Colin asked.

"From where Dali is from—Catalonia," the man said. He sat down at my right. Colin called over a waiter and ordered tea. Field ordered hot chocolate, and Dr. Foz a daiquiri. Dr. Foz, I learned, was an M.D. who didn't practice medicine but worked in a laboratory and occasionally helped Dali with "some things he doesn't know much about." Had he known Dali long? "Very long," he said and smiled. "A very funny fellow."

At that moment Dali arrived carrying a half dozen or so sheets similar to the one on which he had written his explanation of the bank's picture. These, too, were covered with writing, drawing, and decorative doodling, but with a great many more corrections in the text. He shook hands with us all, then moved past Field and Colin and sat down at my left.

"We'll get to your book in a little while," he said to me, "but first I want to look over a few passages of a talk I have to give soon." He spread his papers out on the table and selected one from among them, then began to read aloud, slowly.

" 'Perhaps, and even without perhaps, the most tragic moment in all history occurred in Delft in the year when, in that city located at so-and-so-many kilometers from Gerona and so-and-so-many kilometers from the Perpignan railroad station, were born the two most important and most dissimilar eyes in the world: the visceral eye of Vermeer of Delft and the mechanical eye, the first microscope, invented by—' " He stopped. "By Languedoc," he said finally.

"Don't you mean Leeuwenhoek?" Colin asked.

"That's right," Dali said. "Now—so-and-so-many years had to elapse between Languedoc's death and Dali in order for Dali—" He turned the sheet in another direction. "Ah—all right. Here. 'Perhaps and even without perhaps the most gay and reassuring moment in the entire history of painting occurred on the seventeenth of November of 1964 in the middle of the Perpignan railroad station, which is located at so-and-so-many kilometers from Figueras, where Dali of Figueras discovered the possibility of painting in oil in the third dimension by impressing onto the surface of an oil painting microscopic patterns in the form of parabolic lenses like those contained in the eyes of flies: what amounts to the superposition of the eye of Vermeer onto the microscope of Languedoc.' " He turned over the sheet, then picked up another. "This is confusing," he said. That was as it should be, I reminded him.

"But the part about Napoleon—that should come later on," he said. I could see he was trying to decipher passages he had already scratched out. Colin, looking over his shoulder, pointed to another part of the script. "This one," he said.

"No, no, that's not it," Dali said. "Not that, either. It's already crossed out. Where's that part about Napoleon's soldiers? That was very good. *Enfin.* Here's another one that's very good." He cleared his throat. " 'Already at Le Perthus, thanks to the eyes and the jaws of the flies that came from Gerona, there took place the first levitation of the third dimension in oil painting, the only painting which interests the eye and the jaws of the genius Dali, who deserves to be divine for having invented it all by himself, proving by this invention of the third dimension in oil painting the basic idea of the sublime Jesuit father Tellerand de Chardin—' "

"Teilhard de Chardin," Colin said.

"*Oui.* '. . . Tellerand de Chardin, who wanted to have all the existential anguish of Pascal crumble and disappear, since the insignificant smallness of mankind, instead of destroying itself, submerges itself into the grandiose infinity of the universe as Pascal conceived it. But the exact opposite occurred, because we now learn that the universe, which, moreover, has its limits and is not so large as one had believed, converges in its entirety to produce the most perfect element of the cosmos: the human being, and in the human being the eye, and in the eye—painting in the third dimension. Therefore, let us all be happy, since everything reaches its climax in man, the son of God, just as though the whole cosmos were our dwelling place, freed of its Pascalian terrors in the Perpignan railroad station.' " Dali sat back admiringly. "That is colossal," he said. "The son of God, and then the cosmos without the terrors! Oh, it's wonderful!"

"And the station, too," Colin said.

"Station? Ah, yes. The station, in fact, where . . . took place . . ." Dali fumbled with the other pages, turning them over one by one. "Ah! Here. 'The man who possesses the most paranoiac eye that ever existed—mine—inventing a method of painting stereoscopically—a truly cosmic method, so that with each brushstroke of my new method, man will be able to reinvent perpetually the universe, as Velásquez had already done in his day, but, like Dali, he would never have been able to reinvent it if, like him, he had not felt the imperious and imperial need to come close one day to the periphery of that spot where the entire universe converges—the middle of the Perpignan railroad station.' "

"That's very good: *converge—con* plus *verge,*" Dr. Foz said.

"Naturally," Dali said. "We'll put that in parentheses: *le con et la verge.* You know that Velásquez went to Le Perthus. Now, what I need are scholars to go to work on the details of his journey, when he carried the material for the dress of the Infanta Margarita and afterwards painted the portrait of Philip the Fourth you see in the Frick Collection—the finest of all those in the western world or anywhere else, the one with that magnificent silver sleeve in the king's costume. Now, find out why he went there, the date of his journey, the exact nature of his diplomatic mission. I give all these sublime ideas, but in addition there must be specialists and scholars in fine print to elaborate my text. Like when I talk about ten thousand magnifying glasses because after Languedoc began to make lenses, then he went on to make ten thousand microscopes. I say so, but there should be some specialist who points out that the electron microscope of today grew out of that, and that when those good burghers of Delft polished their lenses they were only continuing the work of the people of the neolithic age, who began by polishing stone and then went on to polish quartz. That's sublime, all that, but I need others to do the hack work. And to find out exactly how many kilometers there are between Delft and Gerona or Perpignan, and so on."

Dali turned over another sheet and then another. "Ah! Listen to this: 'Here is where one understands why the czar of all the Russias, Peter the Great, never had the idea of going to Le Perthus, which would have been the best of all the ideas he could ever have had because once he was there he couldn't have avoided being infected by one of those miraculous flies of Gerona with the only vaccine so far known to be effective against the progressivism of the French Revolution and, as a result, the Russian Revolution, thus eliminating the future Communism of his own country. But instead of going to the spot on which now stands the Perpignan railroad station, he went, Peter the Great, czar of all the Russias, off to Delft and, humbling himself in his role of emperor of divine origin with papal attributes, looked through the microscope of Languedoc and saw for the first time the monstrous swarming of matter which would one day devour his own country.' " He paused.

Colin looked over at him admiringly. "That's more than delirious," he said.

Dali pushed on. " 'And the Russians, with their dialectical Marxism, haven't had their feet on the ground since then. Now they have become astronauts and they're going to fart their way up to the moon.' Ah, here's the part about Napoleon's soldiers. Listen, now: 'Napoleon's soldiers, who had started out joyously to invade Spain and introduce all the latest advances of the Age of Light, just as though their balls were filled with Cartesianism that had caught fire in Delft, now turned back and departed via Le Perthus with their fires banked and their arses chewed down to the bone by the miraculous flies of Gerona. Meanwhile, those same Napoleonic warriors, apparently defeated in Russia, were in reality only frozen, because as soon as they thawed out and started to march again, they were already wearing the uniform of the Red Army to inaugurate the Russian Revolution, which was only their own French Revolution arriving late because of the cold . . .' Oh, that's sublime, sublime." He folded the sheet, unfolded another, and looked at it carefully.

"I call this a résumé of history and of the history of painting," Dali said. "In such-and-such a year, Vermeer of Delft is born. In the same year Languedoc, inventor of the first microscope; then in fifteen hundred and something, Grotius in the Hague lays the foundation of international law. After that, in Gerona, a swarm of miraculous flies released from the well-preserved body of St. Narcissus, patron saint of flies, which had remained frozen at a point where the glacier had prevented him from crossing the Pyrenees, dispersed Napoleon's cavalry. And in 1963 Mr. So-and-so establishes a foundation in Holland for the freezing of human beings. You probably saw the write-up in *L'Express* last week. Now," he said, turning to Colin, "for my talk I want a detailed map, in colors, showing the whole continent of Europe."

"Gerona, Perpignan, and Delft?" Colin asked.

"No, no, no. The whole business. Then I'll wipe out the rest of Europe so that only two places remain—Delft and the Perpignan station."

Colin turned to me. "He began with a delirious idea, and as he worked on it, it became less delirious. Now it's really clear. The curious thing is that geographically he has established a kind of European triangle which explains everything important that has happened in the world—"

Dali broke in. "In the history of the eye—of painting. Because Tellerand de Chardin says that the whole universe, the cosmos, all the galaxies, converge on man, the son of God, and the most divine part of man is his eye. You can't compare man's eye to his ear or his foot or anything else, because the eye is the source *par excellence* of understanding. That's why they do these Pop Art things with moiré patterns, because the eye is simply the brain's ambassador. The brain knows, thanks to the information furnished to it by the eye. So painting is the only thing that matters within the range of a human being, and painting covers a very small area. It has come about only in certain countries and not in others. There's no painting worth talking about in those Scandivanilla countries like Sweden, Finland, Russia, England. Not one painter in the lot who has added anything significant to the history of painting. On the other hand, in Italy, Spain, France, and Holland you have it all. Even in the Ice Age we already had Altamira."

"But what about the parts on farting?" Dr. Foz asked.

"You can take care of that," Dali said. "Just put them in in the right place. I can't write about it because American censorship won't stand for it. You can talk about love, make love, all you want, but you can't fart."

"In public?" Colin asked.

"No, in print," Dali said. "One of the outstanding authorities on farting was one of the greatest Americans who ever lived —Benjamin Franklin—but the censor won't let you write about it. In my book *Le Journal d'un génie* I had a whole annex devoted to farting but in the American translation it has to come out. It's all right for France but not for America."

I told Dali that one of my university classmates had been flunked for introducing that subject into the plot of an English theme.

"Up in Boston? Of course. They're all Protestants. But I'm giving my talk at Fordham. It's a Catholic place and they'll let me talk all I want to about farting. I'll prove to them that throughout the history of Catholicism the Popes were great farters. During the Middle Ages there were important secret societies in which one of the requirements was to be an outstanding farter. I have documentary proof of all this. Even in England, in those days, on Christmas one farted in the presence of the king. In Spain, as everybody knows, they spent whole days farting. But in America you can't talk about it. At least you can't write about it. Thanks to the Protestants."

"I've talked to three Popes, but I never dared to talk to *them* about it," Colin said.

Dali reared back. "Ah, yes, but do you have the Cross of Isabella the Catholic?"

Colin giggled. "Heavens, no."

"That's it," Dali said. "But when one has the Cross of Isabella the Catholic, as I do, anything is permitted. When somebody ordinary begins to talk about farting, everybody finds it scandalous, but when I, with the Cross of Isabella the Catholic, do so, they must respect me. I get right to the point. Which is simply that there's one religion in which one just doesn't fart—that's the Anglo-Saxons'. But Catholics fart all day long. And I'll tell them so at Fordham."

"You'd better get absolution before you go there," Colin said.

"But there's a real tradition for that," Dali said. "In the Middle Ages they thought the soul left the body through the mouth but the devils went out the arse. There's a delicious text by Quevedo called "The Eye of the Arse," and in the Spanish edition of *Le Journal d'un génie* I appended that. They didn't cut a word. Not like America." Dali put aside the large sheets of his Fordham talk and picked up a pile of smaller-sized papers. Colin peered over his shoulder at the one on top.

"What's that?" he asked.

"Oh, it's some woman who's in love with me. I'll have to send her a cable. She's in Bombay, dying of love. She needs a little encouragement. But first read me the letter about hibernation."

From his pile Colin selected a letter and began to read. " 'Dear Mr. Dali, While reading "The Lyons Den" in the New York *Post,* March thirty-first, I came across certain statements you were quoted as making concerning the possibility of immortality through freezing. The organization I represent, the Life Extension Society, is dedicated to the freezing movement. The Society has been in operation for over two years. The steady increase in our rate of growth is profoundly symptomatic of our new and progressive philosophic approach to the concept of human life. We are now in the process of formally organizing in the New York area. We are involved, among other things, in providing opportunities to enable people who are dying right now to have their bodies frozen. You mention an organization for no more death, of which you say you are a member. I have no knowledge of any such organization. I would greatly appreciate it if you would inform me as to the location and activities of this organization. In any case the freezing movement is in its infancy. It is, I believe, the first tangible step leading to immortality, the most meaningful of all conquests. We need famous people such as yourself who are willing to support the idea of freezing, and by so doing, to speed the pathway to immortality. If you are interested, please write to me at my address, advising me . . .' " His voice trailed off. He picked up a clipping from among his papers. "Now here's another group, in Europe. This is from the March twenty-eight *L'Express.*" He read a long article which told of the establishment by a lawyer named K. W. Clausen in the Hague of a foundation for biological research whose members included a banker and an economist. Its purpose was to study thoroughly all aspects of the human-hibernation problem—not only scientific but judicial, economic, and even religious.

"There's a worldwide movement now setting up a basis for communication," Dali said. "No more coffins, no more skeletons. You stay just the way you are. When the doctors get around to finding a way to cure whatever it is you're dying of, they unfreeze you."

"Every man his own Jesus Christ," Colin said.

I asked if there wasn't any problem of brain deterioration.

"At the moment there is," Dali said, "but I talked yesterday with a Nobel Prize-winning biologist. He told me that until very recently there has been great difficulty about lowering the temperature from zero to, say, twenty-five below because crystals formed inside the cells and destroyed them. Just five months ago they found a very simple way to prevent that: by injecting glycerine into the cell. This is the coming thing. It's going to be a big movement. Twenty years ago it would have seemed like science fiction, but today it's an absolute certainty. As a matter of fact I'm going to send a telegram right now to that society."

Colin picked up a pencil and began to write and read simultaneously: "Coincidental with my declarations in the American press about hibernation of man, I salute the creation of the research organization and I hereby offer—"

"*Non, non, non,*" Dali said. He switched into English. "Proveed receive fool leetairature."

"Provided," Colin corrected.

"Provide receive fool leetairature on leest of *biologistes* eenvolvèd." Colin changed his text to accommodate Dali's amendment and read it aloud. Dali nodded in satisfaction.

I had brought with me a photostatic copy of the large sheet on which Dali had written his explanation of the bank's painting. I showed it to him and asked him to translate for me the Catalan nursery rhyme on the right-hand side.

"Ah," he said and began to read it aloud in the original. I recognized it at once from his explosive delivery as the speech he had declaimed at the Galerie Charpentier at the foot of Rutsch's *Monument to Kant*. Then it had sounded like gibberish. Now that I knew it was a language spoken by human beings, it sounded like—gibberish. Reading it seemed to excite him, somehow, and his face reddened a good bit in the process. When he had finished reading, he translated the text into French. From that version I deduced that it was a matter of hens pecking at grain, rich hens eating cakes, over and over again. And now that it was just a thin, repetitious little story in French, I could see it had no more interest for Dali, either. He dropped the sheet and turned to me.

"I forgot your book," he said. "I'll be right back." He left the table. When he returned he was carrying a copy of *Life with Picasso* under his right arm and with his left arm escorting a tall, dark, exceedingly thin young woman whom he introduced as Mlle. Barzini. "The most sought-after fashion model in New York," he told me in an aside. "Her father is a neighbor of yours on the best-seller list, but I'm not one-tenth as much interested in his book as I am in a magnificent beauty spot of his daughter's. It has the shape of a fly."

He sat down at my left, with Mlle. Barzini at his left, and opened his copy of *Life with Picasso*. It was heavily underlined in blue and in red.

"I've marked it page by page," he said, "underlining all the names of people nobody knows or cares about: Monsieur Leiris, Madame Leiris, Picasso's dentist—souls in purgatory. But first I want to take up the matter of this so-called 'ready-made.' " He turned to page 308, on which was reproduced, along with two of Picasso's sculptures, a burner from a prewar French gas stove that looked as though it should have been a Picasso sculpture of a woman. Picasso himself had been struck by the resemblance and referred to it as his "ready-made." He had named it *La Vénus du Gaz*. Dali, I saw, had decorated the photograph with his crayons.

"This is very important," he said. "Mr. Lake presents this object of Picasso's—*La Vénus du Gaz*—and calls it a ready-made." He turned to me. "I beg your pardon," he said, "but you don't know what a ready-made is. That is a term invented by Marcel Duchamp which is applied to any ordinary object which the artist finds and, by choosing it, raises to the level of a work of art. Picasso found that object and didn't change it in any way, but it's something that resembles exactly a sculpture by Picasso, so it's not a ready-made because the principle of a ready-made is that it doesn't resemble anything and people wonder why in the world Marcel Duchamp should suddenly have picked that because it bears no resemblance whatever to a work by Marcel Duchamp.

"If all of a sudden I find Mademoiselle Barzini and she is the very essence of a Dalinian woman, I still can't call her a ready-made. Obviously I didn't create her; she was already that way, but since she looks just like a Dali creation, she's not a ready-made. Now, if Picasso finds an object and says, 'I'm going to exhibit that,' it's because it resembles exactly a sculpture by Picasso. Whether he made it or found it has no importance. Stylistically it's a Picasso and so it becomes one historically. But Duchamp's idea was completely different. He exhibited a urinal and called it a work of art. It seemed such a marvelous thing, all the other painters and sculptors began to turn out their own urinals, but they weren't as well made as a real one. What does that mean? Simply that Duchamp, at a given moment, seized upon a form that corresponded to the preoccupations of a thousand other people and set them to making urinals. But he was the first. He set the example. But the urinal didn't bear any resemblance to a work by Marcel Duchamp. That's the distinction, you see. And therein lies the moral value of a ready-made."

He pointed to the illustration. "That is an extraordinary thing. It's so like Picasso that you can say it *is* a Picasso—a signed Picasso, one hundred percent, recognizable from across a room: that head, the circular form in the middle, and all the rest. But it's not a ready-made, and people are going to say Mr. Lake didn't understand what was the real intention of Duchamp or the Dadaists or Dali when they did a ready-made."

I told Dali it was too bad Picasso couldn't be with us, because he was the one who had labeled it that. He brushed that aside.

"That's just one example of what I mean," he said. He turned back to page 299. It had red and blue underlining and marginal annotations as well. "All right," he said. "Éluard is an important man, but who is Dominique?"

Éluard's last wife, I told him.

"Oh, well, we'll let that go, then. But Golfe-Juan—who cares about Golfe-Juan? More Dominique, La Bravade, St. Tropez, Lee Miller—no interest. Madame Ramié—who is she?"

Picasso's ceramist, I told him.

"All Picasso's ceramists are worthless," he said. He turned the page. "L'Auberge des Maures—who cares about that? Gibraltar. Well, all right. Then God—He's okay. And Rue des Grands-Augustins—very important, because that's the street where so many important things in Picasso's life took place. But Golfe-Juan—no." He moved his finger down the page. "Ah, Christopher Columbus! That's good. Marvelous. Cocteau—all right. Madame Weisweiller. Get rid of her. No good. Mayan culture. No good." I looked at the page and saw that he had stopped at a reference to Picasso's daughter Maya. I asked him if he had read the book.

"Frankly, I haven't got very far with it," he said. "Every time I start to read, I run into a bunch of names of people nobody cares about and it puts me off. If *I* don't know any of those people, how do you expect Americans to be interested? And who cares about Mayan culture?" I explained who Maya was. It didn't make any difference, apparently. "I've given you my advice," he said. "Now you sleep on it. There are too many people and places of not the slightest interest to anybody. Instead of Golfe-Juan you should talk about the railroad station in Perpignan." I promised him I'd do that in the book about Dali. "Have you read Brassaï's book on Picasso?" he asked. I had. "Now, there's a book," he said, "with very important documentation—especially the parts about me. It's completely admirable."

I realized now what lay behind his irrational distaste for almost every proper name mentioned or discussed in *Life with Picasso:* nowhere in its 367 pages does the name Dali appear.

"Some of those things Brassaï tells about me have never been written before," he said.

"Brassaï calls it *Conversations with Picasso,*" Colin said, "but it should have been called *Conversations with Dali.*"

Dali shook his head. "All that stuff you put in about Picasso's dentist and Madame Ramié! Five years after they're dead, even the people who work in the cemetery won't know where they are. And there are probably plenty of things Picasso would rather not see in print. Did you ask his permission to publish the book?"

Certainly not, I told him.

"That was not courteous on your part," Dali said. "To write about some personage whom you respect but without his permission—perhaps even against his will—you shouldn't have done it."

If the only biographies ever written were those their subjects approved of, posterity would have a pretty lopsided picture of most of its great ancestors, I said.

"But Picasso is a genius," Dali said.

I reminded him that twice he had said in my hearing that he—Dali—was the only living genius. How did that leave room for Picasso?

Dali scowled. "No, no, no, no, no, no. I am—I said I am—the only living genius, because Picasso is already no longer living. He has been a genius but then he stopped being one. Or you could say he still is a genius by comparison with the others. Well, all right, I'll say he is a genius still, because at least he has done something unique that the others were incapable of doing. The only thing is, he is diminished by age. That's entirely normal. If someone like Leonardo was able to keep on painting extraordinary things right up to the end, it was because he had a nearly perfect technique. But when a man's genius is based on something completely different, then, at a certain age, he stops producing works of genius. That doesn't apply to me because I have more ideas of genius now than I had ten years ago, that's certain. But in the case of Picasso, that's all the more reason you should have had enough respect for him not to publish this book. First you should have asked him, 'Do you like this or not? If not, I won't publish it.' But if he was so far gone as to say, 'I love it. I want you to print it' —and that is what I assumed had happened—then you go right ahead; that's great. Otherwise you tear up the manuscript. With me it's different. I *want* to be written about, but he doesn't."

I told Dali I was glad to see he was more reasonable in that respect.

He looked at me proudly. "I want everybody to talk about Dali—*even* if they speak well of him. If they speak ill of him, that's marvelous. With me it's the quantity that counts. When my press cuttings come in, I look to see how long they are and how much they weigh, but I never read what they say. But this Madame Gilot—she shouldn't have told you all those things about Picasso."

Mlle. Barzini leaned toward me. "Especially to make money," she said.

I told her I felt certain that was not Mme. Gilot's motive.

"And then as soon as the book comes out, she holds an exhibition of her painting," Dali said scornfully. "When I saw the paintings, I could see she had lived with Picasso without ever understanding what he was trying to do. It's shocking. No, no, no. From the moral point of view I think that anyone who has had the honor of sharing Picasso's life—even if only for fifteen minutes—should be humble enough just to live on the glory and not even try to make a work of art. In any case, no woman should try to create a work of art—they're incapable of it. There never was a woman who did anything of that kind worth talking about."

"Absolutely nothing," Mlle. Barzini chimed in.

"Not in painting or architecture or anything else," Dali said. "So that's the first thing she should have told herself: 'I am a woman; therefore, I'll do no painting, no book—nothing.' "

I told Dali she was a painter before she met Picasso.

"That's even worse, then. Women should never do painting."

"Decoration, perhaps," Mlle. Barzini suggested.

"At the most," Dali conceded. "But they should stick to making children and not try to turn out paintings. There have been a few women painters, but none of them amount to very much —like Rosa Bonheur."

Didn't he approve of Rosa Bonheur?

"Oh, she's not much," he said. "In fact she's very bad. But she's at least better than Marie Laurencin. Or Madame Gilot. Women can influence men—like Beatrice with Dante. They can even be queens, like Catherine of Russia or Isabella the Catholic. But they don't have the creative gift. I went to look at Gilot's exhibition because I thought perhaps she might have done some nice little things."

Colin broke in. "But what stuff! He told her, 'My dear'—

what's her name? Françoise?—'My dear Françoise, I'm delighted to see you, but it's not very good what you do.' "

"No, no, no," Dali cut in. "I said nothing. I had myself carried in to her exhibition in a wheelchair because I had a sore throat. I was waiting for someone to ask me what I thought of her painting so I could say, 'The truth is, it's a piece of shit.' But since nobody asked me, I didn't want to say it. If *she* had asked me, I would have said, 'If all these things, instead of being yours, were Picasso's, that would be marvelous.' But since they were hers, they were a total disaster." Everybody laughed. I asked Dali if he had spoken to her.

"Oh, yes, but not about her painting, because it's horrible. Horrible." He shook his head. "You know, if the book had been called *The Life of Madame Gilot,* I wouldn't mind so much, but to call it *Life with Picasso* is simply capitalizing on Picasso's name."

"Gala would never do a thing like that," Colin said.

"But she's such a completely different kind of person," Dali said. "So pure. An idea like that would never cross her mind."

Dr. Foz spoke up. "I liked the book. My son bought a copy and he liked it, too. In fact most everybody I know who read it liked it very much."

Dali brushed him aside. "No, it's very clear, she's capitalizing on Picasso. There's an enormous public interest in him and none in her. If she had been an extraordinary woman, a queen—"

"Then she wouldn't have done the book," Mlle. Barzini put in.

"She wouldn't have *needed* to do the book," Dali said. "It's capitalizing on Picasso. Do a book, sell copies, hold exhibitions, sell her paintings. The only reason that exhibition ever took place was that she had been Picasso's wife. If she hadn't been, nobody would have taken photographs of her paintings. The exhibition would have passed completely unnoticed."

I remembered then that Dali had had an exhibition of prints

that opened the same day as Françoise Gilot's exhibition of paintings. The New York *Times* had given wide coverage, with many photographs, to the Gilot exhibition. It seemed pointless to suggest to Dali that such high moral indignation sounded strange coming from a man who all his life had made such varied and effective use of publicity.

Dali shook his finger at me. "If Madame Gilot had made love with Picasso in such an extraordinary fashion that no one had ever seen anything like that since time began, then I'd say yes, that's a great legacy for humanity. But instead of that there's only a little gossip about things that occur in every mediocre little household. If they had done something extravagantly erotic or invented things that are priceless for humanity, things such as I'm engaged in working out with Dr. Foz—new ways of producing gooseflesh with certain injections—"

Foz started to explain. Dali cut him off. "No, no, no. Say nothing of all that. Afterwards we'll go into that by ourselves, just the two of us."

Gala came over to the table. Dali jumped up. "Here she is." She shook hands with everyone, then sat quietly over against the wall between Colin and Field.

"And besides, who believes those conversations Gilot reports?" Dali said. "Everything Picasso says is full of malice. He would never say, for example, what he says in that book about Chagall. He detests Chagall. I don't know how she could have told you that. You certainly can't trust a little concierge on the subject of Picasso's ideas about painting. It's ridiculous. She's just an ambitious young girl who worked things out so that this book could coincide with a lamentable little exhibition of painting in which one sees immediately that she never understood what a painting by Picasso is all about. You arranged this because she lived with Picasso and everybody wants to know what a woman who has lived with Picasso has to say about it. Obviously, you took the best of what you found there among what was intellectually valid and interesting, but you should have stayed away from her and approached him from another angle."

I reminded Dali that at our second meeting, in this very room, he had told me, *"Moi, je me livre. Picasso ne se livre pas."* And that was very true—at least the part relating to Picasso. And if Picasso didn't hand himself over, how *did* one get at the man behind the myth?

He seemed uncertain about that so he changed his course. "If she had told you things that were completely unknown— let's say it were a question of Picasso making love with cats— then that would be important and should be set down, because one day humanity will want to know that."

I told Dali I'd put him to the test. In my book about him I would note everything he said or did that came to my attention and seemed to have a real interest for posterity. But I didn't expect that he would then reproach me for my assiduousness and say something like, "Oh, that's true but I'm not sure I want posterity to know it." I wanted to show him at first hand exactly the way he was. I had read the other books about him and thought they were pretty much on the surface.

"Oh, they're all very bad. Fleur Cowles' book is a disaster," he said. "The work of a secretary. And Morse's book is nothing. Nothing."

And *The Secret Life of Salvador Dali?* I asked.

He looked surprised. "But I did that," he said.

Maybe so, I said, but however theatrical it might be in spots, it was not awfully convincing: all those exceedingly detailed and highly imaginative accounts of "critical" episodes of childhood and adolescence that could only be taken—to put it politely—as overextended metaphors. I said I wanted to see him just the way he was—without the literary window dressing.

His face reddened, then he nodded. "That interests me," he said. "That's why I talk to you as frankly as I do."

PART THREE

Toward the end of March, 1965, about five months after
the original publication of *Life with Picasso* in New
York, excerpts from the French translation were scheduled to appear in two consecutive issues of *Paris-Match*. When
the first extract was published, Picasso's lawyer petitioned the
court to have the magazine seized. Certain passages, he claimed,
were "an intolerable intrusion" into the private life of his
client. The judge, M. André Dechézelles, president of the tribunal of the Department of the Seine, read both issues of the
magazine, found nothing in either one of a nature to warrant
seizure, and rejected the request.

A few days later the book itself was published. Within a fort-
night Picasso's lawyer had taken the same legal route in seeking
seizure of the book. Picasso's life, he argued, was his own business and didn't belong to the masses. This demand was made
before the vice-president of the tribunal, M. Fusil. He read the
complete book and then rendered a judgment which French
legal commentators saw as setting a historic legal precedent. He
admitted that "certain passages [of the book] show Picasso as

rather satisfied with himself and indifferent to others, overimpressed by his own value, insufficiently detached from financial considerations, sometimes unkind and unjust to some of his fellow-artists, harsh and without indulgence toward his family and his entourage . . ." but pointed out that "a biography isn't supposed to be a panegyric." Also, in addition to the unflattering passages he had referred to, there were others, he said, that showed Picasso in a very favorable light. As for the "shocking" remarks attributed to Picasso—I assumed M. Fusil was referring to certain of Picasso's acid estimates of some of his contemporaries—any halfway sophisticated reader ought to be able to take them with a grain of salt and attribute them to "artistic pride or exaggeration," he suggested.

His main point he saved for the end: the average man, he said, might be expected to find such a "bright and occasionally deforming light" cast on him to be unbearable. But for an artist of renown who had never fled from publicity and who had constantly offered up, without reticence, his physical and moral image to the public gaze, that was quite another story. No seizure, he ruled.

By the time I reached Paris, *Vivre avec Picasso* was temporarily out of print and the publisher was reprinting as fast as he could. Blocked in their legal actions, the book's enemies turned to the propaganda front. There were several small groups determined to demolish the book. A few English collector-critics, friends of Picasso's, had resented the book's frankness and tried to prejudice opinion against it when it was published in New York and, a little later, in London. The climax of their frenzy was reached in an auto-da-fé in London in which a copy of *Life with Picasso* was burned to a cinder. But in spite of their overheated feelings, commercially and critically the book had wide success in both countries.

When the French edition was published, one month after the British, other pressure groups took up the attack. In the Picasso entourage there were those who had a moral, political, or financial stake in Picasso's good will. The painter Pignon and his wife, she the author of several incense-burning books about Picasso, were among the most vocal.

One of the angriest of this group was D.-H. Kahnweiler, Picasso's dealer. One of the big London daily newspapers tried to reach Françoise Gilot through Kahnweiler at his gallery in the Rue Monceau in Paris. He was rather unhelpful—"vehemently" so, according to the newspaper—and he referred to *Life with Picasso* as "infamous." The London reporter commented that "perhaps the little gray man had a certain justification for his vehemence . . . Kahnweiler . . . like Picasso is depicted with ruthless, not always flattering, honesty in *Life with Picasso*."

The main power behind the propaganda offensive was the French Communist Party, which has benefited enormously and increasingly from Picasso's financial support and his value as a propaganda weapon. For years, the Party has reproduced his image and his work in its newspapers and other media and sold it, in the form of plates and other ceramics, scarves, posters, lithographs, reproductions, and illustrated books, to benefit Party causes. They have elevated him to a level of grandeur reserved to him alone. Their representation of him is in the tradition of the *image d'Epinal:* broad and flat—a lay saint canonized in his lifetime, whose effigy, waved unremittingly before the faithful, is that of a beneficent and indulgent Great White Father working tirelessly for Mankind, Peace, Hope, and all the other uppercase abstractions, and whose art is an expansive, idyllic glorification of Party virtues. To make this image credible the Party reproduces in vast quantity the early sentimental paintings and intermittent neoclassicizing moments in Picasso's later work with their full complement of—in the first case—the poor and lonely, and—in the second—lovers, mothers, children, doves of peace, Arcadian shepherds, and other subjects that lend themselves most easily to simplistic propaganda purposes. They have more than once felt obliged to sweep under the carpet more significant periods and styles of Picasso's work: the suspect formal inventiveness, the recurrent sexual and sadistic outbursts, the distortions of the female face and figure so confusing and/or abhorrent to both Party doctrinaires and the unsophisticated rank and file.

Picasso's sculpture *The Man with the Sheep*, now in the market square at Vallauris, has been almost transformed by the Party into a self-portrait so that Picasso has become the Good Shepherd—the man who stands for Life against Death, Peace against War, Love against Hate, Happiness against Misery—for Purity against the vicious combines of the bishops, the corporate exploiters, the financial manipulators: Public Friend No. 1. As one Communist writer has summed it up: "When Picasso speaks, his sole purpose is to fix on the screen of memory the inexorable aspiration of humanity as it marches toward more justice and toward more beauty."

A book which so flagrantly treated Picasso as a man rather than a god and occasionally showed him as "indifferent to others, overimpressed with his own value, insufficiently detached from financial considerations, sometimes unkind and unjust . . . harsh and without indulgence toward his family and his entourage . . ." could only be a source of extreme embarrassment to the Party. Then, too, the book had indiscreetly shown him making jokes at the expense of some of the sacred Communist cows. So from the moment of its publication in France the Communist and certain other left-wing papers from *L'Humanité* to *Le Patriote de Nice et du Sud-Est*, with a number of interesting way stations in between, began their campaign to bury *Vivre avec Picasso* under mountains of mud. "Scandalous" as the book was in French, there were dark hints that the original edition had been even more "virulent" and more "erotic" to pander to "the American taste."

When the press cuttings began to accumulate, I could see the same phrases—entire sentences—used over and over again, often in the same order, in papers that were widely separated geographically; frequently in stories that appeared to originate lo-

cally, signed with a variety of by-lines. But their common
source was readily apparent.

The next step in the demolition program was a manifesto of
protest signed by 44 painters and sculptors who denounced the
book's *"publicité de mauvais aloi."* A few days after the original
announcement of the *manifeste des 44,* the Communist weekly
Les Lettres Françaises changed the number to 45: Marie-Laure
de Noailles had hopped aboard. If there had been time, hun-
dreds more would have signed, *Les Lettres Françaises* affirmed,
and art critics would have joined *en masse* because "the honor
of all those who write about art and artists has been compro-
mised. For less than that, admission to our professional syndi-
cate of art critics would be refused." This was a nice comic
touch: in France, the Communists exert a good deal of influence in the intellectual world, particularly art and theater.
More than once they had tried to dragoon me into the syndi-
cate. I had always refused to join, feeling that one shouldn't
have to carry a union card of membership in what is essentially
a pressure group in order to practice what is classified in France
as a "liberal profession." They couldn't expel me now because
I wasn't a member, but they wanted to make sure I understood
that if I ever changed my mind, no amount of pleading would
get me in.

The only first-rank artist whose name was attached to the
manifesto was Miró. Two months after the manifesto appeared,
a friend of mine met Miró for dinner one evening. Miró had a
copy of *Vivre avec Picasso* under his arm, my friend told me at
lunch the next day.

"What do you think of it?" my friend had asked him.

"I'll know better after I've read it," Miró told him. "I just
bought it on my way here."

But long before Miró's admission, *Arts,* the leading French
weekly newspaper of the arts, assigned a reporter to interview
the better-known signers. (There was a heavy representation of
Communist militants and of "illiterate Spaniards," one wit ob-

served, "who had certainly not read *Life with Picasso* or any other book ever written.") The apparent promoter of the manifesto was the painter Pignon, an ex-miner and stalwart of the Party's intellectual wing. Pignon was "wild with rage," he told *Arts,* and hence not very convincing in his denunciations. Most of the others interviewed were so vague they gave the impression of not having read the book. Only one, the Surrealist painter Félix Labisse, was honest enough to say he hadn't read it. But he damned it on principle: to discourage other wives and mistresses of painters from putting their memoirs into the record. "If they all do . . . where will it end?" he asked.

So the first petition fizzled out like a damp firecracker, and the committee went back to the drawing board. In time, they came up with another list, this one featuring principally, among a number of miscellaneous names, two distinct groups. One was a family affair: it was led by Kahnweiler and included Sabartés, Picasso's secretary; Michel Leiris, the husband of Kahnweiler's partner and sister-in-law, Louise Leiris; Kahnweiler's friend Armand Salacrou; the painter Vilato, Picasso's nephew; Maurice Jardot, Kahnweiler's assistant; Eugène de Kermadec, one of Kahnweiler's painters; Elie Lascaux, another such (and brother-in-law, as well); and the widow of Juan Gris, of whose work Kahnweiler had been the chief promoter.

The other was a group of International Communism's elite in the arts—some out-and-out Party members along with a certain number of left-wing sympathizers whose names are often found attached to projects the Party sponsors in France: among them, Aragon and Elsa Triolet, Fernand Léger's widow, Nadia, and her new husband, Bauquier, Jean Cassou, Hélène Parmelin, Maria Casarès, Vercors, and the widow of the painter Albert Marquet. And all the way from Moscow and Chile—Ilya Ehrenburg and Pablo Neruda.

To the untutored eye this list looked a good deal more respectable than the first one, and its publication was timed to coincide with a third suit by the Picasso machine in the Paris

Court of Appeals. But the three judges who sat on the appeal were no more impressed with the merits of the case than the first two had been, and the suit was definitively thrown out of court.

At the height of the mudslinging I went to call on Françoise Gilot, at her studio in Neuilly, where we had worked on *Life with Picasso*. I found her much thinner, her face more lined, than when I had left Paris. It was not only the nastiness in the left-wing press, she told me, but there had been vile letters and threatening phone calls; even her picture dealer had been subjected to pressure to remove her paintings from his walls.

"And some of the criticisms are so silly," she said. "They reproach you for not bearing him the children and me for not writing the book. Incidentally, I know, from an unimpeachable source, that Pablo himself hasn't even read the book. He's been dissuaded from it by those around him, who keep telling him, 'Don't read it; it will cause you too much pain.' He lives a little like Louis the Fourteenth surrounded by courtiers and the temple money changers. The sounds of the outside world reach him in very garbled form."

I told her of Dali's fury—real or simulated—over the book. It sounded odd coming from a man who, so often in years past, had said and written very unpleasant things about Picasso and with no more justification than that of any ambitious newcomer who beats and kicks at the gates to the city in an effort to make them open a little faster. After all, Picasso had encouraged Dali from his earliest days and was the one who had lent him the money for his first trip to America—a loan, Dali told me, that he had never repaid in full.

"Dali will find a way of extracting profit from any situation," Françoise said. "Good or bad, he will turn it to his own advantage. But in this case I think he's making those noises for the same reason as most of the lesser fry—they want Pablo to know they're on his side. For years now, Pablo has ignored Dali completely. Now that Dali sits at the right hand of God, the Pope,

and General Franco, I'm sure he'd like to sit next to Pablo,
too."

I asked her if Picasso had ever spoken to her about Dali.
"Never," she said. "Not a word. And I'd never set eyes on
him, myself, until last fall. On my birthday, November twenty-
sixth, at the home of some American friends here, I met Dali's
secretary, a little Englishman named Peter Moore. He said,
'You know, Dali's been wanting to meet you for such a long
time. I wish you'd call on him one morning at the Meurice.' I
turned aside his invitation by telling him I had lots of work at
the moment and very few free mornings. Then, a few days after
that, Peter Moore rang me up. 'You absolutely must come to
call, one noon,' he said. 'I'll be there and I'll meet you downstairs.' I knew you were doing a book on Dali, and since our
book had been out in the States a month or so by then, I assumed Dali knew that and wanted to see me about one or the
other or both. Anyway, before Peter Moore hung up, he had set
a date and I had agreed to be there.

"I got there promptly at noon, as I'd been asked, but no sign
of Peter Moore. I called upstairs and discovered we had our
wires crossed and he was waiting for me there. I went up to the
royal suite and there was Dali, full of compliments and kisses.
He showed me all around, first that enormous salon, then a
smaller room, a bedroom, and a sort of small workroom. There
were crowds of people coming and going although not many
who seemed to have real names attached to them. I remember
there was one young girl—I think a Rothschild—who handles
Pop artists, and then Dali's print dealer. Of course, Dali was
talking all the time, telling me about flies' eyes and then showing me some rather disgusting photographs printed on a kind
of three-dimensional plastic. You move them back and forth
and it gives the impression of a kind of relief. He told me he
was going to use that in painting now. None of that interested
me very much, I must say, but I said, 'Oh, yes, yes, indeed, very
good, of course.'

"Then he said to me, 'I have a very interesting proposition for you. You know they freeze people now, so you can last forever. And it's not expensive. There's an American firm that will do it for fifteen thousand dollars. There are two ways of going about it: either you have yourself frozen while you're still in good health and in that way when you're thawed out you're in just as good condition and you go on to enjoy all the advantages of the greater life expectancy they will have arranged by that time, or else you wait until you see you're on your way out and you have yourself frozen then. In that case they thaw you out when they've discovered how to cure whatever it was that was killing you off. I offer you the very great honor of being frozen with me.'

"I thanked him and said I'd prefer the second course but I'd wait until things were a bit worse before taking the step. Then some other people came and that got him off *that* subject. After that he took me into the cubicle where he was working on his bust of Dante. It was in modeling clay and one side was supposed to be angelic—representing paradise, you see—and on the other there were some hollow spirals representing the different levels of hell. The only thing I liked about it was the crown of laurel he'd placed over Dante's brow, made of little vermeil coffee spoons, courtesy of the Hotel Meurice. It was the only part of it that really came to life, and it made me laugh. After I'd seen that, I decided it was time to go. A couple of days later the print dealer I'd met there called, on behalf of Dali, to ask if I wouldn't like to attend the dedication of a swimming pool at the bottom of which was somebody's tomb, all lighted from under the water. It was an evening affair. I certainly didn't want to go, because with Dali you never know what to expect. I decided it might be all right to see him, on occasion, privately, but in public I'd be better off to stay away. So I told the man I'd go, but I didn't go.

"I heard no more from Dali after that. In fact, with all the preparations for my exhibition and trip to the States I had quite forgotten about him. Then, in March, I went to New York a little before my exhibition was to open. I had been invited to stay with some French friends who were spending the winter there—Mr. and Mrs. Jacques Potin. In the meantime, before I arrived, the Potins had met Dali. When Dali learned they were friends of mine he said, 'We must have dinner together while she's here.' The Potins are very sweet, but they have no conception whatever of how nasty people like that can be. So when I arrived in New York they told me, quite delighted, they had arranged a dinner with Dali for such-and-such a night. I told them I didn't like that a bit, that I didn't care to be seen in public with Dali. To be polite I might possibly— just once—go to see him but I did *not* want to have anything to do with him in public. You never know what he might do to take advantage of others. So I said, 'Can't you cancel the dinner?' 'No,' they said, 'because we thought you'd be delighted and we've invited everybody.' So I said, 'Fine!' After all, it was ten days or two weeks away.

"About three or four days later I was to have dinner with the Sam Kootzes, but before dinner I had an appointment with an old friend, Sir Robert Adeane, who is a trustee of the Tate Gallery. He had asked me to meet him in the bar of the St. Regis. You know how the two cocktail lounges adjoin—well, I was crossing the first one on my way to meet Adeane in the second and who should be there but Dali. And the look he gave me! It was withering. He stood up, though, and naturally I went over to shake hands. He stared at me in this unpleasant way and said, 'You know, I don't like your book at all. And furthermore, who is Mr. Lake?'

" 'Who is Mr. *Lake?*' I said. 'You know *him* a lot better than you know *me*. Mr. Lake is the gentleman who wrote the book with me, as you damn well know. And you know him very well because now he's writing one about *you*.' And then he said, 'You don't know what you're talking about. What are you saying?' That's why I say, Dali is in a class by himself. Always spreading the lie to learn the truth. Just like I'm sure he told the Potins, originally, that he was a great friend of mine. And then they got friendly with him. And behind their back—to some other friends of mine—he said the only reason he bothered with them was that they were related to Félix Potin—you know, all those grocery stores. He speaks well of no one once their back is turned. Anyway, then he said, 'Besides, I don't know whether it's you or Lake or the both of you who are responsible for that book.' I said, 'Since it's signed with two names, we're both responsible for it.' 'In any case,' he said, 'I must tell you I detest that book. It has absolutely no value. It is a completely disgusting book. It's not half so good as Brassaï's.' I said, 'Thank you very much,' and I walked out—furious—to go meet Adeane.

"When I got back to the Potins', I told them, 'You know, it's going to be charming, that evening with Dali next week. I don't have any desire to see him. He's just been most discourteous to me,' and I told them what had taken place. 'But what can we do about it?' they said. 'It's all arranged. We can't call it off now, with all those people coming.' 'I don't care to go,' I told them. But they insisted.

"The day of the dinner, Dali telephoned to Madame Potin saying, 'I've pulled my Achilles' tendon. I can't walk a step and I won't be able to come to the dinner, but Gala will come.' I felt very relieved. Half an hour later he called back and said, 'Gala can't come, either, but Peter Moore, my secretary, and Rock, my model, will represent me. In any case I don't want Françoise to think I wouldn't have been absolutely delighted to dine with her this evening, so for her I'm sending my ocelot.' So we went to Roma di Notte for dinner with lots of people and an ocelot but no Dali.

"Then, about two days after that, I had the vernissage of my exhibition at the Findlay Gallery. In the light of everything that had happened, I thought surely Dali won't set foot in my exhibition. My dear, not at all. Actually he didn't set foot, because he arrived in a wheelchair to make sure no one missed his entrance. There was such a mob that day, I was sick with fright and had gone to hide in Mr. Findlay's office. I was there when Rock, Dali's young French-Canadian model—he's very nice, by the way—came in looking for me. 'Come on,' he said. 'Dali wants to kiss you.' I went out and there was Dali, sitting in his wheelchair, surrounded by people and clutching an enormous gold scarab, like a crucifix, that reached from his Adam's apple to his belly button. He kissed me—my hands, both cheeks; oh, my God, it was quite touching, believe me. 'Dear little Pablo Gilot,' he said, 'how I love your painting.' And thereupon he left. I've never set eyes on him since."

Later that day, as I thought back to Françoise's remark about Dali sitting at the right hand of the Pope and of General Franco, a bell began to ring faintly, somewhere in the back of my mind, and I dug around in my Dali archives until I came up with a clipping from the Madrid newspaper *A B C* dated November 13, 1951, which carried an extended account of a lecture Dali had given on the previous Sunday. His subject had been "Picasso and I," and some of the things he said, as I read them over, took on new significance in the light of his behavior toward Françoise and me. And I understood a little better than I had before the nature of his love-hate relationship with Picasso, too.

"As always"—he had begun—"to Spain belongs the honor of the greatest contrasts, this time in the persons of the two most widely divergent figures of contemporary painting, Picasso and I. Picasso is Spanish. So am I. Picasso is a genius. So am I. . . . Picasso is known in every country in the world. So am I. Picasso is a Communist. Neither am I." ("Loud applause and laughter," the editor inserted at this point.)

Picasso's Communism, Dali went on, had two explanations: the first, a basic taste for misery—guilt?—on the part of this multimillionaire. The second, he felt, could be traced to the offer of a group of "Red intellectuals" to make Picasso director of the Prado museum at the beginning of the Spanish Civil War. That had touched Picasso deeply, Dali said, in view of the fact that up until then his countrymen seemed to have forgotten all about him. And then he added a third reason: the fact that Cubism had never been well received in Spain.

"Whence comes this sensational divorce between our great universal painters and the homeland?" he asked. "It comes from a mentality that denies local fame to the great artists whose work has had resounding success in the wider world outside Spain. In our age of mediocrity, everything great and important has had to be done outside the current and occasionally against [it]. In fact, in these times of authentic crisis and spiritual decadence, every great individual automatically is an eccentric who does everything exactly the opposite from his immediate predecessors, and . . . Generalísimo Franco is the first to have conducted himself in this fashion. Before Franco, every politician and every new Government did nothing but increase Spain's confusion, lying, and disorder. Franco breaks resolutely with this false tradition, introducing clarity, truth and order into the country at the most anarchic moment of world history." (Great applause.) Dali then clarified his own intentions:

"As my name 'Salvador' indicates, I want to save modern painting from laziness and chaos. I want to integrate the Cubist experiment with the divine proportion of Luca Pacioli and sublimate atheistic Surrealism, the final residue of dialectical materialism, into the grand tradition of the mystical and realist painting of Spain."

He was counting, he said, on "that great painter, that anarchic and explosive Iberian who is Picasso, the man who, because of his very mania for exaggeration, has destroyed but has not created, to give up Communism and consider himself once more a part of Spain and its immortal spirit." And to encourage him along that path he proposed to send him the following telegram, which he invited Spanish intellectuals to sign:

Pablo Picasso, Paris.

The spirituality of Spain today is what is most diametrically opposed to Russian materialism. You know that in Russia, for political reasons, they purge even music. We believe in the absolute and Catholic freedom of the human soul. Know, then, that in spite of your present Communism, we consider your anarchic genius as a patrimony inseparable from our spiritual empire and your work as a glory of Spanish painting. May God keep you.

Nov. 11, 1951.

Salvador Dali

Then followed a paragraph telling all those who might want to add the weight of their "signatures and titles" to Dali's telegram how they could do so. The article ended with details of a luncheon in Dali's honor at the Palace Hotel that noon and listed the appropriate "illustrious personalities" of the Franquist Establishment who would be there to fete him. It began to look as though Dali's role in the bidding for Picasso's favor was that of a government spokesman. However, he had to convince not only Picasso but a skeptical Establishment as well, and his argument was cunningly tailored to that end:

To recapture Picasso from the Communists seemed a logical objective. He had already done them more good than they deserved, and Franco's Spain badly needed a universally respected figure to confound its intellectual critics. How had the Communists managed to slip Picasso into their pocket in the first place? (1) He had a great sympathy for misery and the poor. These stood high on the Communist priority list and Spain had always been the land of vested privilege and *mañana*. But Franco was removing the confusion, lying, and disorder that used to characterize Spain and replacing them with clarity, truth, and order, in such an original and revolutionary manner that Spain's achievements now compared favorably with Communism's. (2) Picasso had been offended because Cubism had

never caught on in Spain. Why not? Because some Spanish intellectual circles looked down on foreign success. How could
this be overcome? Quite simply. By rewriting history. And this
Dali promptly did—so effectively that the Madrid paper's sub-
editor made a headline of the result: "Cubism—[Dali] said—
considered for years as French patrimony, is a most Spanish
aesthetic phenomenon, invented by [two Spaniards] Picasso and
Juan Gris." Surely no Spaniard could argue with that. Of
course, Dali's overlooking the role of Cézanne could be attributed to his basic tenet that Cézanne was the worst of all French
painters. But what about Braque? Dali had said more than
once, "Braque and I nod to each other but we don't speak." So
why bother to give Braque his due here? By then Spanish intellectual circles must have forgotten about Cézanne, Braque,
Léger, and any other unmentioned French components of the
"Cubist experiment," and Cubism must have become, ipso
facto, a most Spanish aesthetic phenomenon which, along with
its two Spanish inventors, could finally be honored in Spain.
How could Picasso not be placated?

In his preliminary outline, Dali had referred to the group of
"Red intellectuals" who had softened up Picasso by offering
him the directorship of the Prado. That had "touched his soul,"
Dali said. If so, perhaps that should have been the Franquists'
gambit, too, but they settled for the telegram Dali read and
signed, and unnumbered other illustrious Franquist personalities countersigned. Picasso received it but he never answered
it. Nor did he leave the Communist fold. Not even the Hungarian Revolution, five years later, was able to budge him that
far.

Dali reached Paris soon after I did, and I went to see
him. As I walked into his salon at the Meurice, he was
sitting on the divan in his shirt sleeves, an unusual condition for him. A hand microphone, wrapped in a linen towel,
lay on a small, high table in front of him. He was squeezing a
long paintbrush—a Sennelier C4, I saw, as I drew nearer. A
plump, pink boy with dark, curly hair sat near him, astride a
narrow high-backed chair. Across the room, near a window, a
sound engineer, wearing earphones, adjusted his recording
equipment. Over in the right-hand corner I saw the photographer Robert Descharnes and the publisher Joseph Foret,
whom I had met the year before in New York when he was exhibiting his *Apocalypse,* "the biggest, most valuable book in
the world," as Dali had called it. Beside Foret stood a tall,
blond woman, a full head taller than either of the men. They
were all laughing.

"We were just talking about you," Dali said, "you and that
awful book you wrote with the concierge Gilot. It should never
have been written. If you had to write it, it should never have

been published. Now that it's been published, at least it should
be banned."

I asked Dali if he had turned Communist.

He looked surprised. "No. Why?"

"That's their line," I told him. "All the Party militants and
the illiterate Spaniards who signed the manifesto are saying the
same thing."

"I am happy to find myself in agreement with the Communists," Dali said. "I have no quarrel with them. Politically I am
neither pro nor con—I'm zero. In fact I always found Stalin a
very amusing fellow."

Something about the fatuousness of that statement brought
me back to an evening at Alice Toklas' and a conversation that
had started with her baritone declaration, "I'm rather fond of
Franco." I told Dali about that.

He scowled. "Who?"

Alice B. Toklas, I said. Gertrude Stein's friend.

"Ah!" He looked as though he were reliving an unpleasant
moment. "I remember her well, Mademoiselle Stein," he said
finally. "Quite a farter. She farted all day long. Not physically,
you understand. But she was pretty ordinary—run of the mill.
And all those Picassos, piled one on top of another, right up to
the ceiling! I remember the little dark one, too. What was her
name?"

Toklas, I told him. Alice B. Toklas.

He shook his head. "No interest at all, either one of them.
Frightful rubbish. Just good for burning. Well, let's get back to
work." He began speaking, quietly, with occasional prompting,
on the origin of the beauty spot, or mole, tracing it back,
through Paracelsus, to a period twenty thousand years ago
"when men ground small instruments, designed for weapons,
in the form of laurel leaves."

My mind wandered back across the years to a long and funny
passage in Gertrude Stein's *Everybody's Autobiography* in
which she tells of a visit Dali and Gala had made to her, at Pi-

casso's urging. Picasso had told her he was coming too, but the Dalis arrived alone. Gertrude Stein and Dali had talked a great deal, but neither one listened very much to what the other was saying. Some time after that she met Picasso and Braque at Paul Rosenberg's gallery and reproached Picasso for staying away. He had lately been writing poems in a kind of automatic writing then much in vogue. He was rather proud of the results, and especially proud of the praise they had drawn from André Breton, whose quality as a poet no one—except Gertrude Stein —would disparage. Gertrude Stein didn't think very highly of Picasso's poetry and she had implied as much to Dali during his visit. After all, writing belonged to *her*. Dali must have told Picasso something of their discussion because when Gertrude Stein reproached him for not accompanying the Dalis, he explained his absence by saying that he knew that she would tell Dali what she thought of his poetry but that she wouldn't tell *him*. Why? She sidestepped that one neatly, if somewhat illogically. Because one discusses things with stupid people but not with sensible ones, she said. When the book's French version— *Autobiographies*—was published, Dali doubtless read it—at least the pages that concerned Dali. The fact that she said he had the most beautiful mustache of any European hadn't gone far, I gathered, toward making up for some of her other remarks.

The bedroom door opened with a creak, bringing me sharply back into the present. Gala came into the salon, her coat over her shoulders. The sound man waved her back with a "sh-sh." She looked at him in astonishment. She scowled, stuck out her tongue, and made several other faces, even less pretty. At the sight of Gala, Dali moved forward in time. Gala's beauty spot, he said, was on her left earlobe. Picasso had one in the same place. They had touched ears. "Picasso is my father," he said. "One of my fathers, because I have several, against whom I have rebelled, like my father the notary." There was another reference to Mme. Gilot, "the concierge," and soon the recording session was over. The men packed up their equipment and the onlookers began to drift out into the hall. M. Foret came over to me, extended his hand, and said, "Foret," then introduced Mme. Foret, the tall blonde who had been standing with him. He looked pinker and less worried than he had appeared in New York.

Dali moved quickly around the room, whistling, tidying up the slight disorder. Two men came in and began talking with him about filming his life story. Dali listened for a moment, then said, "It will, like all such things, end badly, but I'll do it on one condition: that you agree to use another actor—another Dali."

"I didn't know there was another Dali," one of the men said.

"For the purpose of your film there is—one much better than I," Dali said. "One of the handsomest boys I've ever seen. Everyone thinks so. Even Fellini." He rummaged through a pile of photos on a table, then came back with one that showed a slender male model of about twenty with dark, wavy hair and, beside him, Dali wearing a heavily brocaded jacket and a curly black wig.

"We'll have this boy play me as a young man," he said. "Then I'll come in later, wearing a wig, to play myself now. That way you get two Dalis for the price of one. But first I want to ask you one question: Do you have plenty of money? These things always cost much more than one plans on." The other man began to talk about money in an assured but unconvincing way. Gala came over to the group.

"You have a proposition for me?" she asked. Dali introduced the men: "the director" and "the decorator," he called them.

"I have some ideas," he said to Gala. "We'll talk about that later; it's not the moment right now. They're going to make some tests. If the tests pan out, they'll have the money and we'll bring William over." Gala looked pleased.

"He has a marvelous face, this boy," the director said.

"You couldn't find a better one," Dali said. "Naturally, his trip over will have to be paid for."

Gala turned to me. She seemed to be trying to make up her mind whether she recognized me. "You remember Mr. Lake," Dali said.

"*Ah, oui,*" she said uncertainly. "Your work is still going on?" I told her it was. "It's been a long time," she said. "Two, three, maybe four years. I'm not sure."

Dali escorted the two film makers to the door. Gala shook hands with me, said "*Au revoir*" to Dali, and left. Dali picked up his large paintbrush and walked over to a commode against the wall facing the divan. Propped up on it was a sheet of translucent plastic about sixteen inches square and an eighth of an inch thick, its surface engraved with slightly irregular oval-shaped concentric forms which expanded to the size of a pullet's egg. The egg-shaped forms, one beside another in every direction, gave a rippling effect to the flat surface of the plastic. On it Dali had painted a crucifixion seen from the rear, with the head and long, blond hair of his Christ hanging forward. He was now painting the cross in brown. He worked quietly for a minute or two, occasionally breaking the silence by whistling or humming. Someone knocked.

"*Entrez,*" he called out. It was the sculptor Christine Forani. She came in, followed by a boyish, cheerful-looking photographer. She peered over Dali's shoulder.

"Is that for a new painting?"

Dali kept on working. "It's another illustration for Monsieur Foret's *Apocalypse,* but with some three-dimensional phenomena." He pointed out the egg forms. "There are the parabolic flies' eyes."

Mme. Forani moved closer to the painting. She nodded. "It throws back a lot more light."

Dali turned toward her. "Don't touch it," he said. "It's not dry. Everybody wants to touch it and then leaves his fingerprints on it." He opened the top drawer of the commode and took out a sailor's cap, its band labeled S.S. UNITED STATES. With

L'artiste est l'instrument de forces inconnues visibles et invisibles qui se réalisent.

Il n'existe pas de lois ou de communes mesures pour l'œuvre d'art ; celles-ci sont dépassées par la vérité originelle de la création.

Chaque œuvre d'art porte en soi ses propres lois, qui restent à découvrir éternellement.

La vérité de l'œuvre d'art est potentielle et non actuelle.

L'exagération de l'originalité tue la vérité.

Le souci de perfectionnement d'esthétique et d'achèvement du style trouvé, trahit la vérité de l'éruption originelle dans l'œuvre d'art authentique.

En osant l'impossible, on crée le possible.

Il faut plus de courage pour abandonner le style que pour le garder.

Le génie dépasse les frontières du style et de la personnalisation, pour atteindre l'universalisation de toute vérité première.

La création est la victoire sur le néant.

Grâce à l'art, nous dépassons notre sort.

RUTSCH.

Aphorisms by Rutsch; editing by Dali. Photograph by Barney Burstein.

Dali's manuscript analysis of his painting *Galacidalacidesoxiribunucleicacid (Homage to Crick and Watson)*. Photograph courtesy New England Merchants National Bank.

Picasso ready-made: *La Vénus du Gaz.*
Photograph by Marc Vaux.

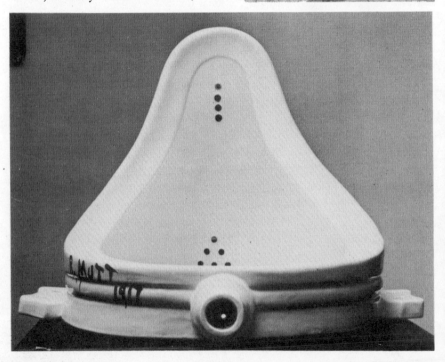

In 1917 Marcel Duchamp sent his ready-made *Fountain*—an upside-down urinal, signed "R. Mutt"—to the first exhibition of the Society of Independent Artists, of which he was one of the founders. The Society refused to exhibit it, and Duchamp resigned from the group. Photograph by Bacci, courtesy Galleria Schwarz, Milan.

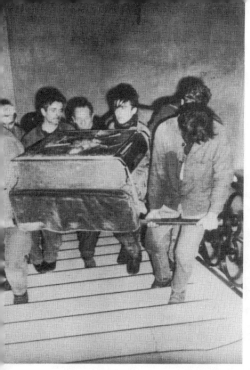

Joseph Foret's edition of *L'Apocalypse*. "...the heaviest book in the world." Photograph courtesy Joseph Foret.

Joseph Foret's edition of *L'Apocalypse*. Bronze cover by Salvador Dali—his first sculpture. Photograph courtesy Joseph Foret.

Salvador Dali. *La Pietà*. Watercolor on engraving, with illuminated border, for Joseph Foret's edition of *L'Apocalypse*. In addition to the conventional techniques, Dali utilized a hand grenade and a charge of nails from a shotgun in incising his copperplate. Photograph courtesy Joseph Foret.

ree lithographs from Salvador Dali's
stration of Joseph Foret's edition of
n Quichotte: "Don Quichotte Ac-
>lé." Photograph courtesy Joseph
et.

Dali. *Don Quichotte:* "La Bombe
Atomique." Photograph by André
Micheau, courtesy Joseph Foret.

Dali. *Don Quichotte:* "L'Age d'Or." Photograph courtesy Joseph Foret.

Salvador Dali. *The Discovery of America by Christopher Columbus*, 1959. Oil on canvas. The Huntington Hartford Collection, Gallery of Modern Art, New York.

Salvador Dali. *Portrait of Gala*, 1935. Oil on wood. Collection, The Museum of Modern Art, New York. Photograph by Soichi Sunami.

Meissonier. *Friédland 1807*. Watercolor and gouache. The Huntington Hartford Collection, Gallery of Modern Art, New York. "...what counts is the movement." Photograph by Peter A. Juley & Son.

Picasso turned down Philipp de Rothschild's request tha he design an emblem for h Mouton Rothschild. But ne Dali. Photograph by Barne Burstein.

it he wiped the brown paint from his fingers, then pointed to the panel.

"That's a cross. Is it clear enough?"

"It certainly is," Mme. Forani said. "And a very original idea to paint it that way." She moved around to look at it from the other side. "By the way," she said, "can the secretary of the Salon de Mai come see you tomorrow? She tells me that every year they invite you to participate but you never answer."

"Never. Never," Dali said.

"This year Picasso has sent in twelve paintings—that's unheard of for him. She wants to come here and invite you personally. I think you should accept."

"It's a little late for that now," Dali said, "but bring her here anyway. At noon."

I asked Dali what had become of the big picture he had told me about that was based on the dollar sign.

"It's already installed in the exhibition at the Spanish Pavilion at the World's Fair. It's the same size as the bank's painting, but much more expensive. It stays at the fair until next October and then moves over to Mr. Huntington Hartford's Gallery of Modern Art for the big retrospective of my work: three hundred canvases—all bad, unfortunately." He began to whistle, briefly, then said, "They're going to ask the bank to lend their picture, too. I hope the bank will agree. That way I won't have to work so hard this summer."

He reached for some paint on his palette, and the buckle on the strap of his vest gave way. He asked Mme. Forani to tighten it for him. As she adjusted it, he went on painting, humming a doleful song. When she had finished, he stepped back and surveyed his Christ.

"Do you see the Christ behind or in front of the flies' eyes?" he asked. Mme. Forani looked at the picture from several angles.

"Behind, I think," she said. The phone was ringing and Dali went to answer it. When he returned she said, "Sometimes it looks to me as though the Christ was in front. Then the pattern shifts. His body recedes and the other things advance."

The photographer agreed with her and pointed out a similarly shifting pattern in another area. Dali indicated with his brush one or two egg shapes near the body of Christ.

"If you concentrate on the flies' eyes, the body of Christ disappears," he said.

"That's a very clever idea, a crucifixion seen from the rear," Mme. Forani said. "I've never seen that. It's always seen front-to. But this way it's tremendous."

Dali looked doubtful. "I'm not sure it's as good now as it was before. Maybe those flies' eyes don't come forward enough. I think it's the cross. I don't like it. It's too prominent. There aren't enough flies' eyes in that part. I'll rub out this cross and put in another one—for the same price." He took some cotton wadding, poured on a bit of linseed oil, and began to wipe away the cross. The photographer asked him if the plate came that way or if he engraved it himself.

"Oh, no, it comes like that," Dali said. "They're going to improve it for me so that every one of these eyes is at a different distance from all the others. That way the image is created in front of the picture but each time you move you'll see things shift."

"The fourth dimension," the photographer said.

Dali nodded. "That's right. I'm going to do *The Judgment of Paris* on it. It will be marvelous." He went on rubbing out the cross and whistling his gloomy tune. "This is going to be very good," he said, pointing to one of the egg forms. The attenuated brown color from the cross had heightened the optical illusion. "You see, that's the basis of moiré. I discovered the whole thing one day while I was shitting in the King of Spain's water closet, which had a moiré pattern on the seat. Then, in the Perpignan railroad station, I got the idea of adding the flies' eyes. Now they're putting out the results commercially."

Mme. Forani moved closer to the painting. "And it gives different tones in this light," she said.

"Ah, that's because they messed up the plate," Dali said. "If they'd done the job evenly, I wouldn't have got the same effect, but since it's irregular, when you look at it—stand back here and look—you see there are forms here on the sides that are larger, and in the middle they're narrower. When I do *The Judgment of Paris,* that will let me put my figure who gives the apple here in the foreground and farther away there will be two girls holding each other by the arm, with their breasts and bellies, thighs and arses, undulating all over the place."

Mme. Forani laughed. "That's very funny," she said. "And all because of those balls not being on the same plane?"

"Absolutely," Dali said. "The surface is irregular and so some areas stand out ahead of others. But by composing the picture with that in mind, I can put all the elements in different planes, almost like in a sculpture." He measured off with his fingers the distances between adjacent egg forms. "And each ball will be on a different level. It's sublime. You create in painting what looks like a sculpture that stands out in front of the canvas, and when you move away and look at it from far off, you see the sculpture has turned into a nose." He went back to rubbing his cross, then stopped and stood off at a distance to study it. "No, it's still too dark," he said, "but it's beginning to look better."

"I have a new bottle of paint remover downstairs in my car," Mme. Forani said. "Don't you want to try it?"

"No, no, no." Dali kept on rubbing with a gentle circular motion. After a while he said, "It comes off hard, though."

"You'd better try it," Mme. Forani said. "I'm parked very close by."

Dali kept rubbing. The color had thinned out to a soft beige moon shape that covered uniformly the larger part of the plaque.

"That's pretty," the photographer said.

Dali shook his head. "It's still not light enough."

"I'm going down and get my bottle," Mme. Forani said firmly. "At least you can try it."

"It won't ruin the plastic?" Dali asked her.

"Of course not. It's brand new. I just bought it."

Dali conceded. "All right. One should always take advantage of chance." Mme. Forani left and he went back to his rubbing. "The color gets into those little holes," he said. "That's the trouble. I can't let it dry because once it does, it's finished." He worked at it a bit more, then stopped. "It's taking the shine off, too," he said, "and that was very nice. Just like a mirror." He rubbed it some more. "It will come back, though." He had put too much linseed oil onto his cotton wadding; a few light-coffee-colored streaks began to run down from the lower edge of the moon shape. "Ah, that's good," he said. "I like those dribbles."

Mme. Forani was back, bottle in hand. "Thanks," Dali said briskly, "but for the moment I won't use any. I don't know what effect your product might have and now I've got some dribbles running down that are going to be very nice."

Mme. Forani looked over his shoulder. "Those *are* nice," she said.

Dali took his sailor's cap from the drawer of the commode and wiped his hands on it. "Later on I'll work more oil into some of the other parts and make them lighter."

Mme. Forani held out her bottle. "You could try just a little of this on a corner," she said. "If it doesn't work—"

"Let's talk about something else," Dali said. He finished wiping his fingers and tossed the cap back into the drawer.

Gala came back into the room. A short, bearded Spanish boy who had been sitting quietly by himself in a corner went over to her. He was holding a rolled sheet of paper. He explained that it was a poem written by a friend of his, a young Spanish poet, and dedicated to her. Could he read it to her?

"There's no point in it," she said. "I don't understand Spanish."

Could he, perhaps, bring the poet one day to meet Dali?

"You'll have to take that up with Dali," she said. "Telephone some morning next week and ask him. Dali's work and appointments don't concern me." She walked into the bedroom. The boy turned to leave. As he opened the door leading to the hall a short, thin man in his forties with wavy, brown hair and a small mustache came in. He was wearing a tight-fitting dark-gray suit with a red boutonniere and leading an ocelot with a jeweled collar.

"*Ah, Capitaine, bonjour,*" Dali called over from the divan. This, I assumed, was Dali's new secretary, the Captain Peter Moore Françoise Gilot had told me about. He nodded, in a general way, to everyone, tied the ocelot's leash to the leg of a table behind the chair I was sitting in, and went over to a bottle of Perrier on a small table beside the bedroom door. He drank two glassfuls and then crossed over to the opposite corner of the room. Halfway across he paused to study Dali's *Crucifixion.*

"Don't touch, *Capitaine.* It's not dry."

"No, no," Moore said and went along to the farthest corner. There he picked up two bundles tied together with light string. He separated them and unwrapped one. He took out a collapsible rubberized plastic object and began to inflate it. It was a model of a baseball player. When Captain Moore's lungs reached the end of their chore and he stood the model up, I saw that it was a three-foot-high catcher, mitt extended, cap reversed, in the customary crouching position and labeled YOGI BERRA. Moore set it up on a window ledge behind him.

Mme. Forani went over to the commode, holding a cloth. "What's that?" Dali asked.

"A cloth from my car," she said. "Why don't you try it?" She held out her bottle and Dali poured some of the liquid into a dish.

"You're sure this isn't going to eat the surface off my material?"

"But it's solid, isn't it? It's not just a thin layer of plastic on top of another base?"

Dali began to scrub at the traces of his cross, with more and more vigor. The round beige moon grew paler. After a moment he tried to pick up the picture. It slipped away from his fingers, down behind the commode.

"Now look!" he said. "It's ruined." Mme. Forani leaned down and reached behind the commode.

"Don't touch it. Don't touch it," Dali said excitedly. She picked it up carefully by the upper corners and held it out to him. "There's nothing wrong," she said. "It slipped through without touching."

Dali scrutinized it. *"Ah, bon.* All right, then. *Capitaine,* put down something to support it in back here." The Captain dropped a second Yogi Berra, uninflated, which he had just taken out of the other package, and brought over a book. He placed it against the wall. Dali moved the picture up against it and tested its solidity. He handed the cloth to Mme. Forani.

"You finish taking off the brown. But be careful not to touch the rest." She finished the job quickly and neatly and held it up for Dali's inspection.

"Excellent," he said. "We'll leave it like that."

"It's still a bit cloudy," she said, "but with a little more rubbing, it will all go."

Dali looked at it dubiously. "Yes, but will it ever glisten again?"

She nodded. "A lot more than it does now. But it's nice even like that. Look how the balls have taken on that faint coloration that makes them almost iridescent."

Dali moved to left and to right studying the plaque. "There are two sources of light," he said. "From this side there's nothing, but from over here I get the same shifting effect once again. I'll have to work on those balls some more. Well, let's go." He walked over to the second Yogi Berra, now inflated and standing on the floor. He knocked it down and it bobbed back up again.

"What's that?" the photographer asked him.

"Come back Tuesday afternoon," Dali said. "You'll see then."

The Salon de Mai, one of the best of the Paris annual art surveys, was scheduled to open the following week. Its tutelary divinity was Picasso, and he had sent an unusual entry formed of twelve separate compositions amalgamated into one curious rogue's gallery of nine heads (men and children) and three reclining female nudes.

For the first time since I had begun to cover the Salon's activities more than a decade before, I received no invitation to the press preview. I might have thought the omission accidental if I had not already had other indications that I was *persona non grata* in certain art circles as a result of the publication of *Life with Picasso*. The Louise Leiris gallery—the public face of Picasso's dealer, Kahnweiler—had dropped my name from its invitation list, but I had half-expected that. I had found it more surprising to be removed from the rolls of the Musée National d'Art Moderne, the government-sponsored museum of modern art then directed by Jean Cassou.

So when I found myself excluded from the Salon de Mai, too, it seemed a logical accompaniment to the other actions. All the

more so since Picasso's good friend Pignon was a member of the
committee that directs the Salon's activities. As I thought it
over, I decided it might be fun to be with Dali when the secretary of the Salon de Mai arrived to issue him a personal invitation to exhibit with them. When I arrived at his hotel the
next morning, I found Dali, Mme. Forani, and a nervously
pleasant, balding man named René Barotte, who writes about
art in the newspaper *Paris-Presse*.

As soon as he saw me, Dali jumped up. "And here is Mr.
Lake, who wrote the book," he said. "I'm completely against
it. As far as I'm concerned, genius has all the privileges, and the
mediocrities, none." He turned to me. "That Madame Gilot is
a concierge, isn't she?"

I told him I thought he was confusing her with the present
Mme. Picasso, who, it had been reported in *Paris-Match* at the
time of her marriage to Picasso in March, 1961, was the daughter of a concierge in the Rue Pierre-Charron.

Dali looked pleased. "Very good. I knew there was a concierge mixed up in it somewhere. You'll see, now, I'm prophetic: Gilot will become a concierge, too. And the book will
be a great favorite with concierges. It's good reading for them."

Barotte seemed pained. "No. Françoise is a very nice girl. Her
mistake was in using that book as a means to make money."

Dali opened his eyes wide. "Not at all," he said. "If you
want to make money, all methods are legitimate—stealing, col-
lusion—but it's ridiculous to pretend that it was done for the
good of humanity or posterity or to publish things about Picasso that weren't known."

Barotte, I could see, was eager to change the subject. "Speaking of Picasso," he said, "you know he has sent a sensational
picture to the Salon de Mai. It is made up of twelve pictures
combined in one, and I thought you might find it amusing if
we all got together in front of his picture and—"

Dali wasn't sure whether he was having any of *that* red her-
ring. "Monsieur," he said to Barotte, "each chance I get, I at-

tack the Gilot and Lake book with the greatest violence." He paused. I could see the wheels turning as he looked at Barotte. "What do you offer me as a present?" he asked, finally. Barotte looked nonplussed. "A gift," Dali said. "A cane or something like that. I think these people from the Salon de Mai should give me something."

Mme. Forani interrupted. "The Salon de Mai will be here soon, but this is for the press, not for the Salon."

"Oh, well, all right, then," Dali said. "No present."

"Now," Barotte said, "suppose we devote a half page to the Picasso. Dali *in front of* the Picasso would be very amusing. With Gala, if possible."

"That's difficult," Dali said. He thought for a few seconds. "Well, then, I'll have to say that I consider Mr. Lake's book very bad."

Barotte looked uncertain. "That's another question," he said.

"*Ah, non,*" Dali said. "No gift, if you wish, but those are my conditions: either I say Mr. Lake's book is very bad or it's all off."

The phone rang and Dali left to answer it. Barotte looked over at me in great embarrassment. I told him not to let Dali's comments on the book bother him; they didn't bother me. He seemed relieved. When Dali returned, Barotte said, "What about Monday morning at ten?" Dali thought that hour was already blocked out. "Why don't we do it now, then?" Barotte asked eagerly. "If the Picasso is already in place. That way you'll have it off your mind."

"The secretary of the Salon de Mai will be here any minute," Mme. Forani said. "We'll ask her."

"*Parfait. Parfait,*" Dali said. "Shall I wear a wig or not?"

Barotte looked at him, puzzled. "But why?"

"Because you're bald," Dali said, "and I'm going to be. Oh, I can do it without the wig. Or perhaps we'll try it both ways and see how it works out."

Barotte hurried on to another subject. "The thing I always

enjoyed about the story of your first trip to Paris was when you went to see Picasso and told him you had come to see *him* instead of going to the Louvre. That pleased him a great deal. Perhaps it isn't true, but it's in all the books—in Brassaï's, too."

"No, it's not really true," Dali said. "The first thing I did was to visit all the whorehouses in Paris. By taxi. Then I went to call on Picasso. And then the Louvre."

In *The Secret Life of Salvador Dali*, Dali says he did only "three important things" on that first trip: he visited Versailles, the Musée Grevin, and Picasso. The whorehouses, according to the book, he saved for his second trip, when he was not accompanied by his aunt and his sister.

"How about Versailles?" I asked him.

"Oh, Versailles was much later," he said. "But where is this woman from the Salon de Mai so we can get on with this thing?"

"There's no rush," Barotte said soothingly. "I suggested doing it now, but there's no great hurry. There's no paper today, and tomorrow is Sunday." (It was May 1, a legal holiday in France.)

"But I insist on talking about Mr. Lake's book. That is the only condition under which I will go."

"I don't like to have you speak badly about Françoise," Barotte said. "I've known her almost since she was a baby."

"In that case I won't talk about her," Dali said. "Out of respect for your feelings I will talk only about Mr. Lake. He's the villain. It's obvious that if it weren't for Mr. Lake, there wouldn't be any book. So today I'll attack him exclusively. She'll be in the background."

Barotte looked somewhat relieved. "That's better. I've known her so many years and she's really a nice girl."

"Of course she is," Dali said. "I've seen her here. She's very nice. But if you start to be weak with people just because they're nice, that's the end of everything. As far as Lake is concerned, you can water down what I say about him if you want

to—I give you my permission—but I'm going to say it anyway."
I asked Dali if he was trying to incite me to say bad things about *him*.

"I want everybody to talk about Dali—*even* if they speak well of him. If they speak ill of him, that is sublime," he said. The phone rang. Dali answered it. "Ah, Madame Jacqueline Selz. *Très bien*. Send her up."

In a minute or two, Mme. Selz appeared—a plump little hen, bright-eyed, with gray hair. Mme. Forani introduced her to all of us.

"It appears I'm about twelve years behind in answering your invitations," Dali said.

"Oh, at least that," Mme. Selz said, laughing.

"That's a habit of mine," Dali said. "And I don't even know, now that you're here, that I'll give you anything this year. But I'm coming to pay you a visit this afternoon, anyway. Is that all right with you? What time?"

Mme. Selz seemed bewildered. "Ah, ah, ah—five o'clock?"

"Wouldn't four be better?" Mme. Forani asked.

"No, no. I prefer five," Dali said.

"All right," both women answered in unison.

"Let's say four thirty, then," Dali said. "Where is it?"

Mme. Selz explained that it was at the Musée d'Art Moderne de la Ville de Paris—not to be confused with the Musée National d'Art Moderne, next door.

Barotte edged nearer to Mme. Selz. "I thought it would be a good idea to make a big spread showing Dali with the Picasso."

"What's-his-name—Philippe Halsmann—made a montage, half me, half Picasso, each of us with the face of a monster," Dali said. "I've got a print of it in Cadaqués but you'd never find one in Paris. Unless, maybe, at La Table Ronde, since they published the French edition of *The Secret Life of Salvador Dali*. They didn't publish that photograph in their edition but they must have it."

"Why don't you make a new montage? I have lots of good material," Mme. Forani suggested.

"Or else," Dali said, "there's something that would be historically colossal. I think no one ever published it. It was done at the time Picasso and I collaborated. We made an engraving: that is, while he was doing a nude woman, I was adding fried eggs to her breasts. The copperplate was at Lacourière's atelier when war broke out, but nobody's ever seen it since. I tried for two years to trace it."

The placement of the fried eggs appeared to embarrass Barotte. "I can try to find the other montage at La Table Ronde," he said, "but I've always had bad luck with montages. I once knew a second-rate painter called Jim Frey, who also worked as a lion tamer. I don't remember now just what my purpose was, but I had the bright idea of showing him painting in the lions' cage for some kind of page I was planning. He didn't object, but the owner of the circus did. 'Nothing doing,' he said. I didn't want to drop the idea, so my photographer said, 'Leave it to me.' He took one photo of Frey painting in the empty cage and another of the lions alone in their cage. He made a montage that was so realistic you would have sworn it was just what you saw. In fact, when the owner of the circus saw it in the paper, he was convinced Frey had gone through with the original plan against his orders and he fired him."

"Those things always work out that way," Dali said. "Whenever I've done any kind of fashion stunt in the show window of a big department store, I always make it a point to ask the workmen who help me, 'Are you ready to lose your job?' If they say yes, then I'm ready to start."

"Oh, I don't care about that," Barotte said. "I'm on the threshold of retirement, anyway."

"There's one thing we *could* do," Dali said, "but I'm afraid there's not enough time: take a photograph of Picasso standing, cut it in half down the middle—that's perfectly legitimate—then

I'll be sticking out from behind it—half of me—half-hidden by the remaining half of Picasso."

"Wonderful," Barotte said, looking very relieved, "and if we get any complaints, we'll say it's just one of your jokes and the photograph came from your private collection. That way we'll stay out of trouble. After all, you certainly have the right to have a collection of photographs of yourself."

"All right," Dali said. "Today we'll work with what we have. We'll start out with that one basic idea. Between now and the time I get to the museum, I'll have fifty new ones. While I'm getting in and out of the taxi, I'll find other elements. So we'll meet there at—"

"At five," Mme. Selz said with preciseness.

"You'd better come pick me up at quarter to five," Dali said to Mme. Forani.

"Let's think about that montage," Barotte said to her. "Do you have whatever you would need for the Picasso half?"

"Oh, not for Picasso," she said.

"For the Dali part she has something very good," Dali said. "Dali dressed as a clown. So we'll take half of that—no, all of it so it will be visible behind the half-Picasso." He stopped and looked over at me. "But a better idea would be to take one of the photographs of Picasso from Mr. Lake's book—the one where you can count all the hairs on his chest."

Barotte seemed determined to play peacemaker. "You had words with Picasso once, but I guess that's all blown over now," he said. "I should think you could get together again. Do you ever write to him?"

"Every year," Dali said, "in the month of July I send him the same message from Figueras: 'In July, neither women nor snails.' He never answers."

"I'm a little put out with him," Barotte said. "I met him through Gustave Coquiot years ago. In those days I got to see him whenever I wanted to. Recently, when they put on the big

Picasso exhibition in Marseilles, I went down to cover it and
I tried to see him—I needed to. He wouldn't receive me."
Mme. Selz sat up on the edge of the divan. "Oh, no. He's *so*
kind."
"He may be charming with you in your official capacity as
secretary of the Salon de Mai, but down there he's inaccessible,"
Barotte said.
She looked affronted. "Oh, no, no. Pignon goes there often.
Oh, no. He's very kind. So very kind."
"But Dali is kinder," Dali broke in.
Mme. Selz laughed. "Of course."
"You think so, too, don't you?" Dali said, turning to me.
"After all, Picasso brought suit over your book." I said that
what I found even more strange than Picasso's suit was Dali's
eagerness to run to his defense, after quarreling with him for
so many years.
"I don't give you any advice," Dali said sharply. "If I ever
did, it would cost you a lot."
Barotte rushed in with another olive branch. "There's an aw-
fully funny story in Mr. Lake's book. Oh, there are many, but
this one—"
Dali grew very red. "Everything in it is false. Every time I
pick it up, I see something else that's all wrong."
"Absolutely all," said Mme. Selz.
"Imagine," Dali fumed, "Picasso saying Chagall is the great-
est colorist of our time. It's not possible."
Mme. Selz seemed on the verge of shock. "Oh, no, no, no!"
"But the parts about Matisse," Barotte said.
"No, no," Dali said. "No, no, no." He hesitated. "Well,
maybe. He was very preoccupied with Matisse. But Chagall—
no, never, zero, zero."
"But there are mistakes in all books," Barotte said. "Now in
Brassaï's—"
"*Ah, non,*" Dali said. "First of all, Brassaï's book is wonderful
because he has a lot to say about Dali. It's sensational—Picasso

expressing himself on the subject of Dali. And the things Brassaï says about me are extraordinarily intelligent, things that show how close Picasso and I were. I even learned things about myself that I had completely forgotten. It's passionately interesting. But the other book—all that rubbish about Monsieur Leiris, Madame Leiris, the doctor, the dentist." Mme. Selz continued to nod sagely, clucking at appropriate intervals.

"But there are some things about engraving in there that certainly aren't false," Barotte pleaded.

"The biggest lie in the world has to be founded on some element of truth," Dali said.

Mme. Selz continued to shake her head. "All false. All false."

I asked her if she had read the book. "Oh, goodness, no," she said. "When do you think I get a chance to read with all I have to do?"

Mme. Forani leaned toward her and whispered in her ear. I caught enough to understand that she was telling her I had written the book with Françoise Gilot. In spite of the previous conversation, Mme. Selz, apparently, hadn't realized that. Her eyes widened and her mouth opened. She stared and reddened.

I asked Dali if *he* had read the book yet.

"Why *should* I read it?" he asked. "I'm not interested in all those people. And it's so vulgar. A girl who had the honor of knowing Picasso—and of bearing him two children, as well— she should look upon Picasso as a god and have the proud and sublime resignation not to publish such a book. He's a genius. Like Socrates."

I said history would be the richer for having Xantippe's story.

Barotte looked unhappy again. "I insist you make peace with Monsieur," he said to Dali.

"With whom?" Dali asked.

Barotte pointed to me.

"But this *is* peace," Dali said. "It must be; now he's writing a book about *me*. But the best way to keep him in line is to give him a kick in the arse every time I see him. If he stands up under it, that means he's functioning. If he doesn't, he's not worth bothering with. As it is, I'm afraid he's going to speak too well of me, so I do all I can to provoke him into writing a book *against* me. That's the only kind of book I like."

I asked Dali if that was to be interpreted literally. "But of course," he said. "I even say all kinds of bad things about myself, such as if you compare me with any Renaissance artist, I know nothing about painting. I even say I'm incapable of making a sketch the equal of one by Meissonier. People laugh. They think I paint better than Meissonier. That's not true. If you gave me a painting by Meissonier to copy, I just couldn't do it. I think he's the greatest French painter that ever lived—not Cézanne."

Barotte's mouth dropped open. "You certainly don't expect anyone to swallow that!"

"What are you talking about?" Dali said. "Some people in New York just paid thirty thousand dollars for a painting of Meissonier's for a museum. Of course he's the greatest French painter. And Cézanne is the worst. There's no doubt about it. That's why we have Pop Art and Op Art: they're a return to the object and the maximum of illusionism. And that sums up Meissonier's art. That's heresy to you and Lake and the rest of the art critics—the kind of people who never understood anything, who think Cézanne is great and Modigliani and all that rubbish. The art critics have always been wrong, at every period, even in the Renaissance. You can't give me the name of one specialist in the field of art who has said, even by accident, a single thing in the past fifty years that makes sense."

Barotte made a face. "In a program I was on the other day, they were asking us what we thought about the sale of Cézanne's *Grandes Baigneuses* to the English," he said. "Some said that it's just as well off abroad, since we have twenty-four Cézannes in the Louvre, and that the version in the Barnes Collection is much finer than this one. But, my God, even so, that's a painting!"

Dali looked at him scornfully. "It's a painting, all right," he said, "not much doubt about that—but such a bad painting. Poor old Cézanne. I always think of that story of Michel de Montaigne, about the man who shit in a basket, then put the basket over his head and covered himself with shit. Cézanne's painting is shit, pure and simple. All the awkwardness of modern painting stems from Cézanne. If you study, from the point of view of draftsmanship, the proportions of his figures, their arms and all the rest, they're all fucked up. That's what brought on Cubism and the whole bag of tricks of modern art. Cézanne himself was a very honest fellow. He wanted to do a good job but he was so unskillful that everything came out wrong. He wanted to paint like Poussin but he just couldn't. You know, when his mother died, he sent for someone else to make a sketch of her on her deathbed and the fellow said to him, 'But, maître, why don't you do it yourself?' He said, 'I couldn't make it look like her and I want to have a good likeness.' During the time of the Royal Academy they'd have required him to take a drawing examination to make sure he knew how to put things where they belong, like a nose. He just didn't know how. He had a great desire, he had the temperament for it, and he worked with a great deal of intensity, but what he did is very bad. He was a tragically honest person, but after him all the indolent good-for-nothings of the modern period began to make bottles and tables that couldn't stand up and to copy all of Cézanne's defects. And they've made miles and miles of post-Cézannism by imitating all those defects that Cézanne would much rather not have had. You know, he was totally incapable of turning out an apple that was round. He *wanted* to make them right but they always turned out square. Sometimes I ask these Pop artists, who are mostly pretty open-minded people, what they think of Cézanne's *Montagne Ste.-Geneviève*. They all say the same thing: 'Who can look at that? It's a piece of shit, all fucked up, bad color—the greatest disaster that ever happened.' "

Barotte looked pale and shaken. He leaned toward Dali. "And what about his *L'Estaque?*" he asked.

"Bad," Dali said. "All bad. All."

"But Picasso owns one of the best of them," Barotte said.

"And if he does, he must believe in it."

"What do you expect?" Dali said airily. "Picasso is an even worse painter than Cézanne." At this, Dali's audience began to peep, cry, and howl. Barotte seemed doubled up in pain.

Dali appeared to be reconsidering. "Oh, but I admire Picasso a great deal," he said with a side-glance in my direction. "He's got more meat than Cézanne. But the fact remains that modern painting as a whole is an awful disaster—including even me. The only thing is, I consider myself a *little* bit interesting because the others are so bad."

Gala came into the room with a lean, gray-haired man with an aquiline nose. Barotte stood up. "I'll meet you there at five," he said to Dali, edging toward the door. Mme. Selz and Mme. Forani started out with him. I asked Mme. Selz if it would be all right for me to attend the ceremony, too. She seemed stunned by the idea.

"Ah, no, no, no," she said, her voice rising with each syllable. "I'm sorry. It just isn't possible."

But couldn't I be there as an anonymous observer? I said I felt sure Dali wouldn't object.

Her eyes were darting wildly around the group. "Oh, no, no. It's not possible. If you insist, the whole thing is off. No. No. Please don't ask." She seemed almost frantic. She turned to Dali. "You can come with Christine and Barotte only. *He* mustn't come. Otherwise I won't go through with it. No, no, no. It's not possible."

Dali waggled a finger at me. "Don't insist," he said. I desisted. "I think I'll wear a wig," Dali said to Mme. Selz. She laughed nervously. I could see tiny beads of perspiration on the down of her upper lip. She left at once, Barotte and Mme. Forani trailing behind.

Gala came over to Dali and me. She asked Dali if I was the one who had sent her the flowering plant.

"No, no," Dali said. "That's somebody else. What *did* you bring her as a gift?" he asked me. I told him I hadn't brought anything. "You have to think of those things," he said. Then he added, in a mock-ferocious stage whisper, pointing to Gala, "You have to be careful; she's a lion from the Siberian forest. She roars almost as loud as the M-G-M lion when she's angry."

"I know it's something about Picasso," Gala said hazily.

"That's right," Dali said encouragingly. "He did the Gilot book. We don't always see eye to eye, but he's a nice fellow."

"Ah, yes, yes, yes," she said slowly. "I know you've been working here for two or three or four years." A bellboy brought her a special delivery letter. She sat down to read it. Dali went to the other end of the room. He sat down at a flat-topped desk, put on his glasses, and whistling sadly, began to brush in rapidly a large wash drawing on a pad before him. From time to time he leaned back and held it away from him in order to see it from a different angle. The gray-haired man who had been talking with Gala sat near him, discussing details of a book he was planning to publish with illustrations by Dali: the size of the edition, the number of plates, cost per copy.

"I'll be able to do something for you during the summer," Dali said without looking up from his drawing, "but I'd rather not give you any exact figures."

Gala put down her letter. "I don't think you should go into all that now. We'll talk about it in Cadaqués."

Dali nodded but continued working. "You'd better listen to the Siberian forest lion," he said to the publisher.

"I've told you you'll have something," Gala said, "but this isn't the time to talk about it. We'll see how Dali's work progresses, you'll come pay us a visit for two or three hours, and in the space of half an hour we'll arrange all the details. But I don't want to see Dali go on working more than anyone else on this earth. There isn't one chief of state, one businessman— anybody, anywhere—who works as hard. And it's stupid."

The gray-haired man nodded. "I wonder, sometimes, how he stands up under it."

"We've *got* to have more free time," Gala said almost savagely. "I'm beginning to rebel. I've been turned into a businessman. I might as well be in Wall Street."

The publisher smiled. "You'd better buy yourself a pair of horn-rimmed glasses."

"I don't buy anything," Gala said, "neither glasses nor shoes —not even an appointment with the coiffeur—because I don't have the time. I'm going to cut off a lot of people because Dali has just too much to do. It's ridiculous. He will have to get more and give less, and do the things he wants to do, whether they are things to sell or not, but do them of his own free will. So, *cher monsieur,*" she said, standing up, "when you pass by Cadaqués you come to call, and in ten minutes we'll have all those details taken care of." The publisher bowed—and desisted.

Dali set his sketch against the wall. It showed a long, leggy girl in a bikini, her hair trailing behind like a train and held up by a crutch. There was a peculiar hump on her back like an oversized pair of water wings.

"That's the latest fashion," he said as he came over to me. "I've just created it."

I asked him what the sketch represented.

"If you're here on Tuesday, you'll find out," he said. "Bring all your friends. Champagne for everybody."

CHAPTER XVIII

On my way to Dali's fashion and champagne party Tuesday afternoon, I picked up a copy of *Paris-Presse*. Dali—in the flesh and accompanied, after all, by Gala—and Picasso (on canvas) covered most of the back page.

"Lilies-of-the-valley for Picasso. At the Salon de Mai Dali sacrifices a pot of flowers to his old adversary and friend," the headline read. The article was signed René Barotte and was accompanied by two illustrations. The larger one showed Dali holding out a pot of lilies-of-the-valley, the traditional French May Day good-luck gift, in front of Picasso's painting, whose title, according to the article, was *Twelve Canvases in One*.

Dali had first deposited his bouquet at the foot of Picasso's painting, but the effect, according to one witness, the painter Félix Labisse, had been too "funereal." Dali had responded by pulling the plant out of its pot and throwing it up to the ceiling. When it fell to the ground, it had made "a very handsome still life, whereupon everyone was invited to take a sprig of good luck and think of Picasso."

This gesture, Dali had explained to Barotte, was his way of

compensating Picasso—"the friend of my youth"—for the "moral injury" he had suffered as a result of "the recent work of Françoise Gilot and Carlton Lake. . . . One should never disturb the peace of geniuses and kings." But as soon as I reached the Meurice lobby, I could see that Dali was actively disturbing the peace of vast numbers of more ordinary mortals. The party was well under way in a parlor off the far end of the lobby, flash bulbs were popping, and although it was a sunny afternoon, blinding spotlights were trained on Dali, whose head loomed up at the center of the crowd. As I reached the entrance of the room, a girl seated at a desk pointed to an album that lay open in front of her. I signed my name, received a sheaf of publicity handouts, and joined the party.

Inside the room a low runway covered with a red Oriental carpet ran diagonally back toward the left-hand corner. Dali had disappeared from view, and the bulk of the crowd—small clusters of the exotic fauna that inhabits the world of high fashion and its various publicity channels—had shifted its attentions to an opulent buffet that filled the back of the room. In the center of several of these clusters stood an oval-shaped bed, all in white, looking like an enormous peeled egg with a horizontal slice taken out of the middle to make room for a sleeper. Above its canopied top was the gilded head of a giant cuckoo bird, and beneath its padded underbelly, short feet like ostrich claws. Chained to one of the uprights that supported the top was Dali's ocelot. Next to the ocelot, fondling him, sat a modern Theda Bara wearing white textured stockings, a shapeless floral-patterned dress, many long strands of fake pearls, baroque Mexican silver earrings, and wide swaths of blue eye shadow.

A waiter captain in tuxedo, carrying a sweating ice bucket, steamed past me. *"Attention, s'il vous plaît,"* he called out and barely avoided colliding with two perspiring white-jacketed waiters who were circulating through the groups with trays of drinks. I retreated to a neutral corner to look over the publicity handouts. They related the rapid rise to fortune and eminence of Jack Winter, a Milwaukee manufacturer of women's sportswear who, it appeared, had placed Dali under contract to "create and design . . . a 'Dali Collection' . . ." The deal, I learned, gave Jack Winter, Inc., "exclusive rights to a series of Dali fashion wear sketches from which the collection would be created." Dali would "design the collection from A to Z and create the styles, select the fabrics, and design the prints, in collaboration with Jack Winter." Dali's sketches, according to the contract, were to become the property of Jack Winter and would, at some unspecified future date, tour the United States. This arrangement was to cover an initial period of two years but the contract gave Jack Winter an option on "additional Dali creations up to a ten year period." Dali had promised to remain faithful to Jack Winter during the ten years and to undertake no other fashion assignments.

I was particularly struck by Mr. Winter's analysis of his interest in Dali: "The sense of fun and whimsey of which Dali is so capable has long intrigued me as a manufacturer of sportswear. The artist's astute manipulation of all schools of art has assuredly captivated the world. His artistic understanding of the total woman is way ahead of modern trends. This relates to our fashions, which are designed for today's total woman and all of her daily activities."

Dali, in his turn, was quoted as having "always admired the youthful spirit embodied in the Jack Winter line. When it was our mutual decision to cooperate in the design of a fashion collection, I was delighted." As well he might be. Jack Winter, according to one paragraph, was "currently doing an annual volume in excess of 35 million dollars." And moving fast: fifteen pages later the figure was given as "in excess of 40 million dollars." The company was now a publicly owned corporation as of the previous November "when a Wall Street firm financed the sale of stock to the public in a multi-million dollar offering."

There were other, equally fascinating pages of background

data on Mr. Winter and his company. He had gone into business in 1933 as a manufacturer of men's pants. During World War II he broadened his line to include "slacks," which became popular among women working in defense plants. After the war he decided "the 'slacks' should be done in a more sophisticated way," and he redesigned "the baggy garments of that area" and the term "slacks" along with them. He pioneered the "development of fashion pants for women which flattered the female figure through exact fit, fine tailoring and utilization of fashion principles" with such success that "the sale of Jack Winter pants, 'the pants that *really* fit,' began climbing immediately." From there it was a short step to a "line of tops (blouses, shirts, tunics) which coordinated with the pants . . ." Then ski wear and, late in 1964, "a complete line of swim suits, pants, tops, halters, parkas and similar garments . . . for all occasions in, on or near the water."

I skipped lightly over the paragraphs relating to the numerous manufacturing plants and the newly completed central distribution center, unique in "its innovative techniques for handling garments," among which the central pressing facility, to reach the biographical data concerning the man himself: a "somewhat unique figure in the fashion field . . . very nearly a walking advertisement for the fashion business. Tall and handsome . . . impeccably attired at all times . . ." and blessed with what one of his associates has called "the 'quick pick' eye. He amazes people who have seen the speed with which he selects fabrics and designs. Even more amazing is his accuracy, as testified to by sales." And to top it all, "he is a non-conformist in many ways . . . not committed to traditional methods . . ."

In succeeding paragraphs I learned about Mr. Winter's business philosophy, his wife (Muriel), their hobby (fishing), their two sons ("vice-presidents in the business"), his ". . . innate restlessness, perhaps typical of successful businessmen," and future plans (". . . additional acquisitions and internal generation of new product lines"). The eulogy ended on a note of ringing determination: "The Jack Winter growth story is far from a completed one."

Just as I reached the final line, a slim, long-haired young man wearing a shaggy violet jacket bounded up onto the runway and clapped his hands for attention. First in French with an English accent, then in English with a French accent, he introduced Mr. Jack Winter. Mr. Winter himself mounted the runway and immediately put to rout whatever cynical reservations one might have had about his publicist's encomiums. He *was* "tall and handsome," and "impeccably attired," with pleasant, relaxed features and slightly graying hair, with not a trace of that odious "quick pick" eye; without any doubt, a "walking advertisement for the fashion business." In straightforward American he apologized for not being able to speak French but made up for it at once by paying all the traditional and appropriate American tributes to Paris. The noise around him kept growing louder, and by the time he introduced Dali, the gang at the buffet was enjoying his hospitality so boisterously that it was difficult to catch more than one word in five.

Dali stepped onto the platform, fresh from the coiffeur, his mustache curled into electric spirals, his hair waved and pommaded, his face smoothly burnished. He was carrying a slender new cane with a curved amethyst handle. He held out his arm to a tall, emaciated model wearing white bikini pants, a white bandeau tied tightly across her chest, and she stepped onto the runway beside him.

Over the hubbub I heard Dali define the keynote of his new collection: ". . . to do away with breasts. They are only in the way in any situation, so we must get them out of the way. With the help of Jack Winter's money I have turned my mind over to the problem and found a solution which gives women the appearance of angels. From now on breasts will be worn in the back and will be collapsible. With the aid of a helium tank they will rise as desired." He turned the model toward him and held his cane—its amethyst handle under her chin—against her front.

I craned my neck, along with everyone else within range, and
saw that there was a definite concavity between the line formed
by Dali's cane and the model's bandeau. Everyone cheered. Dali
looked triumphant and the model, pleased. They both stepped
off the runway.

In a minute or two Dali was back with another model, pret-
tier than the first but pectorally even more recessive. Over her
chest she was wearing a rectangular placard. The top and bottom were of a moiré pattern that wobbled as she walked, making a succession of clownlike noses and mouths surrounding a
pair of very realistic eyes in the center, each eye covering the
spot that in a girl of more immodest proportions would have
been a breast but in her case, at the very most, might have been
a rather large freckle.

"For once, instead of men looking at breasts, breasts will be
looking at men," Dali said.

"With two women like those you'd have the makings of a
sandwich if there was any filling," a Frenchman standing behind me, holding a highball, whispered to his companion.

"They'll never sell it to the Americans," the other fellow
said. "Over there everybody drinks milk."

Everyone cheered again. Dali looked almost benign. The girl
scurried away, through the crowd, into the dressing room. Dali
followed her. Soon he was back, accompanied by the first model
still wearing her bikini triangle and bandeau, but with the addition of oversized white-framed sunglasses and carrying a
white plastic umbrella or, as Dali called it, "a counterum-
brella," to be used, he said, not for keeping off the sun's rays
but for spraying on a fine mist of perfumed suntan lotion.
Slung over her bony shoulders, upside down, was one of the inflated plastic Yogi Berra figures I had seen in Dali's salon several days earlier. Yogi's feet stuck up above the model's shoulders and his knees projected forward underneath her armpits.
He seemed to be intent on climbing down her bare back but
was restrained by crossed black thongs that emerged from

around her spindly thighs. His head, its catcher's cap backwards, reached just below what, in a more nearly total woman, would be called the buttocks. Resisting the pressure of the black thongs, only Yogi's mitt, held firmly in front of his face, kept him from making a spectacle of himself.

Dali, his face glistening under the spotlights, tugged and pulled at Yogi's shoulders, trussing him in a little closer, down a bit farther. Photographers crowded along the sides and the far end of the runway. Dali's secretary, Captain Moore, adjusted the translucent white plastic umbrella to a jauntier angle over the model's shoulder. He attached a tube leading from a water jar to the top of the umbrella, crouched down behind her and began to activate a small plastic hand pump. Water ran off the umbrella, some of it onto Dali. The model started down the runway. Dali drew back, slightly dripping, to her left rear, far enough behind not to mask the profile formed by Yogi's humps and bumps, which, whether by design or a kind fate, fell in just the right places: his buttocks oozed out from the model's shoulder blades in a triumphant demonstration of the efficacy of helium (or Captain Moore's lung power), Dali's creativity, and Jack Winter's money. His head, snuggling close to where the model's buttocks should have been, provided just enough of a bustle to make Dali's prophecy almost convincing. As the model moved along the runway, several of the photographers shouted, "Stop. Stop. More profile." She stopped. Dali moved closer, adjusted the umbrella. Captain Moore crept up behind, reattached his hose, and pumped up another shower. This time Dali was caught in a downpour, but instead of pulling out he drew closer and spat out a few lines of his favorite Catalan tongue twister. The cameramen kept snapping. "More profile," one of them shouted. Dali turned the model's head toward him and lifted up her chin. There were more cheers.

Finally Dali led his model back to the dressing room. Captain Moore darted in behind them carrying his plastic hand pump. The show seemed to have ended. At the back of the room the buffet began to fill up. I saw short, red-faced M. Foret, the publisher of the heaviest book in the world and, beside him, the shapely tanned legs, lean jaw, and chopped-off straight blond hair of Christine Forani. Then, through a break in the crowd I caught a glimpse of a tall, long-nosed Englishman talking to a small, dark-haired girl. She turned slightly toward me and I saw that it was Marina Lussato. Her Dalinian spiral hairdo seemed somewhat diminished, but she had made up for the loss by wearing very high heels.

She and her escort began to weave their way through the crowds toward the lobby. As she came alongside the runway, she saw me and smiled. I went over to her and asked her why I hadn't seen her since Dali's return to Paris.

"I never come here anymore," she said. "Except maybe to a thing like this. And not often, even then." I wondered why. She had been in constant attendance the year before and Dali himself had told me she was *"une jeune fille très dalinienne."* She must have realized I was puzzled by her explanation—or lack of one—but she didn't carry the conversation any further.

"I want to see you," she said, "but I'm leaving Paris for a few days. I'll call you as soon as I get back." The tall Englishman had pressed ahead and was now looking in all directions but the right one to discover what had happened to Marina. She shook hands with me, then slipped off through the crowd to rejoin him.

As I approached the elevator that was to take me up to
Dali's apartment the next morning, I saw one of the
Meurice *chasseurs* pushing a massive easel, dark brown
and glistening and more than ten feet high, into a setback of
the hotel corridor. It was such a large and solid one, I could
almost imagine Courbet painting his monumental *Burial at
Ornans* on it. When I reached Dali's suite, I found the usual
people—Descharnes, Christine Forani, M. and Mme. Foret, and
a crowd of journalists, photographers, and film makers—clustered around *le Divin*. He looked up at me.

"You saw it—the easel?" he asked.

I told him it couldn't be missed.

"Aha! That is the easel at which Meissonier worked. It is my
manifesto for the big exhibition in New York next winter. Now
that you've seen it, you will understand the moral question it
poses for the art of our time."

Moral question?

"Exactly. That object is basic to Meissonier's art. He had it
built to his own specifications, and his paintings were prede-

termined by its structure. And that is where the moral question comes in. Today almost everybody paints on canvas that lies flat on the ground. They throw blobs of paint on it, drip all over it, walk on it. But an easel like that is an ethical structure in the highest degree. To use it a painter needs brushes, liquid amber, all sorts of precious things. And most of all he needs to *paint*."

The phone rang. Descharnes answered it. "It's a man from *Paris-Presse* who made some photographs and sent them to you."

"He's here?" Dali asked.

"No. He's telephoning to find out if you liked them."

"I like all photographs of all photographers," Dali said. "Especially the ones he sent me."

"He wants to know if he can send you his bill."

"Ah. That's another matter. In that case, I don't like them." Dali turned away from the conversation and back to Meissonier. "This easel is my war-horse," he said. "I'm going to exhibit it at a press conference on Monday, along with a *Crucifixion* I painted for Monsieur Foret's great book *L'Apocalypse*. And on Tuesday it leaves for Cadaqués."

"Did somebody lend it to you?" one of the photographers asked.

"Oh, no. It's mine. It was a gift. Everybody gives me gifts. I'm having a special room built for it in Cadaqués. It's going to be photographed stroboscopically. Did you notice that it opens out like an angel's wings to form a kind of triptych?"

Peter Moore came into the room, his face slightly glowing. "Gentlemen—my military attaché, Captain Peter Moore," Dali said. "He's just been waxing the easel. And now Robert Descharnes will take you downstairs and show it to you. And then, perhaps, you will understand that painters need to work with apparatus like that in order to paint. If they did, it would reestablish the ethics of painting, because you can't paint pictures like Meissonier's without an easel like that."

"But what about the big exhibition?" a serious-looking young girl asked him.

"The exhibition will be called 'Homage to Gala and to Meissonier,' " Dali said. "It will be my homage to *pompier* art, my way of demonstrating that the greatest French painter is not Cézanne but Meissonier. It will include Meissonier's masterwork in watercolor. We have blown up parts of it in photographic reproduction. You can see in the waving grass in the foreground an absolutely unbelievable dynamism, just like a painting by Georges Mathieu. If you isolate the beard of one of the cavalrymen, it looks like something by Yves Klein, brushed in with the greatest violence. There's Tachism, there's anything you want, and yet it's historical painting: you see the dirt on each face and at the same time some absolutely hallucinating things."

I assumed Dali was thinking of Franz Kline, since Yves Klein's brushstrokes are pretty nearly indistinguishable from one another; in fact, he rarely used a brush. Dali suddenly glared at me. Had he been reading my mind? "But the world makes up its mind in these matters on the basis of the total incomprehension of art critics like Mr. Lake," he continued after a moment, "even though they are the people who are destined to be wrong about everything they write on. As a result, thanks to the Lakes and the other cultivated people of that period, nobody ever understood anything about Meissonier. But they were persuaded that Cézanne was a great painter. Nowadays people know better. Anyway, go downstairs with Robert Descharnes and look at that easel. Then you'll understand why, long after people have forgotten all about Cézanne, Meissonier's paintings will still remain the glory of French art."

"But what else will be in the exhibition?" the girl asked.

"Chiefly a picture I shall paint this summer, the first painting in the third dimension. And then two or three hundred more."

"That you'll do this summer?" the girl asked.

"No, no, no," Dali said with a scowl. "It's a retrospective."

The crowd began to file out into the corridor. Dali followed them to the door, then came back to me.

"Wouldn't you like to go to a party?" he said suddenly.

"What kind?" I asked.

"Teen-agers. All very Dalinian. They adore me. It's at La Locomotive, up in Montmartre."

"A nightclub?"

"A day club. Right near Le Moulin Rouge. I'll be there at four. Why don't you come? It will do you a lot of good."

I was there a little early. I hadn't been in Montmartre for years, but it would be almost as hard to miss Le Moulin Rouge as the Eiffel Tower. Beyond it, on the left, was the Self-Service Moulin Rouge, a chicken restaurant; beyond that, an exposed theater lobby. Toward the left end of the lobby was a snack bar. A crowd of stony-faced Montmartre types stood watching a football game on a TV set suspended above the bar. Beyond them I saw a marquee labeled LA LOCOMOTIVE.

I had been watching the football game for a few minutes when Richard, Dali's turtle expert, came in off the sidewalk with a blonde on his arm. As he introduced me to her, I saw, over his shoulder, Dali and his court approaching—first, Gala; next, a middle-aged statuesque blonde whose hair was ornately arranged in an eighteenth-century manner; then Peter Moore, accompanied by a bright-eyed, pleasant-looking brunette who spoke to him in an English that was clearly American. They were followed by a dark young girl with large, dead eyes and long, straight hair, wearing jodhpur breeches and snapping a thick wad of chewing gum; a thin, pert blond German girl; a fellow who resembled the photographs I had seen earlier of the boy who was to play the young Dali in the film of Dali's life, and a tall bronzed photographer wearing a red sweater.

I followed along in their wake. At the door Dali was greeted by an ingratiating manager, who escorted the party down a few steps into a large verandalike enclosure off to the right. Down a few steps more was a dimly lighted large rectangular dance floor and beyond that, a brightly lighted stage where a rock-'n'-roll quartet was performing. The floor was packed with shaking and jerking teen-agers, bottom to bottom. After a few deafening rounds the music stopped. A master of ceremonies came out of the wings and made an announcement about a combination called Les Zombis, at which there were wild screams, about the Beatles (more and wilder screams) and about "the Master Salvador Dali." A spotlight was trained on Dali. He rose and bowed in two directions. Whistles and more screams. Finally the noise subsided, the stage curtain was drawn in front of the quartet, jukebox music was piped in, the lights were dimmed further, and the mass wiggling and shaking started once more.

Christine Forani came in and sat down and then a blond girl in a white suit whom I recognized as the one who had called for Dali the day of the luncheon at Marie-Laure de Noailles'. I asked Richard to identify the other women around Dali. "The tall blonde with all the hair is a very special friend of Dali's, someone he calls Louis Quatorze," he said. "The young blonde and the dark one with the straight hair are two of his favorite models. The dark one—her name is Onda—works with a snake, and what she does with it you wouldn't believe."

The heat and movement from the dance floor had penetrated into the veranda. The girls around Dali were beating out the rhythm, first with their feet and hands, then swaying their bodies from side to side. Finally the snake girl jumped to her feet, grabbed Peter Moore's American girl by the hand, and they began to dance, weaving back and forth toward and away from each other in the center of the veranda. The American girl's cheeks were flushed, and Onda's eyes had taken on a fierce glow. Finally the American girl dropped down into a chair. A tall boy with high cheekbones moved into her place and began to shake frenetically in front of Onda. Onda matched his movements tirelessly until finally he, too, seemed to have reached a climax. In one last burst of energy he picked her up, squeezed her, then dropped her onto the floor. She scurried back toward Dali.

"Bravo, bravo," Dali shouted, clapping as she sat down beside him. There was a commotion behind me. I turned and saw a pair that looked as though they might have come out of a French modern-dress version of *A Midsummer Night's Dream:* a short, stubby fellow in his early fifties with dyed pink hair, puffy eyes, a long green silk handkerchief overflowing his tight-fitting racetrack jacket, followed by a tall, slender boy with shoulder-length hair, a very skinny fellow in a quasi-nautical St. Tropez outfit, and a short, fat man with dyed black hair. The red-sweatered photographer jumped up, the man with pink hair squealed, and each of them smothered the pseudo-sailor with kisses. They kept filing in, some recognizably male, a few unmistakably female, and a certain number unidentifiable. I heard one of them ask for Andy Warhol.

"I called his hotel. He's not there. He must be on his way," said a long-legged girl wearing tight trousers and a suede jacket, and smoking a curved-stem clay pipe. She turned toward me. "Hel-*lo!* How are *you?*" she said, and her eyes opened wide. "My fire's gone out," she said. She held her pipe between her teeth and extended it in my direction. I tried to light it for her but it didn't take. The manager applied his cigarette lighter to it with no greater success. He took the pipe from her mouth, drew on it rapidly, and lighted it, then handed it back to her. *"Ici on rend tous les services,"* he said, winking at me.

There was no room left and less air. I got up and, waving good-bye to Dali, started to leave. He spoke rapidly to Peter Moore. Moore came over and put his hand on my shoulder. "Wait just a minute," he said. Dali rose, took Gala by the arm, and, followed by his court, left the Royal Box. Moore smiled. "It's all right now," he said and tagged along after *le Divin.*

Out on the street I saw Dali and his retinue grouped around the black Cadillac convertible. A few photographers snapped pictures as Dali clutched his stick, looking soulfully at Gala and libidinously at some of the younger members of his entourage. Then, as the chauffeur held open the door, Dali escorted Gala aboard and climbed in, himself. The inner circle, in strict order of priority, took seats to the extent of the car's capacity. The overflow stood loyally by and, as the car started down toward the center of Paris, waved bon voyage until it disappeared from sight.

As soon as I reached the Meurice for Dali's press conference the following Monday afternoon, I could see—
even from across the lobby—that Dali's war-horse was
champing at the bit. Hooded by a billowing French tricolor,
Meissonier's easel rose up above the intervening crowd from a
rectangular dais in the center of the salon. Standing stiffly below it was a portly, distinguished-looking attendant whose black
formal wear and heavy silver neck chain gave him the air of a
wine steward crossed with an *ordonnateur* at an expensive
French funeral. Mme. Foret, freshly blonded, and M. Foret in
his shirt sleeves were arranging small tables and chairs into conversation groups, as if for a tea party.

I sat down in one of the chairs. A plump brunette came over
and asked for my name and address. I asked her what the official purpose of the party was.

"It's for Monsieur Foret's great book, *L'Apocalypse*," she
told me.

The heaviest and most expensive book in the world?

She nodded solemnly. "Dali has painted an additional illus-

tration—a three-dimensional one—for it in appreciation for
what Monsieur Foret has done for him."

And that was?

"Monsieur Foret was responsible for Dali's doing his first
lithographs, which he published in his edition of *Don Quichotte;* and his first sculpture, too, which is the cover for this
book." She handed me a colored postcard that showed *L'Apocalypse* inside a giant Plexiglas bubble mounted on a bronze
pedestal. "The most expensive book $1 million . . . a remark-
able meeting of art and the mind," I read. Even more remarkable, I thought, was its spectacular rise in value to two and a
half times the figure M. Foret had quoted to me in New York
a year earlier. It was "composed of 150 selected parchments" in
a "format 31 inches by 34¼ inches," and Dali's bronze cover,
"enriched with gold and precious stones," brought its weight
up to 460 pounds.

I asked her where the book was.

"On exhibition in Pau. It's been all over France. It's four
years now that Monsieur Foret has been exhibiting it. First in
France, then all over Europe; after that, America and now
France again."

Dali and Peter Moore came into the room. They were followed by a bustling functionary who went over to inspect the
buffet at the far end of the salon. Dali and the Forets—M.
Foret now completely dressed—posed for several photographers
in front of the easel, then Dali carefully lifted back one side
of the flag. Behind it I could see an unpainted sheet of plastic
material similar to the one on which he had been painting the
crucifixion a week or so earlier. Under his direction two of
the photographers trained their spotlights on it from various
distances and angles. Finally he seemed satisfied and replaced
the tricolor.

On a projecting crosspiece on the back side of the easel,
shielded from the growing audience, Dali now set up his painting of the crucifixion. Several yards behind the easel was an

ornate marble mantelpiece. On that he stood up a curious-look-
ing collage about fifteen inches high and eight inches wide. The
composition was formed by superimposed layers in blue, yellow, and red of the *trompe l'oeil* material with the pattern of
large tapiocalike drops he had shown me during one of our
early meetings at the St. Regis. Just above the center of the
composition he had pasted a picture of Gala's face in which the
eyes were the dominant feature. It appeared to have been cut
from a color reproduction of one of his paintings. Above it was
a cross on a background of yellow, and above that, an area of
blue. Swatches of red and yellow extended downward from
Gala's face, flanking a blue painted segment in the lower left-
hand corner. I went over and stood beside him. He was muttering to himself as he fussed with it. "That's better," he was saying. "It's more mysterious." Then he ran out into the lobby.

It was a hot day. I sat down at a table directly facing the
easel. Christine Forani came over and sat down beside me. I
asked her where Dali got all his pep.

"I think he sleeps late mornings," she said. She reflected. "Of
course, in Cadaqués he gets up very early, but down there he's
all the time in the sun and the water. He must stockpile enough
energy from that to last him through the winter."

Gala came in, escorted by the young man who resembled the
cinema version of the young Dali. He was wearing a tight-fitting houndstooth check jacket. Behind them came the very
regal Louis XIV wearing a pale-pink suit and accompanied by
a tall, effete, sunburned blond fellow. I asked Mme. Forani if
she knew Louis XIV.

"*Comme ça*," she said. "She's from the south of Spain, the
Marquise of something-or-other." The two couples took seats
at our left, near the buffet. Two of the bearded young Spaniards I had seen at the homage to Kant ceremony at the Galerie
Charpentier came in and stood like footmen behind Gala and
her young friend.

The portly man in black with the silver chain had now left

the easel and taken up his stand at the door and was bawling
out the names of the arrivals. Dali and M. Foret stood beside
him receiving their guests with all due pomp. When the line
had dissolved, Dali left his post and came over to us, one hand
in the gold lamé vest, preening. His mustache was tightly com-
pressed and lustrously waxed, its points thrusting fiercely upward.

"The mustache is particularly brilliant today," Mme. Forani
said.

Dali caressed it happily. "It's all right, is it?"

"It's marvelous," she said. "Who does it for you?"

"I do it myself," he said, bursting with ill-suppressed pride.

Peter Moore rushed in with the ocelot and handed it to Gala.
Waiters began to serve them champagne and canapés. The photographers clustered around. When they had taken their pictures, Moore led the ocelot away.

Dali climbed onto the platform. *"Bonjour,"* he said gravely.
The room grew gradually more quiet, and Dali began to speak,
slowly and distinctly.

"This press conference is historically the most important
ever held by Salvador Dali because at this very moment painting is going through its death agonies. But it is about to take on
a new biology thanks to this object." He laid his hand on the
shrouded easel. "This is the easel—you are about to see it—of
the most sublime of all French painters—Meissonier. Without
exception art critics have made the mistake of believing that
Paul Cézanne, the clumsiest of all French painters, was the
great one. And all while they were babbling their nonsense
about Cézanne, the great painter has never ceased to be—Meissonier. Now I am going to uncover his easel—and my war-
horse." A *valet de chambre* came forward and lifted up the
French flag. It had been too tightly secured at the upper left-
hand corner and refused to come away. He struggled with it
for a minute or two and finally succeeded in removing it. He
gathered it up carefully and carried it away. Meissonier's easel

stood exposed in its full height, width, and grandeur, its two brass handles glistening under the spotlights. In front of the tall, blank rectangular piece of plastic, a small silver egg stood on end. Peter Moore came back with the ocelot and set him into a kind of cradle between the easel's legs. Dali smoothed the ends of his mustache and went on speaking.

"Last night I saw Godard's latest film. I found it very interesting, but he paints the cybernetic future of humanity in sinister tones. However, I am happy to announce to you today that everything will work out all right, thanks to three things which will preserve the spiritual future of mankind. The first of these is the gaze of Gala, my wife." He pointed in the direction of the collage dominated by Gala's eyes which he had set up on the mantelpiece, then paused. "Well, clap," he said impatiently. They clapped. "Who," he continued, "as the great Surrealist poet Paul Éluard wrote, has 'the gaze that pierces walls.' It is thanks to Gala's gaze that Dali is the only living genius of our time." He bowed, waited a moment for applause, then continued: "Your humble servant has discovered, for the first time, in the center of the railroad station at Perpignan, by superimposing layers of the parabolic eyes of flies, the possibility of creating the third dimension in painting." He pointed to the blank sheet of plastic. "In just a moment you will all be able to approach this plate and, if the lighting is adequate, see some things that look like eggs, with another form somewhat resembling high-quality atomic bombs advancing on them. And herein lies the greatest paradox of our time: thanks to two friends of mine, great American scientists who have worked out the mathematical equation of moiré, it will be mechanically possible, by a jesuitical programming of the computer, to impress onto the plastic, tiny, almost microphysical eggs, each one at a different distance from every other. As a result, for the first time in history a painter will be able, by painting, to create sculpture in space and to quantify every one of his little brushstrokes with the same violence that one of the painters I like

best, my friend Georges Mathieu, brings to bear on the macrocosmos." He opened his eyes wide. "Everybody else, the whole
wide world, a bunch of cuckolds. The avant-garde's latest development, Pop Art, which is a return to photographic likeness,
mixed with Op Art, which is the mescalin, the LSD, and the
maximum of optical illusionism, will bring about the apotheosis
of what I call—and I am the one who discovered it—*Art Pompier*. So Op and Pop were both prefigured and can be summed
up in the art of Meissonier, who built this easel, which I consider the archetype of all moral and ethical objects because
when you paint on an easel like that one, you need really to
dominate the action quantum of Max Planck. And as Crick and
Watson have said, I shall repeat in closing—" The cords in Dali's
neck tightened, his eyeballs began to roll, his face grew red, and
he blurted out once more, in all its violence and incomprehen-
sibility, the Catalan nursery rhyme with which he had accompanied Mlle. Yvonne's turn at the Galerie Charpentier. His expression grew more grotesque and his face more red as he pro-
ceeded. His right hand came up tensely and its contorted fingers seemed to be clutching for something just beyond his
grasp. He reached the end of his tongue twister fiery red and
quite breathless, looking fiercely out over the heads of his audience. There were a few seconds of silence and then the crowd
began to cheer, clap, and shout. In spite of the element of buf-
foonery, I couldn't help being reminded of the prewar news-
reel shots of Hitler haranguing *his* public.

The crowd began to disperse, some moving toward the exit,
more heading in the opposite direction, toward the buffet. I
made my way around several small groups and, near the back
of the room, turned to look at the sheet of plastic Dali had set
up on Meissonier's easel. The blank sheet had been replaced by
the one on which Dali had painted the crucifixion. It now had
a brown border. At the center, the brown paint he had diluted
to pale beige and eventually wiped away with Christine Forani's help had been replaced by a predominantly bluish-mauve

tint surrounding the white cross and the body of Christ. Beneath the paint the eggs-cum-atomic-bombs wobbled spasmodi-
cally. How much of this activity was due to reflections from the
lights that bounced off the silver egg standing in front of the
plastic I wasn't sure. As I stood there, I felt a tug at my arm.
I turned and saw Marina Lussato looking up at me, bright-eyed
and very tanned.

"I'm back," she said. "I thought I'd find you here."

"The last I heard from you, you were in Palma bound for
Cadaqués to visit Dali."

She made a face. "I never got there. I was just about to leave
for the mainland when I wrote to you, and then a friend called
me to say that Gala had gone to Turin but Dali had stayed on
in Cadaqués and there were crowds of all kinds of strange people there with him. I didn't want to get mixed up with them,
so I canceled my trip."

"And you never come around anymore when he's here."

She shrugged. "Sometimes. Not often. I used to come see
Dali every day. Even twice a day. But now he demands too
much. I still like him. I find the milieu *sympathique* but . . ."
She smiled wryly, then looked away. "I say I like him but I
suppose I mean I admire him. And even there I have to ask myself how and why. I don't think I admire the man; I admire the
artist. Although with him it's sometimes very hard to separate
the two. And even the artist I admire less than I did. Whether
that's my fault or his I don't know. I have an idea, though, that
the man is pulling down the artist." She began to laugh. "Oh, I
suppose it doesn't sound very clear, but how can anything be
very clear with Dali?"

Dali loomed up suddenly on my horizon, in conversation
with a slender, graying, carefully groomed man somewhat older
and shorter than he. Dali beckoned to me. I pushed my way
through the crowd and went to them.

"I want you to meet Monsieur Raymond Loewy, who has

made me an offer for a piece of my mustache the day I decide to cut it off."

"Not a piece—the whole thing," Mr. Loewy said. "Both sides."

Dali looked surprised. "Ah, but I thought—"

"Only *one* side?" Loewy said, just as surprised. "Certainly not. Both."

Dali thought a moment. "Well, it depends on the price." He craned his neck. "Captain." He looked behind him. "Where is my Captain? Oh, well, you'll have to negotiate with my military attaché. See Moore about it. But there's no hurry." Dali turned to me. "This is not a joke. His is the first offer that I have taken under serious consideration. I can't tell you the amount. For the moment it's confidential." He turned away to speak to someone else.

"I told Dali if he accepted my offer, I would pay the money to the Red Cross," Loewy said.

I said I'd be surprised if Dali went through with it, in that case.

He laughed. "So would I," he said.

The movement of the crowd heading for the bar separated us. I looked back to see if Marina Lussato was still there and found myself looking into the eyes of Onda, the model who had worn out both her dancing partners at La Locomotive a few days before. Her straight, dark hair framed an olive-shaped and -tinted face still in its teens. The eyes were large and dark and without expression. She was dressed in the same manner: riding breeches and a sleeveless blouse. But one thing was new: around her waist and arm and neck was coiled a small python about seven feet long whose head emerged from between her hands. Its eyes were smaller but brighter than hers. Dali saw her at almost the same moment.

"Ah, my snake charmer, Mademoiselle Onda," he exclaimed, and she and her python were soon swept up in the surging mass around the bar.

Later I found myself seated beside Onda on the divan in Dali's salon, this time without her python. I asked her where it was.

"A lady snake cast a spell over him and he slipped away," she said. I commiserated with her. "That's the way it happens," she said. "It's the season."

A nervous young television interviewer was speaking to Dali. *"Maître,* would you explain the different meanings you attach to the word *parade?"* I heard him ask.

Dali frowned. "The first meaning that comes to my mind is the one that Pablo Picasso utilized in a ballet that created a good deal of scandal in Paris. In its monarchistic sense, *parade* means a maximum of exhibitionism and panache." The interviewer pressed him for other meanings. "The Larousse dictionary needs to be completely redone," Dali said, "and I'm in the process of redoing it because there isn't one definition in it which is really right. So I do twenty-five words a day in order that people who want to know the Dalinian meaning of words will have a source they can look to with confidence in place of that Cartesian monstrosity by Larousse. *Parade,* in a physical sense, is the action quantum of Max Planck: that is, the package of energy which, instead of following the Newtonian course, would stop abruptly and describe a kind of nuclear exhibitionism." Dali stopped, then looked at the boy. "This is all very well; but I thought you wanted me to talk about Lorca. What is the connection between *parade* and García Lorca?"

The boy looked startled. "You're asking *me?"*

"Why not?" Dali said. "If I can make an ass out of *you,* then Mr. Lake, who spends most of his time studying *me,* will begin to understand how I function."

The boy grew more nervous. "You mean the production?"

"What production?" Dali asked.

"Of the ballet *Parade."*

"No, no. The connection between the word itself and Lorca."

By now the boy was thoroughly rattled. He mumbled something incomprehensible. Dali cut him short.

"No, there *is* a connection," he said. "For Lorca, *parade* meant a brand of cigars—Romeo e Giulietta. First of all, opening the box and seeing that image, soft and colored, all those pinks and blues, and then delicately lifting up the cover and seeing the tips of those twenty cigars—that for him was the essence of *parade*. And for me the death of Lorca was the supreme *parade*. I consider his tragic destiny such a success that in spite of the fact that he was my best friend, the day a fellow Spaniard came to tell me that García Lorca had had the honor of being shot to death—because every great Spaniard, if he is not shot to death, lacks something—I shouted, '*¡Olé!*' "

A girl standing beside them spoke up. "*Maître,* we noticed when you were at the circus the other day that the performers seemed to look upon you as one of their own and—"

Dali interrupted her. "I am one of the greatest clowns of my time. That should be obvious. I have said in speaking of the books I have done—the most artificial as well as the most philosophical—that no one will ever know, not even I myself, whether they were written seriously or as a joke. And very often the things in my life that I consider gags, done only to make journalists or friends sit up and take notice, I see after a while as the most extraordinarily tragic and important of all. Whereas sometimes things I work very hard at, that I think are very serious, like my painting technique, I eventually come to see as childish nonsense, of no value at all.

"Charlie Chaplin is a truly sublime clown," Dali continued. "He has been received by the Queen of England. The whole world takes off its hat to him. But if, in addition to being the marvelous clown that he is, he could paint and draw like Dali, then he would *really* be something. Another word for clown is harlequin, and in Greek, you know, harlequin is synonymous with Hermes. And since money is what I love most in the world and Hermes was the god of commerce, I am a true harlequin.

Furthermore, Hermes had the gift of turning discord into peace." Dali pointed to Onda, still sitting quietly beside me. "You know that Hermes frequently handled snakes, just as Onda, who is in love with them, does. One day he saw two of them fighting in the road. He put his cane between them and they entwined themselves like lovers around it. That is the sign of his magic power and that is the power of Harlequin."

Someone asked Dali the name of the French writer for whom he felt the greatest admiration.

"Without any doubt whatever," he replied crisply, "it is Raymond Roussel, because he is the first one to have created a cybernetic epoch." But by now he had lost interest. "That's good enough," he said. "You've got your money's worth." He wandered over to a well-groomed, well-behaved young couple seated on the other side of the room.

"It's an abominable book," I heard him say, after a moment. "And I say so every time I see Mr. Lake. It has a side—I can see it now that I have begun to study it—that makes it just the kind of book to appeal to concierges. I'm *for* people—when they are kings and aristocrats—but I have no use for the bourgeois or the great middle class. And the only way concierges are acceptable is when they're down on their knees in front of the aristocracy. And very clean. It's all right for kings not to wash—I myself never do—but concierges must be models of cleanliness. And that isn't often the case. So we use the whip on them." He raised his arm and slashed back and forth.

At the other end of the divan a solemn-looking young fellow with glasses was setting up electrical equipment. I asked him what he was up to.

"I have marionettes," he said. "They're unique. They raise their upper lip when they talk. I told Dali about them and he wants to do a film with them."

Dali looked over at us. "You two should get together. Maybe you have already."

The fellow looked up at me. "Do you have marionettes?" he asked.

"Yes," Dali answered. "He has a little marionette called Madame Gilot."

The boy nodded. "I see," he said, but it was obvious that her name meant nothing to him.

"Why be that unkind?" I asked Dali.

"But everything I say is unkind," Dali said. "I'm a very unkind person. In fact I'm very cruel. I'm straight from the court of Philip the Second—cruel with everyone. Except people like Onda. But with her I'm very good because there aren't twenty-five people of her quality in the entire world." He came over to the divan. He took out of his pocket two small cubes of metal. He handed them to Onda. "Try to bring them together," he said. She tried. It looked simple enough but it just didn't work. She looked up at him, puzzled. "I've invented the most extraordinary erotic object," he said. "Just wait." He put the cubes back into his pocket. "You see how good I really am," he said to Onda. "As a result of coming to see Dali, Mr. Lake is going to become much more intelligent. He's a very lucky fellow. All these things that go on around me are very good for his health—especially from the moral point of view. Later on, when he has become a thoroughgoing masochist and just adores having me spit on him, then he'll have become a Dalinian." The puppeteer looked more confused than ever.

I told Dali I thought he should make his little speech about Françoise Gilot to her face, not behind her back. But if he did, I couldn't guarantee she would take it with a smile. In fact if he went too far, she might even—who knows?—bite back.

"Bite what? My hand?"

I told him I couldn't be sure about that.

"If she bites me physically, I have the Captain, who will kick her arse."

Moore looked over at me. "And there's the tiger, too," he said, with a nod in the direction of the ocelot.

I told him I thought her at least a match for the three of them.

"Physically I fear nothing," Dali said fiercely. "I'll give her a kick in the arse or anywhere else she wants one."

"No," Moore said soothingly, "she'll be received very politely."

"Yes," Dali said, calming down somewhat, "I'm very gallant. I'm Spanish and whatever I say I'll say with a certain gallantry. Bring her here tomorrow morning."

I telephoned to Françoise that evening and asked her if she wanted to debate the matter with Dali.

"Under no circumstances," she said firmly. "I don't want to have anything to do with that man. I don't trust him."

When I called Dali to tell him the debate was off, it was Peter Moore who answered. After we had chatted a moment, I heard Dali at the other end of the room shouting, "Lake is a cuckold." Gallantry for gallantry, I thought, and so when Dali came to the telephone I told him Françoise had gone off to England and wouldn't be back soon.

"It doesn't have the slightest importance," he said. "It makes no difference where or when. The idea is good. I'll carry it out when the occasion presents itself, perhaps when I return in the fall. Or perhaps sometime she'll come to Spain or we'll meet at a painting exhibition in New York. And then I'll convince her that she was wrong. I won't be unpleasant. I'll say it gallantly. But at least she'll know how I feel. That's the important thing."

Dali had suddenly decided it was time to leave for Spain, and his salon at the Meurice was crowded with people who had come to say good-bye. I was seated in an armchair facing him as he reminisced about the homage to Kant at the Galerie Charpentier. The door from the hall opened with a squeak, and a short, dark man poked his head inside the room. Dali looked up.

"*Entrez un peu*," he called out. The little man came in, followed by two others. He was not only short but very young, I saw as he came nearer. He had a close-cropped dark beard and wore glasses and a derby hat. A long zoot-suit chain swung across his trousers: he was obviously Toulouse-Lautrec made up for a burlesque skit. His two cohorts were dragging a pair of large, bright, spiky paintings that looked like Wilfredo Lam working in combination with Rufino Tamayo.

"Over there, against the wall," Dali directed. The rear guard followed his indications and the little man sat down behind me and began sketching Dali in three-quarter profile on a large pad he held on his knees.

A tall, emaciated girl with dyed brown hair, a pallid complexion, and eyes heavily shadowed with kohl came in. Dali jumped up.

"Ah, Mademoiselle Ginesta," he exclaimed. He introduced Richard, the American photographer ("the Turtle"), me ("Mr. William Blake"), Mme. Foret, and a few others to her, then seated her on the divan, picked a long-stemmed deep-red rose from a large bouquet on the coffee table, and handed it to her. He took her order for an orange juice, sent a waiter to fetch it, then returned to me.

I told him I had just been reading an article which claimed that Pop was finished, Op was on the decline, and the new art would be pornographic.

"But absolutely. That's what I've always said. After the apotheosis of *l'art pompier,* we will have the frank expression of all the things that were sublimated in the academic artists. Bouguereau is full of breasts and arses and cunts, but tamped down by the conventions of the times he painted in. Today it is different. All modern expression has a brutal side to it and the conventions no longer hold. Look at these." To our left, standing against the wall, were half a dozen apparently nonfigurative watercolor sketches. Each one appeared to be made up of two oval cloud shapes in pale blue with a darkening center between the two main masses.

"These are arse imprints in the raw," he said. "I have a great number of them. I won't give you any names, but they're all made by beautiful girls—nude, of course."

Made how?

"I soak the paper with water, lay on just a little color, then I have the girl sit down on the paper. When she gets up, she leaves a negative for me to work on. Sometimes she makes angels, sometimes demons, and other times all kinds of strange things. Sometimes I utilize a product they use in fingerprinting. Then I get a wonderful precision. You can see every pore in her skin."

Mme. Forani came in. Dali called over to her. "Where is Nefertiti?"

"Couldn't come," Mme. Forani said. "We'll see about another time."

Dali got up and walked over to the line of drawings. He picked up one of them.

"Look at this one. You see what it is? An arse viewed from the rear. Now look here." He pointed to a tiny spot in the center. "Do you recognize that?" I told him I couldn't swear that I did. He looked at me disgustedly. "The eyes of a fly," he said.

And what was the connection?

"It's closer than you imagine," he said. "You see, God works the way I do. Do you think for a minute that when He made an angel He set up any distinction between the eyes and the arse? He doesn't keep a stock of eyes or of anything else. It's all the same material. It's the act of creation. He made the arse and He made the eyes, and it's not such a long way from one to the other. Different steps in the same process, that's all. They're all elements of creation. And they're all mixed in together. One part isn't any higher or lower, any more divine or more human than any other. It's all part of the same thing. And never forget, He did all that to amuse Himself. People talk about a good God who did everything for the good of humanity. Who said He was good? He was cruel. *He* invented cancer; *I* didn't. In fact I'm more likely to be the one who will cure it."

I asked him if he was actively working on it. He nodded solemnly.

"I have found the way," he said. "It's all tied up with that acid. Not deoxyribonucleic acid, but the other one—the one that carries the little packages containing the cancer to the cytoplasm—the place where everything is made. In the cytoplasm there are anarchists who put the cancer into the packages of this acid—the one that's the messenger, that only carries the packages they give it to carry. What I plan to do is intercept the packages by means of cybernetic machines—that is, all those packages that seem suspect, that aren't just like the others—long before they arrive at their destination. And as we get rid of those, then the acid brings in another batch. So by intercepting all the ones that are suspect, there's a very good chance you'll pick up the ones that contain cancer. But instead of that, the scientists—like the cretins they are—are trying to read what is inside the packages. They should be intercepting them instead, because it will be fifty years before they're able to read the genetic code." He ran into the bedroom and came out with a copy of *Le Figaro*. "Here it is," he said and read the headline: "Exfoliative cytology. A new and sure method for early diagnosis of cancer."

I told him I had read it but hadn't seen any reference to him in it.

"They don't even know me, those people," he said disgustedly.

The waiter came in with a single glass of orange juice on his tray and held it out to Dali.

"No, no, no. Not for me," he said. "It's for La Ginesta." Mlle. Ginesta accepted her drink. Dali sat down between her and a man at the other end of the divan, and began talking in a low voice to the man. Ginesta sat slender and tall, pouting, the pallor of her complexion set off sharply against the deep burgundy of the divan. She held the long-stemmed red rose carefully cupped in her hands like a talisman. Suddenly, without moving, she spoke up in a thin, clear, reedlike voice.

"I don't know why you go on making fun of me. You look only at the outside. You should look at my soul."

"She talks a lot about soul," Dali said to the man. "Like those Buddhists who are always talking about love."

Lowering her eyes, Ginesta brought the rose up nearer her mouth. Her lips parted, and her tongue, narrow and pointed, darted out at the rose. It curled around the edges of the petals, flickering in and out of the rose's deep center as swiftly as a dragonfly. Dali seemed transfixed. Everyone stopped talking and watched.

One of the classics of cinematic eroticism is a scene in one of the films Dali made with Buñuel—*L'Age d'or*—in which the star, Lya Lys, with glazed and dreamy eyes, performs a similar, though less electric, operation on the large toe of a statue. A few years after that, in 1936, André Breton and Paul Éluard collaborated on an essay called *Notes sur la poésie*. It was published as a small brochure with a frontispiece by Dali in which two wraithlike female figures of somewhat decadent pre-Raphaelite extraction hover about a stylized flower and butterfly motif. One of the figures extends her tongue hungrily into a triangular slit between one of the butterfly's wings and the adjacent petal. Obviously, La Ginesta had done her homework.

Finally Dali spoke. "How do you like her? Very pretty, no? Such a sweet little tongue, and so pointed. You noticed?"

Richard, the photographer, was breathing hard. "I noticed," he said and fumbled with his camera.

"The most pointed tongue in the world belongs to a friend of mine named Isabelle," Dali said. "She can stick out her tongue and reach up between her eyes. Extraordinary. Now *she* has a sensational soul."

Mme. Forani broke in. "Where is her soul located? At the tip of her tongue?"

"She can even make the sign of the cross with her tongue," Dali said. "And for a woman, the quality of the soul is in direct proportion to the length of the tongue."

"Does that apply to you?" Mme. Forani asked. "Your mustache is as pointed as Isabelle's tongue."

Dali shook his head. "Not the same with a mustache," he said. "Besides, anyone can wear a false mustache."

"Why doesn't someone invent an artificial tongue?" Mme. Forani suggested.

"It wouldn't sell," Dali said. "Only to Lesbians." He got up and went over to the long table, bumping into the two large, colorful paintings on his way. I saw no sign of Toulouse-Lautrec or his crew. Dali rang up the concierge and asked to have someone sent up to remove the paintings. "They're in my way," he said. "It's terrible. I wanted to encourage him, but he ended by dragging everything up here. I'm going to be receiving Louis Quatorze and all sorts of important people, so you mustn't come in. Besides, I'm painting; there's a nude woman on a pedestal. You knock at the door; we'll open it just a crack and slide them out. Right now." He hung up. The photographer, still short of breath, was trying, I could see, to arrange to photograph La Ginesta. She seemed less eager than he.

"That's very kind, but I can't stay here like that in the sun," I heard her say.

"That's all right," Dali said. "She'll be coming to Cadaqués." He went over to his desk and came back with a large sheet of cardboard covered with names, addresses, and telephone numbers. He borrowed my pen and had her write down her telephone number. "Muy bien, muy bien," he said and escorted her into the hall. The photographer watched them longingly. The room was still buzzing with talk of La Ginesta when Dali returned. A dark young Spaniard across the room spoke up.

"She has such strength in her eyes."

"And such extraordinary immobility," Mme. Forani added.

"Oh, that can be learned," the young Spaniard replied, "but what cannot be learned is that look that comes from a special center deep within her."

"She's a necrophiliac," Dali said. He picked up a large box of white chocolates and passed it around. "It's Menier, the chocolate that grows old gracefully." Someone knocked. Dali went to the door and after a moment returned with a stocky, middle-aged woman who, the conversation made clear, was an Australian journalist.

"What kind of present have you brought me?" he asked her.

"Nothing," she said.

He looked at her in surprise. "But you brought *something* for me?"

"A kiss?" she suggested.

Dali drew away in horror. "No, no, no, no." Everyone laughed.

"You're disgusting," the woman said.

"Even with very pretty women, I don't allow that. But make notes on what I am about to tell you. You'll have to leave very soon because Louis Quatorze is coming."

She looked a little puzzled. "Louis Quatorze?"

Dali began to strut back and forth. "I am going to give you a piece of news for Australia which will delight you."

"Where is the book you promised to give me with your signature?"

"Oh, yes," Dali said. "I always promise things, but I don't always give them. This room is full of people to whom I have promised things, who are still waiting to get them. You have lots of company. That doesn't mean I won't give it to you. You may still get it, but you'll have to wait your turn. However, first of all, go get a copy of day before yesterday's *L'Osservatore Romano*. In it you will find an article three columns long announcing the fact that Dali is illustrating the Bible."

"Pornographically?"

"Naturally. But the important thing is the fact that it is the Vatican which is announcing the publication of the Bible by Salvador Dali."

"The Vatican or the Pope personally?"

"*L'Osservatore Romano*, which is, after all, the Pope's organ."

"Is this a big book or a little one?"

"It's more or less a normal book. A little bigger than *The Divine Comedy*, not so big as *The Apocalypse*." He looked around him. "What time is it, anyway?"

"When are you leaving?" she asked.

"That's a question to which I give everyone a different answer," Dali said.

"When will you be back?"

"I don't know yet. You'll see it in the papers. I think that's all for today."

"But don't forget the book you promised me."

"Immediately," Dali said. "On my return." He held out the back of his hand. "You may kiss me." She kissed his hand. He rubbed it off quickly on his jacket and showed her to the door. When he returned to the center of the room he said, "Extraordinary, these people who come from Australia to say, 'When are you leaving? When are you returning?' But she'll become a Dalinian yet." He rubbed the back of his hand on his jacket once again, then called out to Peter Moore.

"I'm going to do an article, you know, in the new magazine Igor Cassini is bringing out."

Moore looked over at me. "What's the name of that thing? It's just one word."

"Never mind. It will come to you," Dali said. "But the cover will be devoted to *me,* and after an interview there will be a long article called 'The Dalinian Empire': that is, how it is just like an empire, branching out into new activities. It will be a tremendous article."

"I'm afraid that magazine will have rough going," Moore said. "If Mr. Huntington Hartford, with a million a month, couldn't make a go of *Show* magazine—which was very well done—and lost millions on it—"

"But what difference does *that* make?" interrupted Dali. "They're bringing out one number devoted to *me.* It will be very much in view and widely read. That's quite enough. It's like the Huntington Hartford museum. They made it for *me.* I don't know whether it will last or not. And I don't give a fuck."

"Huntington Hartford has put an announcement in the New York *Times,*" Moore said, "asking for a thousand people to pay a thousand dollars each. That makes a million."

"Yes," Dali said. "He asked me about it. It's a good idea. Out in the Corn Belt everybody will want to be a big patron: somebody in Cleveland, somebody else in San Francisco. It's a very good idea." He paused, seemingly deep in thought. "Whom shall I attack in that article?" he said finally. "Ah! I'll attack Mr. Lake's book. But let's not talk any more about Madame Gilot; just Mr. Lake. Ah!" Dali craned his neck to one side and was looking past me. "*Bonjour, bonjour, bonjour*," he said. Marina Lussato came over and shook hands with us. "I thought your brother was coming," Dali said.

"He *is* coming," she said, "but a little later on. He's had the grippe. I've had a touch of it, too. I guess I caught it from him." Dali moved away, as though he felt the germs reaching out for their next victim. He came over to me.

"Ask me something practical," he said with a sudden show of seriousness. I thought of La Ginesta and then of Lya Lys. I asked Dali to tell me about the making of his other film, *Un Chien andalou.*

"I had told Buñuel I had a scenario for him. I didn't have any, and if I had been doing the film by myself I wouldn't have bothered with one, but since film makers think you have to have a scenario, I sat down, fifteen minutes before Buñuel called for me, and wrote the script. I had a shoe box, made out of white cardboard, nice for writing on. I put it down on the bed and wrote the scenario on it. When we got to Billancourt, we rounded up a few fellows in a café. In three or four days the job was done. And now it's a classic." He stopped and thought for a moment. "I must send Buñuel a telegram," he said, "and propose that we make the second part of that film. He wouldn't do it by himself but I think he might be tempted to do it with me because that way it's sure to be a success." I could see his enthusiasm mounting. "After thirty years he'll return to Spain. I'll see him there. And after thirty years we'll make the second part of *Un Chien andalou.* It will be marvelous, with all the new things I've invented since then, to make a film of the same length, that continues—" The phone rang. Moore answered it, then cupped his hand over the mouthpiece. "It's Forani's friend," he announced. "She wants to drop by about six to pick up her drawing." Dali, humming melancholy sounds, went to the telephone.

"*Allô*. Yes. Perfect. You may come at six, but understand that you are going to collaborate physically in the drawing." He paused, then repeated the sentence in a louder voice. "That is, you are going to sit down on the drawing and leave imprints because everything is prepared for it. In that way you will be integrated into the Dalinian mythology. It won't take more than ten minutes. For the imprint, that is. Afterward you may stay as long as you wish. We won't be bothered by people coming and going. Later on I'll have you come to Cadaqués along with the rest of the crowd. *Je vous embrasse. Bonjour.*"

I could see Marina smiling to herself. She saw me looking at her and broke into a wide grin. Dali picked up a covered glass jar filled with small white eggs.

"What are those?" Marina asked.

"Quail's eggs," Dali said.

"Are they good to eat?"

"Of course."

The Turtle looked over at them. "What are you going to do with them?"

"I'm going to insert one in the arse of some young girl and have you photograph it as it slips out again. I'm going to prove to the world that a woman can lay an egg. She'll eat wild strawberries and lay a quail's egg."

Moore laid his hand on Marina's shoulder. "Here's a candidate."

Marina drew back. "Oh, no."

"No, no, no, no," Dali said. "She won't do. I've never seen her nude and I don't know whether she'd qualify. I need someone with the tiniest little pink arsehole."

A waiter came in and took orders for drinks. Dali handed him the jar of quail's eggs. "Before I do anything else with these, I think I'll eat one," he said. "Open the jar and bring me pepper and salt."

Dali went over to his desk, picked up a photograph of himself, and scrutinized it critically. "I don't think much of this one," he said. "I had it taken in a studio we happened to pass one day." He looked at it again. "But maybe it would be a good going-away gift for my chauffeur. I think it's a good photograph for a chauffeur, don't you?"

Moore dipped a short pen into a bottle of India ink. "Your chauffeur's name is Richard," he said.

Dali scratched a noisy inscription, which spattered all over the photograph. "Those are antiprotons," he said. The waiter returned with the drinks and the jar of quail's eggs.

"Is it open?" Dali asked. He lifted off the cover. "Very good. And there's the salt and pepper." The waiter left and Dali picked up a thick quarto volume. "Here's a marvelous book on Meissonier," he said. He set it down on an end table and opened it to a page which carried a reproduction of a detailed sketch, in pencil, touched with white, of the foreparts of a horse wearing a breast-piece. He slapped the page with the backs of his fingers. "Look at that leg. Nobody else could have done that. Not Dürer, not anybody." He turned to another illustration, a landscape. "I'm going to do a book which will trace the history of art through the treatment of skies. Nothing else." With his hand he blocked off areas in several of the paintings reproduced on the following pages. "In some cases—this one, for example—I'll reproduce three or four details in color. Sometimes Meissonier spent two months painting a sky. He had extraordinary patience. Today a painter would slap on some Spanish white, swab it back and forth a time or two, and consider it finished." He pointed to some flecks here and there in a cloud formation. "But Meissonier painted this and that and that slowly and lovingly, day after day. No wonder it's such a marvel." He looked up at me. "If I could ever get that idea across to you, you'd realize that compared to this, Cézanne is worth

nothing. Believe me, that idea will bring about a revolution."
Soon?

"It has already caught on. You ask any young Pop Art painter
and he'll tell you Cézanne is worthless. Look." He picked up a
copy of *Harper's Bazaar* and turned to a photograph of a sculpture, a seated male figure by George Segal, looking almost like
the inhabitant of a modern Pompeii, fixed for eternity by a
downpour of white plaster.

"You look at this and then look at Meissonier. It's the same
idea. You see it?" Suddenly Dali smiled. "It's wonderful to be
as intelligent as I am," he said. "Each day that arrives, I'm more
enraptured by my genius."

"You're going to find yourself all alone," Moore cautioned
him. "The most intelligent man in the world is the most solitary."

Dali saw it another way, apparently. "Solitary," he said
proudly, "and then, with an imperialist influence like Cézanne's. Everybody obeying me. And what's more, without
knowing why."

"Jesus was the most intelligent man in the world, the most
solitary *and* the most humble," Moore reminded him.

"That's right," Dali said. "Like me, your humble servant."
He picked up the copy of *Harper's Bazaar* from the table.
"Look at that Segal thing again," he said. "What are they up
to, these people? They are once again producing images without any kind of stylization—pure objective reality. It's the same
as this." He turned to a page of the Meissonier book which
showed two extremely realistic male nudes. "Two guys, bare-
ass, without any artistic flourishes, just as they were. They
might almost be plaster casts, too. These two characters mod-
eled for the fireplace in his atelier. They were living models.
Today nobody cares about that. In Cadaqués I'll have Meissonier's easel. I think I'll reconstruct his fireplace in the same
room. Anyway, the point is, this and the Segal are in the same
spirit. I'm sure Segal prefers Meissonier to one of those way-out

sculptors where you can't see anything because there's nothing to see. Naturally, Meissonier is at a much higher level than Segal, because Meissonier was a great artist and these Pop Artists are very little ones. But the important thing is that they aren't attempting to stylize something out of existence or make an interpretation of something or show how much the artist is suffering. What interests them is to show things as they are. Praxiteles never deformed anything. And yet he expressed everything he wanted to. But then along came the cuntheads who caricatured everything because they felt that in order to express their ideas they had to elongate legs, twist bodies, and instead of painting a face flesh color, do it in green or blue. Since the public didn't understand, the art critics wrote articles to make them believe it was very good. And that's the story of modern painting."

The phone rang. Moore answered it. He turned to Dali. "There's a Monsieur Banquet from some student paper."

"Does he have an appointment?"

Moore put the question, then said no.

"All right," Dali said. "Since he doesn't have an appointment, I'll see him."

I quoted to Dali Maillol's verdict on the *Hermes* of Praxiteles: "It's pretentious, horrible. It looks as though it had been carved out of laundry soap."

"That shows you what a jackass Maillol was," Dali said. "Praxiteles was a whole lot better than Maillol. What you should find out now is what Meissonier thought of Praxiteles."

I asked him if he thought Segal was of any importance.

"Oh, no," he said. "The important thing is the trend. All through the history of the modern movement there are crosscurrents like that, interesting from the moral point of view. Segal isn't an artist, but he's no worse than the next fellow. Expressionism is the phony thing, and this is a return to order— against Expressionism. These Pop people are very mediocre, even bad: there isn't an artist among them. But they paint

things as they are and in that sense they are in the classical tradition." He shook his head. "That's very interesting, that crack
of Maillol's about Praxiteles. What an arsehole. But everything
is like that. Everybody. One day a group of young avant-garde
painters came to visit me. I had a reproduction of a painting
by Raphael on the wall. They were all praising Miró, and when
they saw the Raphael they thought I had put it up as a joke. It
simply shows the stupidity of our times, when people can think
that Miró is more important than Raphael. Oh, Miró is interesting enough—it's better than a badly painted boat done by
some painter up on top of Montmartre—but it's folklore. And
yet there are plenty of young people who think Miró is a genius
and Raphael's no good. And all that is the fault of people like
you, Lake. Up until now the people who wrote about art have
been people of no culture at all. They sprang from the same
background as the painters. Look at all those Montparnasse
painters—that so-called École de Paris crowd. What do they
amount to? Nothing. They were people who knew nothing
about anything. And those who wrote about them—Maurice
Raynal, André Salmon, Monsieur Zervos, too—they're all people who knew nothing about anything that mattered. Perhaps
a little about things that resemble modern art, the caricatures.
Monsieur Zervos is a Greek, and in his *Cahiers d'Art* he features the primitives, Negro art, all that sort of stuff. But never
in the world would he print an article about Praxiteles. Those
people have a terrible responsibility because they have built up
a whole body of literature on the latest fashions in art and on
some very obscure and valueless painters who, when you compare them to Meissonier and Bouguereau, look pretty sick.
There's just one thing in all this modern period that is interesting, and that is a state of mind: the spirit of revolt. But it's
all a very tiny fragment of the history of art."

Gala came into the room. "A quail's egg for Gala, Captain,"
Dali called out. "We'll see whether she likes it."

"What's that?" Gala asked, as Moore spooned out one of the eggs.

"A quail's egg—to see if you like it," Moore said. He sprinkled it with salt and pepper.

"That won't poison me, will it?" Gala asked apprehensively. Moore looked uncertain. "Someone who took one did faint a little while ago," he said, "but I don't think he died. They're aphrodisiac."

"Oh, I don't need an egg," Gala said, but she took it. Moore ran to answer a knock at the door. He returned with a long-legged, dark, thin boy wearing glasses and introduced him to "Maître Dali." Dali's eyes were fixed on an oblong folio volume the boy was carrying under his arm. I recognized it as a monograph on Dali's painting published by the New York Graphic Society.

"So you're bringing me a book," Dali said. The boy smiled, blushed a little, and started to say something.

"Thank you," Dali said and took the book from him.

The boy started to explain that he had brought it for Dali to sign.

"No, no, no, no," Dali said. "I'm taking it because I need it. It's an amazing coincidence. I really do need that book for this afternoon. I'm going to give you a quail's egg." He salted and peppered one for himself, then offered one to the boy. "They're very good. Aphrodisiac, too."

The boy looked surprised. "Is that true?"

"Why? You have difficulty with your erections?" Dali asked. "Do you have normal erections or are they a little bit . . . well . . ."

The boy looked embarrassed. "I'm all right," he said and kept his distance from the egg.

"No, but that's very well known about quail's eggs," Dali said, pushing the jar toward him. "Quail's eggs, rhinoceros horn, those are things that produce . . . well, what can we offer him, then? How would you like a photograph of me?"

"Monsieur wanted to ask you for an interview for his paper,"
Moore reminded him.

"I don't want to disturb you," the boy said, eyeing his book.

"Ah, no. Not at all. Not at all," Dali said. "Just imagine, I
would have spent the entire afternoon looking for this book,
telephoning everywhere. Let's go."

The boy asked a question about one of Dali's recent television appearances, and Dali's *délire* was launched on a sea of
molecular structures, genetic codes, deoxyribonucleic acid, the
persistence of memory, the eyes of a fly, cybernetic machines,
and painting in the third dimension. I slipped out of the inner
circle and made my way over to a table at the end of the room,
where I had left my briefcase, and took out two books that I
had decided to give to Dali. I wasn't sure when I would see
him again and I thought I should make some kind of going-
away gift, in the circumstances. They were first editions of two
of the works of his favorite writer, Raymond Roussel, *Impressions d'Afrique* and *Nouvelles Impressions d'Afrique,* each of
them one of a small number of large-paper copies on *japon im-
périal.* During a lull that followed a telephone interruption of
his interview, I gave them to him, telling him I thought he
might like to have them. He looked at them, turned the pages
briefly, then looked up at me, his mouth agape.

"You're *giving* them to me?"

Why not? I said. He'd given me a liberal education.

He looked incredulous. "But that's magnificent," he said.
"That's something I *really* like." He went quickly over to Gala
and showed her the books.

"*Ah, oui. C'est ça,*" she said vaguely and went into the bedroom. Dali came back to me and thanked me again. He started
into the bedroom, then returned to me once more.

"You understand, Lake, I'm pure," he said. "I never touch
a woman. My only interest in this question of tongues stems
from the fact that I plan to design jewels for the tongue—cover
it with a kind of stocking of fine gold mesh. I've dressed the

other parts of the body. Now I'll dress the tongue." He left me and returned to his interviewer.

Off to the right, Marina Lussato was talking to a man I didn't recognize. She saw me and came over to the door. We walked out together. I asked her where she had been since M. Foret's party.

"Back in England," she said, and shuddered.

And what was wrong with England?

"It's not amusing. And I've been there for such a long time this year. But I've married an Englishman and I must get used to England. So I try. People tell me I should read the books of Anthony Powell; that would help me. I've had *At Lady Molly's* on my night table for three months now and with the best will in the world haven't been able to get past page thirty. Each time I pick it up, I fall asleep." She sighed. "There's one consolation, though. I don't need sleeping pills anymore."

I asked her if her husband was a Dalinian.

"Heavens, no," she said. "Not at all." She smiled ruefully. "And I'm less and less one all the time. I did enjoy being with him, but as I told you the other day, he demands too much."

We walked out the Rue de Rivoli entrance and crossed over to the Tuileries.

"In the beginning there was a certain intellectual excitement in being with Dali," Marina said. "The first time I met him was at a lecture my brother had organized for him at the École Polytechnique. It was a very exciting evening. The great amphitheater was filled. I sat in the General's loge. The press, radio, and television were there. Dali was greatly stimulated by the crowds. The students asked dozens of questions and his answers were brilliant. Afterward we went down into the catacombs and christened with champagne the Rue Salvador Dali.

"After that, Dali came to our house in Paris and then I began to visit him at the Meurice and he invited me to go everywhere with him. He isn't really crazy, but he does have his psychological problems. He has his complexes and on top of that he wants to play a certain role. And he has worked so hard to create the character to play that role, he has finally become that character."

I asked her how she would define the character and the role.

"Well, his sexual neurosis is at the base of it all. But I can't believe he's a true paranoiac. He tells everyone he is and he writes about it in all his books. But if he really *were* one, he probably wouldn't be aware of it. Or if he had even the slightest inkling of his condition, he would struggle against it and wouldn't for the world want to show it. I've known paranoiacs before. If ever you try to tell them about themselves, they react violently, but Dali wants everyone to believe he *is* one. It's like what he tries to do in his painting, I think: to confuse people by emphasizing the tremendous contrast between the content of the painting and its manner. It is carefully drawn and meticulously finished—impeccable from a technical point of view because he's a first-class technician. But behind it there is always something disturbing and rather unhealthy. But the question of genius . . ." She shrugged. "It's not an easy one to settle. He often says he doesn't consider himself a genius as a painter."

I had heard him say that, too. Did she think he meant it?

"You think he's playing a game when he talks that way?" she asked. She hesitated. "There may be a little of that in it, but I think he knows deep inside he's not one of the great ones. No, when he says that, I believe him. But you have to take him as a whole—because *that* is where he believes his genius lies. And that brings us back to his sexual neurosis. Because that is the real basis of the man. And therefore of the work, too."

I asked her to give me an example.

"Every year when he returns to Paris, he seems to be obsessed by some erotic idea. Two years ago, while he was away, I had become engaged, and when he returned I was about to be married. That idea and all it implied took on a kind of symbolic significance for him, and one day when I arrived at the Meurice I found a long tube made of a deep-red cloth about the color of a Bordeaux wine stretched across the full length of his salon. It was held in shape by a series of eight or ten plastic hoops at regular intervals inside. It had a diameter of about—" She touched her hips, then held her hands up to show me the dimension. "When I asked him about it, he told me it was for my initiation. He said he was sure I would be very happy with it. He had me get down and climb through it from one end to the other. It was a very tight fit and I could barely squeeze through. And he was so excited! I had never seen him so excited. He had me go through it again and again, and each time it seemed to excite him more. He liked the way the hoops held me very tightly so I could just squeeze through, slowly, with great difficulty. Sometimes he would set the stage very carefully. One time when I went there, the room was all in darkness. He had me walk back and forth around the salon, then he had me go down into the tube. He told me, when I got to the end, to stick out just my head and stay still. He stood there, looking at me, terribly excited. Afterward he explained to me that he wanted to reverse the usual process: instead of man coming out of the sex of a woman, he wanted to see woman emerging from the sex of a man. He wanted very badly to take the tube back to Cadaqués with him, but Gala said no. He kept insisting right up to the moment they left. The car was waiting for them, and there he was with this immense red thing. There was no room for it but he couldn't bear the thought of leaving it. Finally Gala put her foot down and Dali had to give in.

"But he is always looking for figures and representations of some kind of sexual deviation, like the things you see in his early pictures of the Surrealist period. Now he paints different things, with scientific and religious symbols. But the impulses are the same and they have to take shape somehow, so they come out in one form or another in his daily activities instead of being channeled off into the painting."

We sat down in the shade, in painted metal chairs overlooking a small circular basin with a fountain at its center. Children were sailing boats along the perimeter. Marina tapped her head. "Dali has a little hole here, you see?"

I told her I thought he had more than one. In fact, I remembered his referring once to the "total Swiss cheese" of his personality.

She sighed. "You see, then, why I go to Dali less often now. I don't shock easily but it is annoying."

In any case, Dali's activities hadn't seemed to interfere with his health or slow him down in other ways, I said.

"Oh, but he's very passive," Marina said. "And he doesn't drink anything stronger than Vichy water. He watches his health ever so carefully. And then, you see, he has that little *tic* inside him and he *must* exteriorize it in some way. And he doesn't only exteriorize it; he emphasizes it. It's almost as though someone had six fingers and instead of hiding his hand because he's ashamed of it, he's proud of those six fingers and he shows them to everybody and even earns a rich living from them. He turns bad fortune into good by building on it and playing it up. But if Dali suppressed all his little games, then I think he would become psychotic."

She laughed. "It is very strange, isn't it? And he always looks for new things. He wants to invent. He wants to discover himself. You see, he really does not believe he is a great painter. The painter is only a part of him. He plays, he searches, and he does not know, really, whether he is serious or not. But when he is dead—and sometimes, when he is most crazy, I think it is because he sees himself die—there will only be left the painting. What will it look like then? Will people understand why it is like that?" She smiled and shook her head. "Not if you write the kind of book Dali would like you to write. Please don't."

Dali had beat the drum for his forthcoming retrospective often enough to fix it firmly in my mind as the art event of the season. Over the years, I had seen a number of small exhibitions of his drawings, paintings, jewelry, and prints, but the chance to see a full-scale retrospective had never come my way. There had been an early one, at the Museum of Modern Art in New York in 1941, which I had missed, but even if I had been there to see it, it had scanted the early years and stopped too far short of the Dali of today to be of much help now. Then there had been the one in Tokyo that Robert Descharnes had helped organize in 1964, but that had been too far out of my orbit. So when winter came and Huntington Hartford's Gallery of Modern Art presented the largest of them all —"Salvador Dali: The Years 1910–1965"—I saw to it that I was in New York. More than four hundred works were shown, from Dali's first painting, a small oil on cardboard done when he was six, to several he had just finished—chief among these, the dollar painting he had told me about in New York nearly two years earlier, during one of our first conversations. In print, the dollar painting had become *Salvador Dali in the Act of Painting Gala in the Apotheosis of the Dollar in Which You Can See on the Left Marcel Duchamp Masquerading as Louis XIV Behind a Vermeerian Curtain Which Actually Is the Invisible Face but Monumental of Hermes by Praxiteles.* Crowded into that painting, and into the years that separated it from his first, there was everything—including the kitchen sink.

Visitors to the exhibition were required to take the elevator to the fifth floor of the museum and from there work their way down through the eleven galleries that housed the show. I made the trip three times, on three different days, and when I had finished, I felt I had a much clearer idea than before of the whole spectrum of Dali's painting and its significance.

The exhibition had been assembled in accordance with the old mass-merchandising technique, on the principle—no doubt sound—that in that way there should be something for everybody. But even before the end of my third visit I had decided that the net effect on me, at least, was simply to invert the Miesian cliché: More is less, I found myself muttering.

From Glasgow had come the *Christ of St. John of the Cross*, which Dali had painted in 1951. In April, 1961, according to a press release the Gallery issued, "the painting was damaged by a stone thrown by a young man who was later admitted to a mental hospital." Had that really happened, I wondered, and in just that way? If so, was Dali himself somehow connected with the incident? He had been so fascinated by the fate of Millet's *Angelus* and of the *Mona Lisa* in similar incidents in the Louvre; how could he not have been involved in such an inspired attempt to move his *Christ* onto the same historical plane as two of the paintings he admires above most others?

In the Glasgow painting, Christ crucified is shown from above a dramatic plunging shot which brings his hanging head and nailed feet within inches of each other. At the bottom of the long canvas, against the familiar Cadaqués landscape that serves as backdrop in so many of Dali's paintings, are a figure borrowed from Velásquez and another from Louis Le Nain. As I studied the picture, I found myself wondering if perhaps we were supposed to think, first, how much better Dali does the foreshortening bit than, say, some ordinary Old Master like Mantegna in such a picture as the Brera Gallery's *Dead Christ Mourned by the Virgin;* then, having applauded the technical skill, to nod, in passing, to the figures from Velásquez and Le Nain, which are, of course, appropriately dwarfed by the Dalinian Christ; and finally, to remember that a hypersensitized, unbalanced viewer in Glasgow, moved by some haunting, piercing, maddening or otherwise unbearably insistent quality in Dali's *Christ,* had attempted, by violence, to exorcise its provocative spell in much the same way that other deranged minds had responded to two other masterworks, one of them the picture the world has been taught to consider almost the greatest achievement in painting, the other the picture Dali has fought single-handedly for more than thirty years to raise from utter banality to masterpiece status. And all the way through the exhibition, I felt, whatever pitch a painting made for one's attention or interest was invariably based on some similarly adventitious and generally "sensational" feature.

The double image so dear to Dali's heart can, on occasion, be amusing. But in dozen lots, I discovered, it becomes a little boring. Even an otherwise admirable figure like Voltaire begins to seem rather tiresome when, time and again, you catch his "invisible bust" leering out at you from the underside of some paranoiac sister image that shares space with him in such pictures as *Slave Market with Invisible Bust of Voltaire.* And a painting like *Fifty Abstract Pictures Which as Seen from Two Yards Change into Three Lenins Masquerading as Chinese and as Seen from Six Yards Appear as the Head of a Royal Tiger* becomes just one more whirl in a perilously oversustained roller coaster ride of self-indulgent stunting that can have only one outcome: eventual derailment.

More than thirty years ago, Dali set forth his ambitions in

painting: "to materialize with the most imperialistic insistence on precision the images of concrete irrationality." In that way, he said, the "most abjectly arriviste and irresistible illusionism of imitative art, the clever tricks of paralysing *trompe-l'oeil*, the most analytically narrative and discredited academicism can become sublime hierarchies of thought." It sounded good (i.e., outrageously daring) on paper at the height of the Surrealist vogue in 1935. It looked less good on canvas thirty years later. The abjectly arriviste and discredited academic elements were easy enough to find; the sublime, less so.

It has become a commonplace, among both admirers and denigrators of Dali's work, to refer to his remarkable classical technique and style. But essentially, Dali is a *faux-classique:* the style is baroque or Mannerist or, on occasion—and this is a dirty word in Dali's mouth—Expressionist. There were, to be sure, occasional reassuring references to classical subjects, like the *Cosmic Madonna*, of 1958, with its side-glance at Raphael, and the Winston Guests' *Virgin of Guadalupe*, 1959, with the omnipresent idealized Gala in the role of Virgin. There were other echoes of the Renaissance, such as the application of the Golden Section to the composition of *Leda Atomica* (1949). And there were pastiches of Velásquez, of Zurbarán and Watteau and borrowings from almost everywhere: One of the principal components of *Dali at the Age of Six Lifting the Skin of the Water to Observe a Dog Sleeping in the Shadow of the Sea* (1950), is a dog lifted intact from the fifteenth-century *Martyrdom of St. Medin* in the Barcelona Museum. But borrowing images from Raphael or Velásquez or aping the techniques of Leonardo or anyone else has very little to do with the classical tradition: at best it is simply fun and games, and when it takes itself seriously—as it so often did here—it becomes pretentious academic bombast.

But if one simply refuses to take it seriously, the possibilities for fun are not lacking: for example, *Discovery of America by Christopher Columbus* (1959), one of the Gallery's own treasures, should certainly not be overlooked by any art historian compiling a list of the ten most macaronic paintings of the twentieth century. I thought of the two-edged tribute paid to Dali by Mr. Jack Winter, the Milwaukee manufacturer of fashion pants for women: "[Dali's] astute manipulation of all schools of art has assuredly captivated the world."

As for the technique, it was often impressive but sometimes inadequate. Even the much-praised photographic likeness in Dali's work seemed to fail him on occasion. He had often told me that he was not a very good painter; that if he looked good, it was only because the others were so bad. In some way he may have been right: I saw many portraits, so titled or not, of Gala, where the resemblance was, at best, approximate, as in *St. Helena in Port Lligat* (1956)—to say nothing of this Helena's peculiarly unnatural right hand. And there were, now and again, pictures in which the attempted naturalism was actually puerile. A look at the horse's forelegs in the *St. George* of 1962, for example, would make one wonder whether Dali had ever seen a horse. One thinks nothing of the distortion of natural forms in the work of many contemporaries; however, since that is the main burden of the diatribe Dali levels at most of the art of the past hundred and fifty years, it was surprising to see how unsure *his* footing could be at times. But to consider even his best efforts "great" painting, one would too often have to equate artistic value with technical tricks and a slick finish.

Much of Dali's scorn, in his conversations with me, had been poured out against those he refers to as the "caricaturists" of art—such painters as Piero della Francesca, Goya, El Greco. And yet how often the exhibition stressed, particularly in its examples from the late 1930's and the 1940's, that very quality in Dali's own work. The elongated, attenuated figures of *Resurrection of the Flesh,* of *The Broken Bridge and the Dream,* and of so many others are extensions of El Greco.

A painter in the classical tradition, Dali had said, is one who "paints things as they are." The greatness of Velásquez, he had told me early in our discussions, "lies in his not changing anything. His personages are exactly the way they looked. The proportions aren't arranged, any more than in Praxiteles or Vermeer. There is no deformation at all . . ." But Dali, who aspires to continue the tradition, changes whatever suits his convenience: identifiable personages are idealized; composition and proportions are arranged to conform to the straitjacketing requirements of his compulsive *trompe-l'oeil* routines; scale, formal relationships, and functional values are scrapped in the interest of making each major picture a newsworthily exhibitionistic Dali anthology.

Why this discrepancy, I wondered, between what he pretends to believe in most fervently and what he produces? A puzzled viewer could hardly be blamed for concluding that although Dali admires the essential honesty of a Vermeer or a Velásquez, (1) he *must* show off, (2) he has nothing to say, and (3) the incessant stunting satisfies (1) and distracts *us* from thinking about (2).

"When you don't believe in anything, you're not capable of painting anything," Dali had said, in one of our earliest conversations. I had never been able to take very seriously any of his declarations about religion or modern science. He had never convinced me that, in either of those areas, he really had the faith. And painting is nothing if not an act of faith. So if one's faith is limited to the all-power of technique and "illusionism," the results are bound to seem rather brittle.

The most curious thing was that in spite of their busyness and grandiose subject matter, there seemed to be a total absence of emotional content in most of these paintings. One could only assume that Dali didn't feel a thing—and therefore we don't.

Suppose—I thought—one tried to understand Dali through his painting, without knowing anything about Dali, the man. In the early work, of which there was far too much on display, there was a bit of everybody. After the usual post-Impressionist beginnings there were some secondhand Mirós, there was Picasso, there was Derain, and an occasional spot of one of those vague sub-Cubists whose names no one any longer remembers. There was a lot of Chirico, a touch of Tanguy, a whiff of Ernst, and uncounted others. That is no reproach; every artist spends a few years painting out his ancestors. But seeing so many of the early pictures assembled in one place only underlined the fact that nothing Dali had painted before he broke into the Surrealist movement gave any hint of true originality. However, Surrealism and Freud and Dali's own neurosis changed all that, starting in 1929. And if we consider the paintings of the next few years simply as a group of historical documents in the vulgarization of Freudian doctrine and the exploitation of Surrealist themes, they have a definite importance, whatever their excesses. Given Dali's predispositions for the processes involved— *i.e.,* vulgarization, exploitation, and excess—the work had an intermittent cogency and—on those rare occasions when he succeeded, by an uncharacteristic simplicity or directness, in making one feel he was sincere—a quite disproportionate strength. I had known in reproduction *The Spectre of Sex Appeal* (1934), but I had never seen the painting itself. It was surprisingly small, but in spite of its size—6⅜ by 5⅛ inches— more monumental than most of the more grandiose canvases I saw on all sides.

Well before the end of the 1930's Dali's painting grew slicker. The human figures had often seemed to lack any internal structure. Now they became rubbery, willowy, with an ersatz-ethereal sweep and swish. *Tristan as Christ* (1944), a squirming, ambivalent transvestite, might be explained away as a High Camp exercise *avant la lettre* and, as such, just another prophetic joke. Could it be that one was supposed to rationalize on that same basis the full gamut of narcissistic and invert outcroppings that stretched across the eleven exhibition galleries?

It started as early as *The Font,* of 1930, where one idealized nude male figure is down on his knees in front of another, the

standing one reaching out with a protesting left hand and covering his eyes with the right. In *Meditation on the Harp* there
is a similar suggestion. This time the standing male figure is
adapted from the man in Millet's *Angelus* and is holding his
hat over what in Dali's paranoiac-critical interpretation of the
Angelus is an erection, between him and the kneeling figure;
and there is an exceptionally—for Dali—feminine-appearing
nude who seems to be clinging to the Millet figure and restrain-
ing the kneeling one. *Memory of the Child-Woman* has a bust
of an ambiguously painted figure with one female breast and
a curiously anticipatory suggestion in its features of the face of
the Dali of thirty years later. Gala is painted full length wearing shorts in *Cardinal! Cardinal!* Her breasts are exposed but
her shorts bulge at the front in a most extraordinary way for a
woman. The *Hysterical Arch,* of 1937, formed by the body of
a woman bent over backward, holding herself up by her hands,
makes the same point about women as a number of Tennessee
Williams plays. In *The Broken Bridge and the Dream* (1945)
one of the principal figures has the breasts of a woman and the
sex organs of a man. *Dali at the Age of Six Lifting the Skin of
the Water to Observe a Dog Sleeping in the Shadow of the Sea*
shows Dali in the nude as a young blond with long hair and the
sex organs of a girl.

His masterpiece of the genre was a painting of 1954 entitled
Two Adolescents. At left, a slender blond boy, nude, with shimmering flesh, reclines on the ground, his left knee drawn up,
against the usual Cadaqués seascape. His genitals are elabo-
rately laid out for inspection, the penis pink and glistening,
each pubic hair lovingly delineated. The boy's mouth is open
and his teeth have been touched with brighter accents of white
so that they catch the light, as in theatrical photography or Italian calendar art or candy-box buckeye. At right a dark-haired
faceless boy of similar taste, style, and equipment stands like a
fashion mannequin, his left hand on his shoulder and his left
leg drawn back, the toe daintily pointing into the ground.

The references and aspirations in such pictures were obvious: the preoccupation with fellatio, the embellishment of male genitalia, the idealization of the male relationship, sexual ambivalence, the caricatural treatment of woman (aside from the tiresome, repetitive mythologizing treatment of Gala). But the most distressing note was the obtrusive makeup man's technique: the highlights and glints. It was the Hard Sell made flesh.

I decided to look for the results of Dali's recent preoccupation with three-dimensional painting. At the entrance to one of the smaller galleries I came upon something entitled *The Magdalene Before Christ,* painted in black on a whitish version of the plastic material covered with an allover pattern of tapiocalike drops that he had shown me, in its red form, during one of our early conversations at the St. Regis, and later, in Paris, in blue. Understanding his motive in using the material, I swayed forward and back and then to each side, as I looked at the picture, in order to induce the illusion. The drops, or eggs, moved back and forth with me, but the painting itself, cooperate as I might, stayed well within the usual two-dimensional limits. It was under glass, and the two heads appeared to have been painted in a pale-gray wash on the back of that glass. There was a cloudy, translucent area above the head of the Magdalene which, I gathered, had been applied as a kind of filter to enhance the multidimensional possibilities. A meandering line had been drawn through this filter, perhaps with the other end of the brush that had applied the filmy gray-white wash to the glass. It suggested the general lines of the Magdalene's hairdress, and in doing so, it cleared enough of a path through the film around her head to provide a sharper view of the black paint on the tapioca base behind it. But for all the differentiation of the layers, there was nothing really three-dimensional about the painting itself. I wondered why he had bothered.

A bit farther along I came to another, more elaborate, experiment in depth set well back within a shadow-box frame. As background there was a golden sheet of the tapioca material surrounded by an architectural decor painted in gray gouache. Centered within that framework was a smaller swatch of tapioca, this one in white, with the same kind of surrounding gouache decoration. On top of that were two very thin sheets of copper. On the outer one was painted a rear view of a long-haired figure holding some kind of sea monster whose tail curled out from under its right arm. The two copper sheets had begun to come apart from each other and from the white tapioca background and were casting shadows against it and each other. Two paper clips attached to the bottom to hold the sheets together only served to emphasize the flimsiness of the construction and of the idea as well. On the underside of the glass I noticed a vague grayish wash that I assumed had been applied in the hope of heightening the illusion.

There were two more exercises of this kind—small paintings entitled *Nude on Pedestal (front)* and *Nude on Pedestal (back)*. They were dated 1965 and labeled "oil on glass." Both were painted on the same kind of Op-oriented tapioca background within frames whose glass was set about an inch in front of the picture. The first, painted on an opalescent strip of the tapioca material, portrayed a long-legged male nude with dark hair and a girlish face. He held out a stick that was reminiscent of Dali's Victor Hugo cane. His wasp waist was unnaturally high. The scrotum was long and full and the head of the penis lyrically outlined in pink.

The second painting showed a similar figure from the rear, but the hair, instead of being dark, was blond and very long. The stick was the same, but the proportions of the rear view, combined with the long, blond hair, made one assume the figure was female. None of the painting was actually three-dimensional despite the way the tapioca moved as I shifted my head from one side to the other. The fact that the opalescent panel in the first painting was coming away from its ground wasn't at all helpful to the cause, either. The mountain had labored but thus far had brought forth four very small mice, it seemed to me. Perhaps the masterpieces will appear later.

The homage to Meissonier was something of a mixed bag, too. I saw no sign of Meissonier's easel, although Dali had announced it was to be included in the exhibition, but I was glad to renew my acquaintance with *Friédland 1807,* which I had last seen in front of the movie camera at the Cour de Rohan in Paris, between the prosaic defection of Yvonne and the more poetic rebellion of Maria Latour.

Dali had carried out his plan of having photographic enlargements made of the three details that had struck him so forcefully that morning before the camera: the cuirassier's chin, the nostrils and bridle of one of the horses, and the waving grass. Magnified fifteen or twenty times they emphasized the vigor of Meissonier's brushstroke but carried, for me, a good deal less conviction in the grayish monochrome of their isolation than they did in their normal context.

The most effective argument in favor of Meissonier hung nearby: Dali's four-by-eight-foot 1965 oil *Homage to Meissonier,* so successfully sloppy an effort that without Dali's signature it could only have crashed the gate at the Gallery of Modern Art. In it, Dali seemed to be parodying all the dribble, squirt, and swab of the kind of modern art he and his host detest. There was no doubt—Dali the painter was no match for Dali the showman.

I went back out into the adjoining gallery. On the strength of the painting alone, I felt, Dali's message had little impact. The intelligence, the wit, the brilliant impulses, needed the dynamic context of his ceaselessly invented daily life to take meaningful shape. On canvas, no amount of technique could disguise the fact that their transcription was, too often, little more than an exercise in style. Dali's painting, I realized, had passed from the expression of a perversely original rebel to an irrelevant anachronism. He had played out his historical role as painter but could not bear the thought he no longer mattered. And so he did whatever he felt was necessary to bring the spotlight back to his corner. Now he was, indeed, a clown, a performer, with a superlative mental equipment which occasionally gave off sparks no other painter was capable of. Chagall once said of Picasso, "What a genius, that Picasso. It's a pity he doesn't paint." In Dali's case one might wistfully revise Chagall and say, "What a genius, that Dali. It's a pity he bothers to paint."

On my way downstairs I passed again in front of the mammoth dollar painting. It was so overcrowded and diffuse, so deliberately and gratuitously confusing, that I suddenly saw it as the perfect pictorial symbol of our inflationary age. At least in this respect, I thought, Dali was right up to the times, a sort of High Priest of Showmanship as the ultimate Fine Art.

"My painting is the least important thing about me," Dali had told me more than once. As I had often observed before, there was always a grain of truth in whatever Dali said, no matter *how* preposterous his statements might sound at first. That one, I decided, was no exception.

I N D E X

I N D E X

A B C (newspaper), 216
Abstract art, 48, 49, 171
Accommodations of Desire (Dali),
  67
Action painting, 169, 172
Adeane, Sir Robert, 214
Age d'or, L' (film), 69, 278
Alemany, Carlos, 30–31
Alphonse XIII, King, 79
Altamira, 190
Angelus, The (Millet), 53–56, 58,
  91–92, 109, 295, 301
Annigoni, Pietro, 59
Aphrodisiac Jacket, The (Dali), 69,
  79–80
Apocalypse, L' (Foret), 39–40, 220,
  224, 255, 261–62, 280
Aragon, Louis, 65, 66, 67, 164, 210
Arcimboldo, Giuseppe, 72
Arensberg Collection, 132
Arman, 26, 30, 50
Arp, Jean (Hans), 65, 67
Artaud, Antonin, 67
Arts (weekly newspaper), 71, 209–10
Atlantic Monthly, 182
Avant-garde, 51–52, 67, 266

Baez, Joan, 165
Ball, Hugo, 65
Balthus, Klossowski de Rola, 59

Balzac, Honoré de, 48
Barcelona Museum, 297
Barnes Collection, 241–42
Barotte, René, 233–44, 246
Bartholdi, Frédéric Auguste, 97
Barzini, Mlle., 194, 199, 200
Baudelaire, Charles, 66
Bauquier, M., 210
Bellmer, Hans, 67
Belmondo, Jean-Paul, 164, 166, 168
Berlin, Irving, 165
Bernstein, Leonard, 165
Besteguí, Charles de, 157
Bohr, Niels, 52
Bonheur, Rosa, 199
Borrones, 49
Bosch, Hieronymus, 72
Bouguereau, William, 25, 46, 47,
  48, 275, 287
Brando, Marlon, 31
Braque, Georges, 219, 222
Brassaï, Gyula H., 197, 215, 235,
  239–40
Bravura di tocco, 50
Brera Gallery, 296
Bresdin, Rodolphe, 72
Breton, André, 65, 66, 67, 68, 69,
  70, 71–72, 222, 278
*Bride Stripped Bare of Her Bache-
  lors, Even* (Duchamp), 130–32

Broglie, Prince Louis, 52
Broken Bridge and the Dream, The (Dali), 298, 301
Brueghel, Jan, 72
Buffet, Bernard, 39
Buñuel, Luis, 67, 69, 278, 282
Burne-Jones, Sir Edward, 52
Burial at Ornans (Courbet), 254

Caca Dauphin, le, 87
Cadaqués, Spain, 23, 245, 255, 263, 267, 279, 285
Cahiers d'Art (magazine), 36, 287
Calder, Alexander, 69
Caravaggio, Michelangelo Merisi, 46
Cardin, Pierre, 82, 90, 136, 152, 180
Cardinal! Cardinal! (Dali), 301
Cassini, Igor, 281
Cassou, Jean, 210, 232
Cervantes, Miguel de, 21
César, 139, 159, 180
Cézanne, Paul, 51, 52, 53, 58, 77, 172, 219, 241–43, 256, 264, 285
Chafarrinadas, 49
Chagall, Marc, 201, 239, 305
Chaplin, Charlie, 270
Char, René, 67
Chef-d'oeuvre inconnu, Le (Balzac), 48
Chevalier, Haakon, 38
Chirico, Giorgio de, 67, 300
Christ of St. John of the Cross (Dali), 295–96
Clausen, K. W., 193
Cocteau, Jean, 42, 67, 164, 166
Colin, Saul, 31, 32, 33, 182, 184–85, 186, 189, 190, 191, 192, 193–94, 199–200
Communism, 47, 188, 210, 216–17, 218–19, 221
Communist Party, 66, 207–10

Conversations with Picasso (Brassaï), 197
Coquiot, Gustave, 238
Cosmic Madonna (Dali), 297
Courbet, Gustave, 254
Crevel, René, 175
Crick, Francis H. C., 15, 20, 266
Crowninshield, Frank, 95
Crucifixion (Dali), 27, 229
Cubism, 21, 45, 49, 217, 218–19, 242

Dada, 65–66
Dali, Gala, 17–18, 23, 37, 41, 67, 81, 82, 83, 92, 115, 116–17, 121, 122, 135, 140, 144, 147, 150, 158, 183, 200, 201, 215, 222, 223, 224, 228–29, 243, 244–45, 246, 257, 259, 263, 264, 265, 267, 287–88, 289, 292, 297, 298, 301, 302
Dali at the Age of Six Lifting the Skin of the Water . . . (Dali), 297, 301
Da Vinci, Leonardo, 54, 176
Davis, Mafalda, 94–95, 103, 114–15, 118, 125–27
Dead Christ Mourned by the Virgin (Mantegna), 296
Dechézelles, André, 205
De Kooning, William, 60, 102
Delacroix, Eugène, 72
Demongeot, Mylène, 81
De Quincey, Thomas, 89, 137
Derain, André, 300
Descharnes, Robert, 38, 78, 79, 81–82, 121, 124, 127, 135, 137, 150, 151, 156, 220, 254, 255, 256, 294
Desnos, Robert, 67
Dieu a choisi Paris (film), 83, 159, 164, 166
Discovery of America by Christopher Columbus (Dali), 297

Discurso sobre la forma cúbica (Herrera), 21
Divisionism, 49
Domínguez, 67
Dreier, Katherine, 132
Duchamp, Marcel, 25, 69, 130–32, 195, 196
Dürer, Albrecht, 284

Eddington, Sir Arthur Stanley, 48
Edison, Thomas A., 111–12
Ehrenburg, Ilya, 210
Éluard, Paul, 65, 67, 68, 196, 265, 278
Embarkation for Cythera, The (Watteau), 22, 54
Ernst, Max, 67, 129, 133, 158, 159, 300
Eroticism, 54–57, 131, 175, 178, 278, 291–93
Estaque, L' (Cézanne), 243
Everybody's Autobiography (Stein), 221–22
Express, L' (newspaper), 189, 193
Expressionism, 50, 51, 286, 297

Face of the Great Masturbator, The (Dali), 67
Faith, matter of, 92
Fellini, Federico, 223
Femme Visible, La (Dali), 68
Field, Albert, 31–32, 33–39, 40, 61, 74, 75, 82, 181, 182, 184–85
Fifty Abstract Pictures . . . (Dali), 296
Figaro, Le (newspaper), 74, 75, 91, 177, 179, 277
Findlay Gallery, New York City, 215
Fini, Léonor, 39, 150–51, 158, 181
Font, The (Dali), 300–1
Forani, Christine, 95, 97–100, 112–13, 118, 125–28, 135, 145, 150, 224–26, 227, 228, 229–30, 233, 234, 236, 237, 238, 240, 243, 253, 254, 258, 263, 264, 266, 276, 279
Foret, Joseph, 31, 32, 33, 39–40, 61, 220, 223, 224, 254, 255, 261–62, 264
Fortuny, Mariano, 26, 60
Foujita, Tsugouharu, 39
Foz, Dr., 185, 187, 200, 201
Francesca, Piero della, 51, 298
Franco, Francisco, 70, 212, 217, 218
Franklin, Benjamin, 191
French Communist Party, 207–10
Freud, Sigmund, 27, 45, 53, 54, 66, 74, 300
Frey, Jim, 237
Friédland 1807 (Meissonier), 168–69, 179, 304
Furet, Yves, 166
Fusil, M., 205–6

Gala with Bees (Dali), 91, 120
Galacidalacidesoxiribunucleicacid (Hommage à Crick et Watson), 15–18, 19–21, 22–24, 26, 181
Galerie Charpentier, Paris, 65, 70, 71, 72–73, 75, 91, 110, 129, 151, 155, 180, 194, 274
Galerie Goemans, Paris, 67, 72
Galerie Maeght, Paris, 71
García Lorca, Federico, 70, 175, 267–70
Gaudí, Antoni, 96, 118
Gaulle, Madame de, 160
Gershwin, George, 165
Giacometti, Albert, 67, 132
Gilot, Françoise, 179, 183, 198–202, 207, 211–16, 220, 222, 233, 235, 240, 247, 272–73
Glass of Absinth (Picasso), 69

Goya y Lucientes, Francisco José
de, 51, 298
Grandes Baigneuses (Cézanne), 241
Grandville (Jean-Ignace-Isidore Gé-
rard), 72
Greco, El (Domenico Theotoco-
puli), 51, 298
Gris, Juan, 210, 219
Grotius, Hugo, 189
Guest, Winston, 81–82, 297
Guggenheim Museum, New York
City, 24–25, 26

Halsmann, Philippe, 236
Hara Kiri (magazine), 115, 116
Harper's Bazaar, 285
Hartford, Huntington, 52, 104, 114,
281–82
Hartford Gallery of Modern Art,
Huntington, 25, 26, 52, 225, 281,
294–305
Harvester, The (Millet), 56
Hermes (Praxiteles), 51, 286
Herrera, Juan de, 21
Hitler, Adolf, 70, 266
Hogan, Mike, 95
Homage to Kant (Dali), 69, 72, 73,
75, 90, 132, 133, 134, 135, 137,
141, 143, 148, 153
Homage to Meissonier (Dali), 304
Huelsenbeck, Richard, 65
Hugnet, Georges, 67
Hugo, Victor, 96
Humanité, L' (newspaper), 208
Hungarian Revolution, 219
Hypnagogic Clock (Dali), 153

Illumined Pleasures (Dali), 67
Impressionism, 44–45, 48–49
Impressions d'Afrique (Roussel),
289

Ingres, Jean A. D., 44, 48
Invisible Object (Giacometti), 132–
33

Jardot, Maurice, 210
Jarry, Alfred, 66
Journal d'un génie, Le (Dali), 74,
75, 105, 107, 171, 173, 174, 191,
192
Judgment of Paris, The (Dali), 226,
227

Kahnweiler, D.-H., 207, 210, 232
Kant, Immanuel, 73, 75, 84, 89–90,
180
Keeler, Christine, 105
Kermadec, Eugène de, 210
Kern, Jerome, 165
Klein, Yves, 256
Kline, Franz, 256
Knoedler gallery, New York City,
15, 26, 29, 41, 181
Krafft-Ebing, Richard von, 68

Labisse, Félix, 210, 246
Lacan, Jacques, 54, 108–9
Lacourière, Roger, 237
Lam, Wilfredo, 274
Lannes, Jean-Pierre, 101–2
Lao-tzu, 142
Lascaux, Elie, 210
Last Days of Immanuel Kant (De
Quincey), 89, 137
Latour, Maria, 163–68, 170–71, 173–
78, 304
Laurencin, Marie, 199
Lautréamont, Comte de (Isidore
Ducasse), 66
Lavreince (Niklas Lafrensen, the
Younger), 79
Leda Atomica (Dali), 297
Leduc, Stéphen, 43

Léger, Fernand, 210, 219
Léger, Nadia, 210
Leiris, Louise, 210, 232, 240
Leiris, Michel, 67, 210, 240
Leiris Gallery, Paris, 232
Le Nain, Louis, 296
Levy Gallery, Julien, New York City, 25
Liberté élairant le monde, La (Bartholdi), 97
Libro Nero, Il (Papini), 35
Lichtenstein, Roy, 27, 50
Life Extension Society, 192
Life with Picasso (Lake and Gilot), 179, 181, 184, 194, 197, 200, 205–11, 214–15, 220, 232, 233, 234, 239, 271, 282
Linde, Ulf, 132
Locomotive, La, Montmartre, 257–60
Loewy, Raymond, 267–68
Louvre, the, Paris, 46, 54, 56, 74, 109, 163, 241
Lugubrious Game, The (Dali), 67, 72
Lull, Ramón, 21, 102
Luncheon on the Grass series (Picasso), 29
Lussato, Bruno, 124–25, 126, 132, 133, 134, 136, 146, 290
Lussato, Marina, 83, 84, 95, 96, 99, 100, 103, 106, 107, 111, 112–13, 116, 124–25, 126, 127, 135, 137, 138, 146, 150, 151, 152, 153, 156, 158, 159, 179, 253, 267, 268, 282, 283, 289–93
Lys, Lya, 278, 282

Macrocosmos, 48, 266
Magdalene Before Christ, The (Dali), 302
Maillol, Aristide, 287

Mami, Dali, 21
Man with the Sheep, The (Picasso), 208
Mantegna, Andrea, 296
Marie Antoinette, 77
Marinetti, F. T., 67
Marquet, Albert, 210
Marriage of the Virgin, The (Raphael), 58
Masochism, 157
Masson, André, 67
Mathieu, Georges, 39, 47, 50, 171, 256, 266
Matisse, Henri, 46
Matta (R. A. S. Matta Echaurren), 67
Meditation on the Harp (Dali), 301
Meissonier, Ernest, 26, 46, 47, 50, 53, 60, 84, 159, 168, 172, 179, 241, 254, 255, 256, 264, 284, 285–86, 287, 304
Memory of the Child-Woman (Dali), 301
Meninas, Las—The Maids of Honor (Velásquez), 42, 43
Méryon, Charles, 72
Metropolitan Museum of Art, New York City, 27, 169
Meurice Hotel, Paris, 61, 75, 76–77, 101, 161, 220, 247, 261, 274
Millais, Sir John Everett, 52
Millet, Jean François, 53–56, 57, 58, 91–92, 109, 301
Minotaure (magazine), 36
Miró, Joan, 33, 67, 129, 209, 287, 300
Modern art, 33–34, 58, 77, 217, 304
Modigliani, Amedeo, 51
Moiré pattern, 41–44, 80, 103, 226, 251
Mona Lisa (Da Vinci), 54, 295

Monde, Le (newspaper), 71
Mondrian, Piet, 33
Montagne Ste.-Geneviéve (Cézanne), 242
Montaigne, Michel de, 177, 242
Montes, Eugenio, 102
Moore, Peter, 212, 215, 229, 230, 252, 255, 257, 259, 262, 264, 265, 268, 272, 273, 281, 282, 283, 284, 286, 288, 289
Moreau, Gustave, 25, 72, 79
Morse, Reynolds, 81
Mozart, Wolfgang Amadeus, 51
Musée d'Art Moderne de la Ville de Paris, 236
Musée National d'Art Moderne, Paris, 232, 236
Museum of Modern Art, New York City, 21, 33, 35, 36, 294
Mythe tragique de l'Angélus de Millet, Le (Dali), 91, 109

Nacenta, Raymond, 71–72, 142–44, 147, 180, 181
National Gallery, Washington, D.C., 27
Neruda, Pablo, 210
New England Merchants National Bank of Boston, 16
New York Armory Show (1913), 130
New York Graphic Society, 288
New York Times, 201, 281
New York World's Fair, 18, 225
Noailles, Vicomte de, 138
Noailles, Vicomtesse Marie-Laure de, 88, 90, 110, 115, 116, 124, 138, 139–40, 154, 156, 180, 181
Notes sur la poésie (Breton and Éluard), 278
Nouvelles Impressions d'Afrique (Roussel), 289
Nude Descending a Staircase (Duchamp), 130
Nude on Pedestal (Dali), 303–4

Objet 1900, L', 114
Oedipus complex, 54
Oil painting, 44
Onda, 258–59, 268–69, 271
On Murder as One of the Fine Arts (De Quincey), 89
Op Art, 241, 266, 275
Oppenheim, Meret, 69
Osservatore Romano, L' (newspaper), 280
Oster, Gerald, 42, 43

Pacioli, Fra Luca, 21, 217
Papini, Giovanni, 35
Paracelsus, 221
Paris-Match (magazine), 205
Paris-Presse (newspaper), 180, 233, 246
Parmelin, Hélène, 210
Pascal, Blaise, 187
Patriote de Nice et du Sud-Est, Le (newspaper), 208
Pau, France, 262
Pavillon, Le, New York City, 157
Pegler, Westbrook, 95
Péret, Benjamin, 65
Persistence of Memory, The (Dali), 21–22
Petals and Garden of the Nymph Ancolie (Ernst), 136
Peter the Great, 188
Philadelphia Museum of Art, 132
Picasso, Maya. See Widmaier, Maya Picasso
Picasso, Pablo, 29, 32–33, 34–35, 46, 47, 50, 69, 102, 156, 164, 179, 194–202, 205–12, 216–19, 222, 225, 232, 233, 234, 235, 237, 238–39, 243, 246, 269, 300, 305

Pignon, Edouard, 207, 210, 233, 239
Planck, Max, 266, 269
Pointillism, 49
Pollock, Jackson, 169, 172
Pompier art, 26, 47, 51, 114, 172, 256, 266, 275
Pop Art, 25, 26–27, 45, 152, 172, 190, 241, 266, 275, 285, 286–87
Port Lligat, Spain, 37, 79
Porter, Cole, 165
Portrait of Paul Éluard (Dali), 67
Potato Harvest, The (Millet), 57
Potin, Félix, 215
Potin, Mr. and Mrs. Jacques, 214
Poussin, Nicolas, 52, 242
Powell, Anthony, 290
Prado, the, Madrid, 217, 219
Praxiteles, 51, 176, 286, 287, 299
Prévert, Jacques, 67
Proust, Marcel, 27
Prouteau, Gilbert, 83–84, 104, 114, 121, 159, 160, 161, 162, 163, 164, 166, 167, 168, 169–70, 171, 172, 173, 174, 175

Queneau, Raymond, 67
Quevedo y Villegas, Francisco Gómez de, 49, 192

Racism, 70
Raimu, 45
Raphael, 21, 51, 58, 60, 176, 287, 297
Ratton, Charles, 75, 143, 153, 154
Ratton Gallery, Charles, Paris, 69, 153, 154
Ray, Man, 67
Raynal, Maurice, 287
Realism, 48, 50, 59
Redon, Odilon, 72
Resurrection of the Flesh (Dali), 298

Révolution Surréaliste, La (magazine), 109
Rheims, Maurice, 104, 110, 114, 179
Rheims, Philippe, 114, 169, 170, 179
Rimbaud, Arthur, 47, 66
Rodgers, Richard, 165
Rosenberg, Paul, 222
Rossetti, Dante Gabriel, 52
Roussel, Raymond, 66, 289
Rutsch, Alexandre, 86, 87, 90, 125, 132, 133–35, 136, 137, 140–41, 142–49, 151–52, 153, 154–55, 156, 158–59, 180, 181, 194

Sabartés, Jaime, 210
Sacrament of the Last Supper, The (Dali), 27
Sade, Marquis de, 66
St. George (Dali), 298
St. Helena in Port Lligat (Dali), 298
St. Regis Hotel, New York City, 30, 75, 214, 302
Salacrou, Armand, 210
Salmon, André, 287
Salon de Mai, Paris, 225, 232, 246
Salvador Dali in the Act of Painting Gala in the Apotheosis of the Dollar . . . (Dali), 295, 305
Scientific American (magazine), 41–42, 80
Secret Life of Salvador Dali (Dali), 171, 202, 235, 236
Segal, George, 285–86
Séligmann, Kurt, 67
Selz, Jacqueline, 236, 238, 239, 240, 243–44
Seurat, Georges, 49, 57–58
Show (magazine), 281
Slave Market with Invisible Bust of Voltaire (Dali), 296
Small Battle of Tetuán (Dali), 26

Société de Pavage et des Asphaltes de Paris et l'Asphalte, 97
Soupault, Philippe, 67
Spanish Civil War, 217
Spectre of Sex Appeal, The (Dali), 300
Stalin, Joseph, 221
Stanislavsky (Constantine Sergeevich Alexeev), 168, 174
Steiger, Rod, 31
Stein, Gertrude, 221-22
Stockholm Modern Museum, 132
Stravinsky, Igor, 158
Straw-Binders, The (Millet), 56
Surrealism, 26, 38-39, 65-73, 155, 217, 297, 300
Surrender of Breda (Velásquez), 58

Tachisme, 49, 256
Tamayo, Rufino, 274
Tanguy, Yves, 67, 300
Technique, acquisition of, 60
Teilhard de Chardin, Pierre, 102, 105, 187, 190
Thinker, The (Rodin), 119
Toklas, Alice B., 221
Tokyo, Japan, 81, 294
Trémois, Pierre Yves, 39
Triolet, Elsa, 210
Tristan as Christ (Dali), 300
Turner, Joseph M. W., 52, 108
Twelve Canvases in One (Picasso), 246
Two Adolescents (Dali), 301
Tzara, Tristan, 65

Un Chien andalou (film), 69, 282

Van Eyck, Hubert and Jan, 44
Van Gogh, Vincent, 54, 56, 57
Velásquez, Diego Rodríguez de Silva y, 29, 42, 43, 46, 47, 49, 50, 51, 58, 60, 188, 296, 297, 298-99
Vénus du Gaz, La (Picasso), 195
Venus with Drawers (Dali), 72, 73, 74
Vermeer (Jan van der Meer), 27, 44, 46, 47, 50, 51, 186, 189, 299
Vilato, Xavier, 210
Villon, Jacques, 158
Virgin of Guadalupe (Dali), 297
Vive l'Empereur (Meissonier), 84
Voltaire, François Marie Arouet, 296

Waldberg, Patrick, 71, 72, 91, 142-44, 153, 181
Warhol, Andy, 259
Watson, James Dewey, 15, 20, 266
Watteau, Jean Antoine, 22, 54, 297
Widmaier, Maya Picasso, 196-97
Wildenstein Gallery, Paris, 71
Williams, Tennessee, 301
Winnower, The (Millet), 56
Winter, Jack, 248-50, 252, 298
Winter, Muriel, 249
Woman (Giacometti), 132
World of Salvador Dali, The (Descharnes), 38, 78

Yvonne, Mlle., 76, 77-78, 80-81, 82-83, 84, 115, 123, 124, 135, 137, 138, 139, 142, 159, 161, 162-63, 168, 170, 172-73, 304

Zadkine, Ossip, 39
Zervos, Christian, 31, 287
Zurbarán, Francisco de, 297